LIGHT

YEARS

ALSO BY GARY KINDER

Victim: The Other Side of Murder

GARY KINDER

LIGHT

AN INVESTIGATION INTO THE EXTRATERRESTRIAL
EXPERIENCES OF EDUARD MEIER

YEARS

A MORGAN ENTREKIN BOOK

THE ATLANTIC MONTHLY PRESS

NEW YORK

My effort to see this through
I dedicate with much love
To the one who gave more than I . . .

Alison

only she knows

———————————

First Edition

Library of Congress Cataloging-in-Publication Data

Kinder, Gary.
  Light years.

  I. Title.
PS3561.I427L5   1987   813'.54   86-28858
ISBN 0-87113-139-0

Published simultaneously in Canada

Printed in the United States of America

ACKNOWLEDGMENTS

IT IS IMPOSSIBLE TO ENTER THE FIELD OF UFOLOGY WITHOUT TREADING upon many footprints. My research on UFOs and their history has come from books, doctoral theses, vintage newspaper and magazine articles, publications from various UFO organizations, government documents, and correspondence from the files of the National Investigations Committee on Aerial Phenomena. I would like to single out David Michael Jacobs's doctoral thesis, *The Controversy over Unidentified Flying Objects in America: 1896–1973.* I found myself referring to it often. I also traveled to many parts of the country attending UFO symposia and interviewing ufologists. For their time and patience in helping me understand the phenomenon, I would like to thank Sherman Larsen, curator of the now combined archives of the Center for UFO Studies and the National Investigations Committee on Aerial Phenomena; Walt Andrus, head of the Mutual UFO Network, who graciously made me feel welcome at his organization's 1986 convention; Dr. Bruce Maccabee and the Fund for UFO Research in Washington, D.C., especially members Larry Bryant and Dick Hall; Coral Lorenzen and the late Jim Lorenzen of the Aerial Phenomena Research Organization in Tucson; Dr. Leo Sprinkle, organizer of the contactee convention held each summer at the University of Wyoming; and Doris Arnold, whose husband Kenneth started it all.

The primary investigators on the Eduard Meier case—Lee and Brit Elders, Tom Welch, and Lieutenant Colonel Wendelle Stevens (USAF, retired)—have given generously of their time and energy in recalling their experiences with Meier from 1976 to 1982. They will receive a percentage of royalties for introducing me to Meier, and for supplying

v

me with records, correspondence, interview tapes, and their research on the Pleiades, plus photographs, sound recordings, video tapes, and other materials owned and copyrighted by Lee Elders. All materials were provided for me to use at my discretion, and I have maintained total control over the contents of the manuscript.

Jim Dilettoso, who assisted the investigators, also has my gratitude for talking to me of his role in tracking down scientists willing to examine the evidence.

The Swiss and German citizens whom I interviewed are all mentioned by name in the book—Bernadette, Eva, Engelbert, Jakobus, to name a few—and I thank each of them for taking the time to speak with me of their experiences. Elsi Moser and Herbert Runkel were especially accommodating and helpful, as was Timothy Good in London. Popi Meier, who seems more than any other to have grown from the experience, always made me feel welcome in her home, though I was one of thousands to tromp through in search of her husband. A very special thanks goes to Frank Stuckert, who served not only as my translator but became my friend as well; Frank and his wife Frida are warmly remembered for their hospitality.

The scientists and engineers who examined the evidence and agreed to talk with me on the record did so at some risk to their reputations. All are mentioned by name in the book. As they were candid with me, I have tried to be fair in reflecting their complete opinions, including any reservations they may have had. They have made clear to me, and I now make clear to the reader: Their observations and views are their own and in no way are intended to represent the position of their employers. I sincerely hope they will not be castigated by their peers or their employers for having the courage to explore and to wonder.

My editor, Morgan Entrekin, and my agent, Richard Pine, deserve recognition for backing me as I embarked on an adventure that, after much time, energy, and money had been expended, could have led nowhere. They stood by me and had faith that I knew what I was doing when even I did not know that I knew what I was doing.

I am fortunate to have a brother to whom I am close, and who is also in the hotel business. Randy, thank you for making the lonely times on the road first-class. As always my parents, Irving and Peggy Kinder, and my in-laws, the Ernest Evans family of Seattle, have continued their support and encouragement.

And last, Theo and George, I have not forgotten.

PART I

EDUARD MEIER

LATE ON A COLD AND RAINY NOVEMBER NIGHT IN 1976, A Volkswagen and a small German-built Ford wound through the islands of darkened forest in the hills southeast of Zurich. The rain fell so hard for so long that the back roads had turned to mud and the rain dripped from the needles of tall evergreens soaking the forest floor until it was spongy. Then the temperature cooled and large wet flakes of snow now mixed with the rain as the Volkswagen, followed by the Ford, slithered through the mud past the shadowy presence of an old farmhouse and headed further into the darkness. Wearing a gray leather jacket, a man with his left arm severed just above the elbow rode in the passenger seat of the lead car; though the driver could see nothing save the wet path before him pelted by silver rain, the man with one arm seemed able to see past the veil of darkness, to know where he was and where he was going. Above the muffled beating of the rain, he directed the driver through the darkness across a swampy meadow, down a prominent rise, to the edge of another forest, where he told the driver to stop.

The car engine died quickly, and only the rain splashing on the metal roof now broke the silence. Then the headlights of both cars dimmed and went out, and the driver could see nothing in the blackness. Neither he nor a passenger in the

3

backseat had seen anything since the headlights swept past the ghostly farmhouse a few miles back. The man with one arm instructed the driver that they were to wait for him there, that he would return in perhaps an hour, perhaps longer, he could never be sure. Then with no further word he opened the door and they watched his silhouette disappear quickly through the rain into the dark of the forest.

For over a year the driver had accompanied the one-armed man to such sites, a half hour, sometimes an hour, from the village. As months passed the journeys had taken place later at night and the sites had become increasingly remote. For someone alone, waiting in the darkness, they could be frightening. This night the presence of the other people, the man in the backseat, the man and woman in the Ford, eased the fear as he waited.

Outside, the rain and wet snow continued to fall, and the driver realized they would have to mount chains on the rear tires or they would never be able to drive through the deepening mud up the rise and back several miles to the main road. If they bogged down in the mud, they would have to spend the night in the two cars.

The men got out of the cars, and illuminated by the headlights, they stood in the rain and mud jacking up first the Volkswagen then the Ford. The rear tires of each car had to be raised, one at a time, then lowered, and the jack stand repositioned again in the mud and pumped again until the next tire rose inches from the ground. The chains were heavy and difficult to manipulate, especially with fingers wet and numb from the cold. The woman sat in one car then the other, dozing as the men worked.

Before each chain was in place, nearly an hour had passed, and the three men were now soaked to their skins and chilled by the icy rain running in rivulets down their faces. Finally they were satisfied with the tautness of the chains, and as they began stamping about, trying to get warm, they suddenly heard a strange sound above the trees.

"A singing noise," recalled one of the men.

They peered upward into the rain. Except for the constant

flow of water dripping from the pine needles, the trees stood motionless, but still the noise was that of strong wind.

The eerie sound, a high-pitched warble that pierced the falling rain, moved slowly over their heads. They followed its course with their eyes, straining to see; then suddenly the noise began to subside, and the one-armed man stood with them in the light not two feet away.

"We didn't see him or hear him walk," remembered another. "Just all of a sudden he was there."

The noise in the trees had awakened the woman, who got out of the car to see the three men in their darkened and soggy clothes huddled together in the beam of the headlights and looking up into the trees. She closed the door and took one step into the mud, glancing down for only a moment. When she raised her eyes again quickly, what she saw startled her: The man with one arm was suddenly standing in the headlight beam only a few feet away, with his back to her.

"In the time I looked down and up again, a split second," she remembered, "he practically grew out of the ground in front of me."

The man with one arm appeared almost like an apparition in their midst. They stared at him through the rain and saw that his hair was dry; they reached for his hand, and his skin was warm to their touch. As he stood in the bright light saying nothing, they could see the rain and wet flakes of snow just beginning to form dark speckles on the bone-dry leather of his coat.

ONE

History first mentions the village of Hinwil, Switzerland, in a document dated 745. Thirty miles southeast of Zurich, it nestles in a landscape of rolling green hills pocketed by large islands of forest a hundred feet tall, with the Alps rising in the distance. Hinwil itself perhaps would disappoint the tourist looking for the charm of alpine architecture: Though chalk-white chalets shuttered in green rise from the village core and scatter among the hills, many stark buildings constructed of concrete have risen in their midst. They resemble not so much the quaint cottages in travel brochures as they do utilitarian apartment buildings erected in the 1950s and '60s in the United States.

But a short distance from the village center, along the street Wihaldenstrasse, stands a three-story farmhouse built a hundred years ago. During the mid-1970s summer grape vines climbed the sunny south wall of the old house. Flowers filled a stone water trough to the north near the entrance, and small birds fluttered in an aviary built of wood and wire. To the south and east of the house lay a small green field, and to the north and west stood more of the cold, institutional apartment buildings.

The community of Hinwil had acquired the old farm years before and built the surrounding apartments to house

7

senior citizens. Though the farmhouse someday soon would be torn down to make room for more apartments, the community now rented the house for a nominal sum to an unemployed night watchman, Eduard Meier. Meier lived in the house with his Greek wife, Kaliope, nicknamed Popi, and three small children—a girl, Nina, a boy, Atlantis, and the baby, Bashenko. They had been living in the house since December 1973, though they had lived elsewhere in Hinwil for two years.

Meier, a man of thirty-seven, had a sixth-grade education. He was not a very big man, maybe five feet seven inches tall, but he was thick-chested and strong. His face was handsome, set off by unusual greenish-hazel eyes. According to village records, Meier's professions were "birdbreeder, iron layer, night watchman." He held a permit to carry a gun because he had once worked as night security in a factory.

In a former house, a tiny three-room row house contiguous to the Hinwil village museum, Meier had kept a cage out back filled with nearly two hundred birds. He had been employed then as a night guard and consequently was often at home during the day. But many people in the neighborhood avoided talking to Meier because he was "different." He spoke a great deal about Moses and said things other people did not understand. Julios and Erika Kägi knew the Meiers better than other neighbors did because they had a daughter the same age as Nina and the two girls often played together. "He had a terrific fantasy," remembered Erika Kägi, "and I could not agree with his philosophy. But he was not a bad person. He was not even odd; he just had his own ideas and believed whatever he said." Said another neighbor, "Meier lives the way he wants to and does not adapt to anyone else's way of living."

Meier had only one arm. His left arm had been severed just above the elbow in a bus accident in 1965, as he traveled from India, through Turkey, back to Switzerland. Still, when part of the barn adjacent to the small house collapsed, Julios Kägi saw Meier rebuild the wall alone by holding the boards in place with his shoulder stump while he positioned and pounded nails with his one hand. "He was faster with one hand than other people are with two," recalled Kägi.

Again out of a job, Meier now supported his family on the 700 francs provided him every month by the government for the loss of his arm. To supplement their income the Meiers kept chickens in the attic of the old farmhouse, and Popi sold eggs to the neighbors.

To neighbors living in the apartment buildings overlooking the front door of the farmhouse, Meier seemed to be always home. In a culture that values hard work and conformity, the neighbors saw him as a singular and idle man, often lost in thought, as though the weight of the world rested upon his shoulders, and they began to talk.

Then on the afternoon of January 28, 1975, a cold day, but warmer than most at that time of the year, Eduard Meier left the farmhouse on his moped, towing a tiny wagon behind him. He wound through the streets of Hinwil, steering with one hand, the empty left sleeve of his leather jacket jerking in the wind. Working his way out of town, he eventually came to a country road, which he followed for a time, then disappeared into the forest of a nature conservancy. A few hours later he returned to the farmhouse without telling anyone where he had been.

Several days passed, during which the neighbors saw Meier dawdling around the house, seemingly as always without purpose. Then one afternoon he again pulled his moped from a storage room, pedaled it down the driveway until the tiny motor kicked over, and rode through the village out into the country. Soon he was lost from view in another of the islands of forest surrounding Hinwil. When he returned, as before, he told no one where he had been or why he had been there. But the Swiss are observant and curious people, and the neighbors noted his peculiar comings and goings.

Within weeks Meier was traveling regularly into the forest, guiding his moped with one hand, the tiny wagon behind. Each trip seemed to take him along a new path in a new direction through town and out onto the country highways, often for as long as an hour. Later, many of his trips took him into the hills. Sometimes he would disappear in the early afternoon and not be seen again before supper; other times he would sneak from the house at one or two in the morning and not return till dawn.

"He had to go away again and again," Popi remembered. "He would come home for five minutes, fix himself a cup of coffee, and, hop, he was gone again. It was bad at night. You'd be sleeping peacefully and the kids were quiet in bed. All of a sudden he would get up, get dressed, and be gone. You know? You think your husband is lying in bed next to you, but he is gone. I did not know anything. All he said was that he was going to work."

As the weeks passed, Meier's journeys through town and into the forests began to occur three, four, even five times a week. And his frequent departures rubbed against the grain of order and routine so conscientiously observed by his neighbors. The more he disappeared, the more they talked.

"The people in the neighborhood didn't know anything about what was going on," said Popi, "but they were very curious. They could tell me to the minute when he left on his moped and when he came back. It was always the same questions. 'Why did he come home so late?' Sometimes he got up in the middle of the night and left, so they would hear the moped. And when he did this, it was even worse with the people the next day. 'Why did he leave last night?' 'Where did he go?' I would say nothing. I wasn't interested. They are just *Schnuriwiiber* [gossips]."

On clear nights neighbors living in the apartment building just above the farmhouse saw Meier standing in the alleyway to the west and watching the sky through binoculars for hours. On nights when he did not leave the house, neighbors to the east saw a light burning on the second floor late into the night.

A week, a month, maybe two months passed, Popi

could not remember. Then one afternoon, as the two of them stood in the small living room on the second floor of the house, her husband handed her photographs.

"What do you think of this?" he asked.

But Popi only stared at the pictures.

"I was shocked," she recalled, "because I saw something completely new, and I did not want to believe that this existed. He said nothing at all. Didn't explain. Not one word." Her husband merely picked up the pictures and left the room, as Popi yelled at him for wasting his time taking pictures when money for the family was so scarce.

Meier next took the photographs to his friend Jakobus Bertschinger, whom he had met while working at the Piatti gravel pit years earlier. Though Jakobus was twelve years younger than Meier, the two men had struck up a lasting friendship. They spent much time together, talking about Meier's experiences during the twelve years he had traveled back and forth through India and the Middle East. But Jakobus, too, seemed confused by the photographs Meier showed to him. He even laughed, but he promised to help his friend in any way he could.

With a loan from Jakobus, Meier placed a small classified ad in the German publication *Esotera*. The ad solicited people interested in forming a group to discuss natural life, logic, and truth—things "metaphysical."

Several more months passed. Through the summer and fall of 1975, the neighbors along Wihaldenstrasse watched Meier continue his frequent trips into the foothills and forests at all times of the day and night. On his little green moped he often was seen at the edge of the open road, putt-putting along, twenty, maybe twenty-five miles an hour, passed constantly by the much larger and faster automobiles. But then something new entered Meier's routine: One Saturday afternoon a half-dozen cars appeared at the farmhouse and remained till late at night.

The neighbors did not understand why people came to see this man. He was poor and handicapped, with an unkempt wife who spoke little of their language. He did not work and his habits seemed strange. But over the weeks and months, not only did the visitors continue to come, but their numbers increased. In the tiny parlor on the second story, the man with the single arm and unusual hazel eyes spoke to these people for hours. When they left, the neighbors heard Popi screaming at him.

For many months the neighbors watched Meier disappear frequently at odd hours, and saw the cars on Saturday afternoons filling the narrow alleyway running alongside No. 10 Wihaldenstrasse and spilling onto the streets of Hinwil.

TWO

Ilse von Jacobi, a journalist living in Munich who wrote
frequently about metaphysics and the paranormal, had
read about Eduard Meier in a newsletter printed and circulated by a self-study group in Munich in the summer of
1975. Interested, she contacted the young man who edited
the newsletter and through him began to monitor developments in the Meier story as reported by witnesses. A few
months later, after seeing photographs Meier had taken,
she decided to interview him for publication.

When von Jacobi arrived in Hinwil in December 1975,
she found herself one of about eighteen people who had
come to the Meier home to listen to the man speak. She
stayed for two days.

"I was impressed," she recalled. "I was convinced that
he had had the experiences he talked about. The facts he
gave me, the pictures, the personal impression he created,
there was nothing wrong. I wanted to make him known,
and to put his story in the papers, because it was real. But
something made him mad, and he told me I should not
publish anything about him, so I left. But it was for his own
good that he become known."

GARY KINDER

Von Jacobi took her article to *Quick* magazine, one of the two largest slicks published weekly in Germany, with circulation in Switzerland and Austria as well. Hesitant to run such a story without verification, the magazine editors assigned a staff member to Hinwil to interview Meier. When the writer returned with substantially the same information von Jacobi had given to them, the editors set the article for publication on July 8, 1976.

The magazine circulated rapidly through the town of Hinwil, carrying a story that astonished Meier's neighbors. For nearly a year and a half they had observed and disapproved of his constant comings and goings at all hours of the day and night, but not one had confronted Meier about his purpose or attended one of the meetings at his home. The reason he now gave for his behavior made them angry and made them laugh all at once: Meier claimed that he had been telepathically contacted by alien beings from a planet in a star cluster known as the Pleiades. Through telepathy, said the article, the Pleiadians frequently had directed Meier to remote locations near Hinwil, where they landed a seven-meter silvery beamship, disembarked, and met with him face-to-face. Most of Meier's contacts were with a female named Semjase, for the Pleiadians, according to Meier, had found that females seemed to be far less intimidating to earth humans. Meier met with her often, and she allowed him to photograph her beamship as it approached for landing and again as it ascended.

Many people laughed. But others seemed awed by the clear, color daylight photographs of the beamships, and captivated by the thought of space beings alighting on earth in a gentle and peaceful fashion. The July article in *Quick* led to a series of articles in various European magazines that appeared throughout the summer and fall of 1976. *Il Giornale die Misteri* in Italy published von Jacobi's original piece on Meier in August; then in September the largest tabloid in Switzerland, *Blick,* ran the front-page title *"Zürcher verblüffte Erich von Däniken"*—"Zurich Man Amazes Erich von Däniken." More articles followed in the

German magazines *Echo der Frau* in October and *Neue Welt* in November. One of Meier's neighbors had a son living in South Africa who even read of Meier in a newspaper there.

The neighbors scoffed at the articles, certain that Meier somehow had perpetrated a hoax with his strange and seemingly purposeless perambulations about the countryside. But for those who visited the Hinwil house to investigate the claims further, Meier presented evidence that looked convincing. He showed scores of bright color photographs of Semjase's ship hovering just above a jagged line of evergreens or edged into the branches of a giant leafless birch. In his journal he had recorded each of his meetings with the Pleiadians; detailed conversations, some thirty minutes, some longer than an hour. The journal now consumed several hundred pages and continued to grow rapidly.

One afternoon, at their request, Meier took a small group into a meadow completely surrounded by tall evergreens. He told them that several nights earlier he had met with the Pleiadians in the same meadow, and that he and Semjase had sat in the grass by the trees and talked for an hour. The people imagined the scene—a glowing, almost weightless craft suddenly descending upon the meadow, the luminescence from its shell pulsating against the wall of darkened trees; then the alighting of a lithesome and humanlike creature, gentle in approach and filled with wisdom.

And there on the ground where the people now stood with Meier in the daylight they saw three large circles, each equidistant to the others, peculiar flattened swirls six feet across, perfectly symmetrical, perfectly rendered in the tall grass.

Those who heard Meier speak on Saturday afternoons in his home and who read parts of his journal found the writings beautifully conceived, far more complex and sophisticated than a man of Meier's station would be capable of imagining. Semjase, said Meier, had told him of life elsewhere in the galaxy, the history of her people and that of the earth. She had taught him to understand earth humankind's place in the galaxy. Order exists in the universe, she said, more advanced civilizations teach the less advanced, and spiritual evolution must parallel technological progress.

"We, too, are still far removed from perfection and have to evolve constantly," she explained to Meier. "When we choose to come in contact with an earth human, we do so because we feel an obligation to the developing universe, and to life which is already existing throughout the universe. We are not missionaries or teachers, but we endeavor to keep order throughout all areas of space. Now and then we begin contacts with inhabitants of different worlds by searching out individuals whom we feel can accept our existence. We then impart information to those contacts, but only when their race has developed and begins to think. Then slowly we and others prepare them for the truth, that they are not the only thinking beings in the universe."

* * *

Meier claimed that he continued to meet with the Pleiadians in the forests of eastern Switzerland, and that the telepathic signals warning him of an impending contact could come at any time of the day or night.

"It happens like a shot," he explained. "Like a cool wind going across your forehead, very, very weak, though." Following that came vibrations inside his head that produced symbols. "On the one hand, it is like pictures which appear, and on the other hand, it is like a voice. There are no words for it . . . it is as if you heard a voice in the symbols."

Meier could be in a room full of people when suddenly his eyes would close, his skin would grow pale, and he would begin to perspire faintly. He would then go to his room and dress in boots, and a jacket if the air was cool, or a gray leather coat if the weather turned bitter. Popi had made him a warm hat like those worn in the mountains of the Middle East, and she would fix him coffee; but if the

16

coffee was not ready in five minutes he would leave without it. He could be gone a half hour or half a day.

One afternoon Meier told his wife that he was about to have a contact and that she and the children were to come with him. Also allowed would be two others who happened to be at the house, one of whom was Hans Schutzbach, a man in his late twenties. Skeptical of Meier from the beginning and watching him closely, Schutzbach had studied every photograph Meier had taken of the beamships, and had helped him to catalogue the photos. He also had driven Meier on many of his night contacts. Although a few witnesses, including Schutzbach, had seen strange lights at night that could have been beamships, no one except Meier had seen one in daylight.

"I put everybody in my car as usual," recalled Schutzbach, "and Billy went ahead on his moped, empty-handed. He told us to just follow him, and he went every which way. Outside Hinwil we finally came to a little hill filled with trees. It was very exciting."

Meier told them, "All of you wait here." Then he drove off.

"I don't remember how long we were standing there," said Popi, "when all of a sudden Atlantis jumped up and screamed, 'Look, Mommy, over there!' We all got up and there was the ship about a thousand meters away. It was big and circular. We wanted to see more, but the ship soon disappeared."

When the child screamed, Schutzbach jumped up and saw something rising out of the forest into the air.

"I presume it might have been a balloon," he said later, "but I have no proof of that." He tried to take a picture, but he was so nervous that at first he forgot, and then he shook so badly he jerked the camera. "That's why the picture is not sharp," he explained. "All you see is a little dot."

The neighbors were certain Meier was crazy. "No one took him seriously," one of them said later. The mayor of a nearby village said that Meier's stories were pure fantasy because *he,* the mayor, had never seen a UFO in the vicinity. People in Hinwil laughed at the mention of Meier. "He is a *Spinner*," they would say, one who is nuts. Or they called him *"Verrückte,"* a lunatic.

"Are we blind," asked one couple, "or are we stupid, because we don't see these things and he does?"

Now when they watched him searching the night sky with binoculars, the neighbors would snicker and say, "He is looking for his lady from the galaxies."

But the articles that by now had appeared in several European countries attracted dozens of curious people from all over the continent. They came to talk to Meier about the messages from the Pleiadians. To the surprise of the neighbors, these people appeared to be well-to-do, most of them driving Mercedes, many all the way from northern Germany. The neighbors could not understand how such people could be so taken in.

"For us and everybody else in the neighborhood," said Franz Hänsler, who lived in an apartment overlooking the farmhouse, "it was a very questionable situation. We all thought he was a 'fantastist.' The whole house was a strange affair."

Marie Hänsler often spoke to Popi, the only neighbor who did. She bought eggs from Popi and considered her "a very, very nice lady. But," she added, "I wanted nothing to do with her husband!" Often Popi came to her crying, and Hänsler would teach her to sew and knit.

"She was not a woman to be envied," said Hänsler. "She suffered."

Meier himself did nothing directly to offend the neighbors. But his teachings, his telling of fantastic stories that they felt were untrue, would "aggravate" them. And sometimes so many cars trailed from the Meier driveway into the street that they blocked traffic. One of the town administrators, Rudolf Rüegg, thought that all of Meier's stories were "imagined, invented. I think he invented it all." Rüegg received many calls from neighbors near No. 10 Wihaldenstrasse, most of them complaints about the presence of so many cars. Once, a worried mother called town officials because her daughter had gone to the Meier home.

In the beginning Popi tried to talk to some of the neighbors. "But I noticed they didn't believe me," she said, "and I started to ignore them. At that time I had my own problems."

One Saturday morning, as she walked in the village with her two sons, she saw two elderly women in front of the town hall. "I didn't know them," she said later. "The children knew them, I think from kindergarten. So they started to play with the children. Then they asked, 'What's your name?' Bashenko could not yet say his name, so he always said Baschel. Then they asked, 'And your last name?' 'Meier.' One of the women made a long face, and the other one asked me if I was the wife of *that* Meier. And I said, 'Yes.' And she said, 'Are you as crazy as he is?'

"The children even had problems in school," continued Popi, "because the parents of the other children did not believe in all this. Atlantis went to kindergarten and the children always made fun of him. They called him 'Ufo' Meier. He came home crying so many times. I told him to go to the teacher, but the teacher didn't believe in all this either. He told me that my husband and I were doing weird things with UFOs, that this wouldn't be the best influence for the kids. I told Billy it would have been better if none of this had happened."

* * *

That summer, 1976, just before all of the publicity on Meier's alleged contacts with the Pleiadians, Hans Schutzbach had accompanied Meier one afternoon to a secluded meadow not far from Hinwil. There, in the presence of Schutzbach, Meier held out a tape recorder and captured the sounds made by one of the beamships. The sound, an eerie and grating noise, like a high-pitched cross between a jet engine and a chain saw, thought Schutzbach, seemed to emanate from a point in open air about thirty feet above

Meier. When Meier raised his hand and circled it the sound increased; when he lowered his hand the sound softened. Then the two, loud and soft, interlaced in an ethereal resonance. Suddenly Meier made an angry gesture and the sounds stopped altogether. Schutzbach turned and saw a game warden and a policeman, one with binoculars, plus another policeman with a dog and two men on motorcycles.

Before Schutzbach left the scene, he had "a real good look around," combing the nearby landscape, walking to the few trees dotting the meadow and examining their branches. He saw no speakers, cables, or balloons, nothing.

Two days later Schutzbach secretly returned to the same meadow with two friends, and the three of them tried to re-create the sounds using the tape he had made with Meier. They hung speakers high in the trees and used amplifiers, but the apparatus was obvious and the sound weak and distant.

Hans Schutzbach drove Meier to perhaps twenty of his contacts in the forests outside Hinwil, many of them on cold, damp nights. A self-proclaimed nosy person, he watched Meier closely, but never saw him make anything or handle any materials that could have been used to fabricate the sounds or the photographs. Schutzbach's biggest problem, though, was the strange landing tracks. Whenever the beamships left them in the tall grass, he would help Meier measure and photograph them. Schutzbach thought about them often. He saw many people try to prove Meier a fraud by duplicating the tracks, but they always looked much different. "The tracks made by Billy were perfect," Schutzbach said. "The ones by other people were a bad copy."

On the night of June 13, 1976, several people accompanied Meier to a clearing in the forest where he was to have a contact with the Pleiadians. It was 2 a.m. when they arrived. Meier told them that to demonstrate the Pleiadians' existence, Semjase had consented to a light display where the ships would take on color and fly in erratic patterns. Among those who waited was Guido Moosbrugger, the principal of a small school in Austria.

Moosbrugger had first come in contact with Meier a few months earlier when he traveled to Munich to attend a series of monthly lectures on UFOs. At one of the lectures Meier had been invited to speak and to show some of his photographs. "I was so fascinated by those pictures," recalled Moosbrugger, "I sent a letter immediately to him in Hinwil and asked him whether I might visit him." Meier had consented and Moosbrugger visited Hinwil in mid-May 1976. During his stay, Moosbrugger had followed Meier to a contact, Meier on his moped, Moosbrugger and Schutzbach in a car. The three men had driven along a dirt path through a field until Meier signaled for them to stop. Then he had told Schutzbach and Moosbrugger to wait there.

"He took off on his motorbike to where the contact would take place," remembered Moosbrugger. "After he left, I thought to myself, I wonder what would happen if I would follow him to see where he went. When he came back from the contact he said that Semjase had welcomed him with the words, 'You brought two men with you. Mr. Moosbrugger had a thought for a short moment what would happen if he would follow you. It didn't concern me though; that was just his honest interest.' "

The two men had sat in the car waiting for Meier to return when high above the tree line two miles away they saw a fire-red disk "as big as the headlights from a distance of one hundred meters." The red disk moved back and forth, then suddenly disappeared. After a few seconds a rotating silver ball spun into view, then two smaller silver spheres appeared beneath the first, also spinning. At the base of the central and largest of the spinning spheres, a large drop formed and hung lower and lower until it broke free and plummeted, disappearing in two or three seconds. Suddenly all of the lights had disappeared.

"After another pause," Moosbrugger explained later, "the very same disk appeared again, became bigger and bigger, and we thought it flew toward us. Then it shrank and disappeared."

Moosbrugger had seen exotic fireworks displays before, but what he saw that night seemed more solid and vivid, like a color cartoon taking place in the blackened Swiss sky; not little explosions of gunpowder, but more the brilliant illumination of strangely behaving physical objects. Later he wrote, "Of course, I cannot be angry if somebody does not believe this story, if they cannot or do not want to accept it as reality. I don't mind if people call me crazy or say I have lots of imagination, but I do not want to be called a liar."

Moosbrugger knew nothing about using a 35mm single lens reflex camera, but he would not return to Hinwil without one. From a friend he borrowed a Pentax, a tripod, and a telephoto lens and had his friend load film into the camera for him, and set the adjustments for nighttime exposures. Three weeks later Moosbrugger had returned to Hinwil, and he now stood in the dark beneath tall pines at the edge of the clearing, his Pentax and his telephoto lens mounted on the tripod. Out of his sight, Hans Schutzbach and his brother, Konrad, also had positioned themselves in the woods, each with a camera. Nearby, the rest of the group ate cake, sipped hot coffee, and watched the dark sky from a knoll.

Suddenly, over the forest, they saw first a red disk, then a silver disk. The lights hovered, then grew, then just as suddenly disappeared. Moosbrugger got the red disk on film. He then bent over his tripod to adjust the angle of his camera when a third disk-shaped object appeared, this one alternating brilliant colors. When Moosbrugger looked up again, this disk had gone, but immediately, very high in the sky, he saw another silver disk edge on, a bar of intense light, with a "glittering rain of fire falling straight down." Moosbrugger captured this last disk on film, an image that looked like a huge brilliant jellyfish with tentacles drifting across the sky. Before and after Moosbrugger photographed the disk, the intense yellow-white bar changed its form several times, then softened to a glow, and the observers on the ground saw the luminous ball fly slowly away until it was only a bright red speck in the distance. Then it ascended rapidly and disappeared. Meier had had his fifty-fifth contact.

* * *

The articles released in the summer and fall of 1976 persuaded more and more people to travel to Hinwil to see Meier. Every weekend visitors came to the house, sometimes as many as twenty, some of them familiar, some of them new. All of them wanted to see Meier's photographs of the beamships and to hear about life elsewhere in the universe. What is the Pleiadian culture like? Their government? Their society? How advanced is their technology? How do they communicate with Meier? What do they look like? Are their intentions peaceful?

According to Meier, the Pleiadians lived to be one thousand years old; Semjase herself was a comparatively young 330. Her home planet, Erra, was only slightly smaller than Earth, yet was populated by far fewer people, less than 500 million. Upon discovering Erra's hospitable but young environment, the Pleiadians themselves had engineered the planet to support life, and today its landscape looked much like the countryside found on Earth, with hills, grass, trees, and running water. They located production and processing facilities in remote regions, away from the population, and utilized nearby uninhabited planets for mining. The Pleiadians told Meier that were he to travel to Erra, he would find species similar to the horse, cow, rabbit, and fish.

Robots and androids performed most physical labor on Erra. The androids looked and acted so human the only way to distinguish them from humans was by their dress. Each wore a uniform, the color indicating the job the android was assigned to perform. They appeared unusually lifelike because their skin was made of living protoplasm, and their brain, too, was an organism capable of natural responses and conversation.

Families not only existed on Erra, but they were purportedly tight and caring. Though sexually mature in their early teens, Pleiadians did not marry until after they had completed their education, a process that began when they were four years old and lasted until they reached seventy. By that time they would have acquired specific skills in fifteen or sixteen disciplines, or, in the case of Semjase, as many as thirty.

There was no government.

"They have, what you call here, 'spiritual leaders,'" Meier told those who came to see him. "And the highest form that they have for their leadership they call Horralft. It's a form of life that's not hard face and body, and not a real spiritual form. It's a middling between both of them. If you put your hand into them, it will go through. The Horralft will not give out orders. They give out something else, what we call 'suggestions.' And then each one on the planet, by his own wisdom in evolution, tries to do his best out of this."

* * *

With all of the people coming to her home, to see her husband, taking up his time, Popi felt as alienated as she had when she first moved to Switzerland. When she was only seventeen, Popi had met Meier on Christmas Day, 1965, in the city of Thessaloniki, Greece. Meier was then nearly twenty-nine. Only a few months earlier he had lost his left arm. A month after they met, Meier had asked Popi to marry him, and when the girl's mother would not consent, the two of them fled to a small town where they were married on February 13, 1966. For four years afterward they had traveled from Switzerland to India and back again, working and living in Pakistan, on the Isle of Crete, in the mountains of the Middle East, and in India. When they returned to Switzerland, Popi understood little of the Swiss German spoken in her husband's country. A few years later, when the contacts began, she communicated better in Swiss German, but she still knew so little High German that she found her husband's writings about the contacts difficult to read. "I tried to read them," she remembered, "but I just didn't understand anything. So I made myself a wrong picture of all this.

"It got bad," she continued, "when all these people began coming to Hinwil to see my husband. Most of them were women, and he used to take many of them to the contact sites. I was very jealous at that time. Not that I was thinking he would see another woman. It's just that nobody ever said they would watch my children so I could go with him. They just came to him and said, 'Let's go!' So I was very angry."

One of those who now attended the meetings regularly was Bernadette Brand, a computer technician. In July 1976, she was riding the train home from work one evening, reading *Quick* magazine, when she saw the article on Meier.

"I remember saying to my colleague," she later recalled, " 'Another crazy who says he is having contact with extraterrestrials.' He asked me whether I believe that baloney. I said, 'Of course extraterrestrials exist, but why would they come here? If they went anywhere it would be to a place where they could learn something, but not here.' I thought it was awful that somebody said he was having 'contact' and fooling people. You should put them behind bars. All of them."

Brand knew the Schutzbach brothers, Hans and Konrad. When they told her about an invalid they knew who claimed to have contact with beings from another star system, she failed to connect their story with the article she had seen in *Quick*. She said to them, "Another crazy around here!"

Konrad tried to tell Bernadette about Meier, but she would not listen. "Don't be so stupid," she said.

"You don't understand," said Konrad, "you have no idea."

And the two of them argued about Meier for the rest of the summer.

One Saturday evening in the fall, Konrad brought his friend Jakobus Bertschinger to Bernadette's apartment for dinner. "The whole time," remembered Bernadette, "they were talking about some woman, like, 'Don't take her seriously. When she's jealous she makes everybody crazy.'"

After dinner the three of them drove to Hinwil to see a "friend" of Konrad's who lived in an old farmhouse in the middle of several apartment buildings. He did not tell her the friend was Eduard Meier, though as they turned off Wihaldenstrasse onto the long alleyway Bernadette guessed who lived there. By now she was willing to meet the man.

A woman met them at the front door and said, "Wait here. You can't come in yet." Then she whispered to Konrad. When they finally entered the house, Konrad told Bernadette, "We can't go into the living room; there is a discussion going on in there."

In the kitchen, Bernadette brewed coffee for the people in the living room, and while the coffee percolated, a woman ran through carrying a large container of water swirling with coal dust. Most households kept this especially fine grade of coal dust for emergencies, to induce vomiting in children. Bernadette wondered, Has someone tried to commit suicide?

Then Meier himself walked into the kitchen and told Bernadette to come into the living room with the coffee. Immediately, she saw a woman with long dark hair slumped over in a chair, and another woman washing her arms and forehead with cold water and patting her on her cheeks to keep her awake. But the woman in the chair was "white, like snow," her head drooping. Popi had swallowed close to fifty sleeping pills. A second woman replaced the first, continuing to bathe her in cool water and pat her on the cheeks. Bernadette thought, If these people keep on doing it this way, this woman is going to die.

When the second woman complained of being tired, Bernadette offered to take her place. She was not as gentle as the other two. She slapped the woman across the face as hard as she could. Then she slapped her again, and again. The woman started to whimper and said to stop hitting her, her teeth hurt so bad.

"If you keep your eyes open," said Bernadette, "I won't hit you anymore."

But the woman again nodded off, and Bernadette slapped her face hard. She wanted to make her angry. For three hours, Bernadette slapped the woman's face.

Then suddenly the woman leaped out of the chair, grabbed Bernadette, and knocked her to the floor. The woman, though slight, was unbelievably strong, and tossed the 160-pound Bernadette around the living room until Meier stepped in and helped Bernadette subdue her. Then Meier wrestled his wife into a bed and told her if she fell asleep she would have to come back into the living room. But she closed her eyes again, and Bernadette slapped her across the face. The woman hit her back, screaming and cursing her husband. Using only one hand, Meier whipped off his belt, got it around her wrists, wrapped it quickly around the back of her knees, and fastened her to a chair. Popi continued to curse him and the others, then closed her eyes and started to nod off again. Bernadette slapped her. Then again, and again. Suddenly Popi strained against the leather belt and broke it, but just as suddenly she seemed to calm down. It was almost 6 a.m. She had last vomited at midnight, and the toxicology center had told them to keep her awake for six hours after she had emptied her stomach of the remaining pills. Bernadette quit, and the other two women went back to washing the woman's face and limbs in cold water.

One Saturday afternoon a few weeks after Popi's attempted suicide, Bernadette accompanied Konrad to a meeting at the Hinwil house with about fifty other people. Though she had expected to despise Meier, she found him gentle and honest, not the *Schwindler* she had imagined him to be. And this caused confusion, because what the man said of his contacts and his trips into outer space still sounded crazy to her. In a short while she was coming often to the Hinwil house. And late one night, after she had been to see Meier, she was driving home from Hinwil alone.

"As I was driving I got this feeling all of a sudden that I had to stop. I thought, You *are* crazy. All these ships and stuff make you crazy. So I drove on. But that feeling came again, a very strong feeling that I had to stop, so I stopped the car and stayed inside, locking all the doors. Then I waited in the dark, curious what would happen.

"I was looking out the window from my side when I saw a light rise above the forest. It was snow-white, about the width of my hand from where I sat. It stopped for a moment, then went back down, and when it sank back it was fire-red. I thought somebody was playing with fireworks, but this was so precise. Rockets don't do that. I waited awhile and after one or two minutes it rose again. Then all of a sudden it was gone.

"I thought, Should I drive on? No, wait a little longer. And indeed a little farther away, it is hard to estimate, maybe five or six hundred meters, an orange light rose, again from behind the forest. It rose very slowly and it was very big. I would say it was a quarter the size of the moon. This orange light rose and then looked like it was going up stairs, zigzag, and then very quietly it flew away. I could see it for about twenty minutes. From that area you are able to see the Alps, and I saw it disappear in the Alps. It got smaller and smaller."

THREE

On a Friday night in the early summer of 1976, Herbert Runkel and Harold Proch, men in their late twenties from Munich, were cruising the autobahn to Augsburg in an older cream Mercedes. With the windows rolled up they listened to "The White Rose," a radio program from East Germany that aired every Friday at midnight. Each of them held a spicy German sausage in one hand and a liter of Coke in the other. Herbert, who was in charge of quality control at his father's insulation factory, smoked his Camels; Harold, a professional photographer with a neatly trimmed dark beard, cradled a pipe. They had been close friends now for six years. The Friday night drives on the autobahn to Augsburg had become a ritual, a time to talk.

As always they talked of many things, but one thing that Harold specifically wanted to mention that night was an intriguing article he had recently seen in *Quick* magazine about a man living in Switzerland who claimed to have had contact with beings from another star system. And the contacts, said the man, still occurred regularly. The article even mentioned U.S. presidential candidate Jimmy Carter as one who had seen a UFO when he was Governor of Georgia. Harold had had his own unexplained sighting when he was only five years old. He later told the story:

"That was on the island where I was born. We were at the beach one afternoon, and suddenly from the seaside there came a flying saucer, two or three, I don't remember exactly. They stood still, a little bit in motion for about one minute, maybe fifty meters high. They were big, it's difficult to say how big. They were there for one or two minutes and like a shot they were gone without acceleration. Gone. I never forgot that. I asked my mother, I asked other people, 'What is that? This is not an airplane, what is that?' Nobody could tell me. Nobody could explain to me what they were, why they were here, what it meant. That was in the '50s, 1953, 1954. I was so fascinated. I will never forget that picture."

On their Friday night journeys to Augsburg, Herbert and Harold often had "philosophized" about the universe, the existence of extraterrestrial societies, the possibilities of travel into space over cosmic distances. "As many do, we were trying to find a truth," explained Harold, "but without religion."

Herbert, a compulsive reader, had read UFO stories before. One of these was about the most famous "contactee" ever, the American George Adamski. Adamski had lived on the southern slope of Mount Palomar. In November 1952 he claimed he had had a conversation with a man of slight stature and shoulder-length blond hair who landed in the California desert in a "Scout Ship" from Venus. The alien had come to Earth because his people were concerned about "radiations going out from Earth," caused by the exploding of atomic bombs. Adamski had traveled the world, famous as the first person to claim contact with extraterrestrial beings. He, of course, was a controversial figure, and his few murky photographs of the "Scout Ship," Herbert had read, actually were superimposures using "part of an icebox machine" as a model.

"In the other cases," said Herbert, "the people always talk about religion, how the space people are sent by God to help the people on Earth and that's all crazy. For someone who thinks logically, it is nothing. No," he told Harold, "I'm finished with UFOs. I read about Adamski, I believe there are extraterrestrial people, but all these stories in magazines are hoaxes."

"Before you say that, you should look at the pictures from Switzerland," said Harold. "You have never seen pictures with quality like this." A photographer with many years experience, Harold had been impressed with the pictures in the magazine, and he described each one in detail for Herbert.

When they returned from their late-night journey to Augsburg it was early morning though still dark. A night person requiring little sleep, Herbert regularly went to bed at three, four, five o'clock in the morning, slept for a few hours, then was ready to start the day. That night he was not interested in sleep; he went instead to Harold's apartment to see the article that had so impressed his friend. When Harold unfolded the magazine in front of him, Herbert saw immediately why the photographs had caught his eye. The two-page spread featured a black-and-white photograph of a large silvery ship hovering high above a valley near Hinwil. A series of three smaller pictures showed a similar ship in various positions around a tall pine. In another picture in a field of grass stood Meier himself, a handsome man with hair thinning in the front, and a well-developed right shoulder and forearm. The left sleeve of his white shirt drooped and rose, neatly pinned to his shoulder.

When Herbert saw the layout, he grinned. "This is a better hoax than the rest."

In the past, nearly every report of unusual sightings or claims of contact that Herbert had read about had occurred in South America or the United States, nowhere he could conveniently investigate himself. But this time the story was in Europe. Harold spread a map across his desk, and they found the village of Hinwil to be a little southeast of Zurich, no more than a four- or five-hour drive from Munich. The two of them decided they would drive to Hinwil the following weekend and try to find Meier and talk to him. "It was just curiosity to see if it was true," Harold said later.

* * *

On Saturday morning the following weekend, Herbert and Harold left Munich at daylight and headed south, crossing the Swiss border just after sunup. Driving to Winterthur, then down through the villages near the Pfäffikersee, they arrived in Hinwil about ten o'clock. Not knowing Meier's address, they drove to a kiosk in town, where an old woman selling newspapers and candy told them that Meier lived in a large farmhouse at No. 10 Wilhaldenstrasse. "Why do you want to see him?" she asked. "He's crazy."

When Herbert and Harold arrived at the farmhouse Meier was not at home and would not return for at least two hours. Popi invited them inside for coffee, but they declined. At two in the afternoon, with Meier still gone, Hans Schutzbach arrived. A few minutes later Popi came out to the car and told Herbert and Harold that Schutzbach could answer some of their questions, since he knew Billy (her husband's nickname) well and had been on several contacts with him. She again invited them inside for coffee, and this time they accepted.

Inside the old farmhouse, Popi handed them two thick albums filled with photographs. Harold studied several of them closely with his professional eye. "As much as I know about photography," he said later, "I could not say these photos were faked somehow. They looked real to me."

"For ten minutes we could say nothing," remembered Herbert, "because our mouths were open. In the magazine there were only black-and-white photos in two or three different positions. But these pictures from up and down, from here and there, clear and in color, were perfect."

Schutzbach explained to them how Meier had taken the photographs during his many contacts with the Pleiadians. "If you would like to see landing tracks from a ship," he added, "actually two ships, there was a contact fourteen days ago. They are quite fresh, I can show them to you."

The article in *Quick* had mentioned nothing about landing tracks; Herbert and Harold had no idea such evidence existed. A few hours earlier they had speculated on whether they would find Meier, and if they did, whether his story would hold up or dissolve into nothing but unsupported claims as had all of the others. Now they sat in Meier's house, looking at photographs even more incredible than those they had seen previously. And here was a man who had been with Meier on several contacts offering to show them physical evidence supporting the man's story. The more they saw in the photo album and heard from Schutzbach, the more intrigued they became. Shortly after Schutzbach made his offer, Herbert and Harold were back in the car again, following him through the streets of Hinwil, then out into the country, onto a narrow side road to a place where the road ended. There they got out of the cars and began to walk.

"We walked almost one hundred meters through the woods," remembered Herbert, "and then we came to a place where the wood was closed all around and there was a meadow in it. There was very high grass, maybe a little less than a meter. And there were the six landing tracks from the two ships. I took a picture of them, and I thought, That's not possible, I have never seen anything like that. The grass was turned counterclockwise, right? The interesting thing was the grass was not broken. If you break grass it will lie down, but this grass was not broken. I pulled up some pieces of it and looked at it and it was not broken. I could not understand.

"If you stand at a place like that, the first thing you think is, How did these landing tracks get here? He must come in with a car or with a helicopter or something to make them. But that was impossible. The woods were so close you could not go through with a car."

Except for the landing tracks from the two beamships, only a single set of footprints led from one of the tracks to the edge of the woods and back again. Untouched, the rest of the grass still stood stiff and tall around the six-foot counterclockwise swirls so precisely pressed into tracks. And the meadow in which they lay seemed the perfect place to hold a secret rendezvous: Nearby but secluded and quiet, a thick growth of trees formed a wall over a hundred feet tall to hide the landing and departure of a strange lighted craft.

"The pictures were special," said Herbert, "but when we stood in the woods at this surrounded place and saw the tracks, it was special, special, special. I had never seen that before. It's difficult for me to explain."

Standing at the edge of the forest, Schutzbach explained to Herbert and Harold how the Pleiadians guided Meier telepathically to the chosen site, then landed their ship and disembarked to speak with him unless they desired either to teleport Meier into the ship's hold or break him down and reassemble him instantaneously on board. After Herbert had taken several pictures of the landing tracks, some at a distance, some up close enough to see into the swirls of grass, the three men returned through the forest to the cars and drove back to Hinwil. By that time Meier had returned, his wife told them, but he could not meet with them now; he would meet them in the city of Wetzikon at the Post Restaurant near the railway station at 5 p.m.

After seeing the many photographs in the albums and viewing the landing tracks, Herbert and Harold now thought Eduard Meier was far more intriguing than portrayed in the simple article that only several hours earlier had persuaded them to drive over three hundred miles to Hinwil. Each was far from accepting the reality of the contacts, yet the man's story, from what they had seen, had some substance to it. More than before, they wanted to meet Meier and question him to see if this knowledge from the Pleiadians seemed genuine or was filled with the contradictions of one obviously in touch with no source but his own earthly imagination. They drove alone to Wetzikon and arrived at the Post Restaurant just before five o'clock. About thirty minutes later, as they sat talking at an outside table, Meier walked up in the company of the Schutzbach brothers and extended his hand to Herbert.

"I never saw him before," Herbert said later, "only the picture in the magazine. And he came straight to me, extended his hand, and said, 'Hello.' It was a strange feeling when I looked into his eyes, like, 'I know this man.' I don't know his voice and laughter, but I look at the eyes. 'I know this man.'"

For the next three hours on that warm summer evening the five men sipped hot coffee and iced Coke at a table under a shade tree. Harold questioned Meier about the photos they had seen in the albums, but Meier seemed to know little about photography. His knowledge was summed up in the phrase, "I push the button . . . and it works."

Herbert had read many books on astronomy and space travel. He was familiar with some of the mythology behind constellations; he knew about the origins of the universe and that over 200 billion stars now spin in the slowly revolving galaxy known as the Milky Way, and that for every star in the Milky Way there was thought to be an entire galaxy in the universe; he knew, too, about the formation of star systems and the conditions necessary for the evolution of life. He even understood the basic thought behind Einstein's theory of relativity and the problems it presented for faster-than-light travel.

"For three hours I asked questions about these things," he later said, "and all the answers came correctly, quickly, and logically. He would give an answer, and maybe one hour later he would give another answer to another part and it was all correct. All such brilliant logic. I read many books . . . but there is no sequence inside, no logical connection, and that was the first thing I found fascinating about the conversation with Billy. He took his time and always tried to answer a question so I was completely satisfied.

"We talked about his personal life, too, and he said he had only an elementary school education. I know many people who have been only to elementary school, and I've never heard any of them speak like someone with a Ph.D. He speaks like this, and it makes me wonder. When he speaks of certain things I think, There must be some way he knows that."

* * *

A month later, after exchanging letters with Meier, Herbert, this time alone, drove again to Hinwil to continue quizzing the man and, he hoped, to see more evidence. When he arrived on the outskirts of Hinwil, however, he detoured into the forest where Schutzbach had shown him the fresh landing tracks.

Despite two weeks of unusually hot August weather with no rain, the grass that had been pressed into the large flat swirls continued to be green and springy. And though they were now six weeks old, the tracks stood out as distinctly as on the afternoon Herbert had first seen them. Like Schutzbach and others before him, he could not understand how the large counterclockwise swirls could be so precisely pressed into the tall grass without crushing it. But if the grass had been crushed it now would be brown and dry. And since it was not brown and dry, nor crushed or broken, why did it not rise up again? For the next five weekends Herbert would return to that same site, but the grass never stood; it merely continued to grow round and round in a peculiar flat swirl. "Then the farmer came and cut the grass," said Herbert. "The tracks still were fresh. I saw that with my own eyes."

Herbert's second experience with Meier proved as intriguing as the first, and he returned again the following weekend. For hours he studied the photographs and talked to Meier about the experiences. His initial cynicism over the man and his alleged contacts slowly turned to curiosity, and for the next year he traveled every weekend to Hinwil, sometimes alone, sometimes accompanied by Harold. He stayed with the Meier family, sleeping in a small bedroom at the farmhouse and watching Meier closely. He was free to roam all levels of the house, and he spoke frequently with Popi, helping her with her German and explaining the contact notes, which she tried to understand. They developed a close friendship, as Popi relied on Herbert for the moral support and understanding her husband now had no time to give her. But Herbert saw and heard nothing suspicious. Popi, if she kept any secrets, divulged nothing. Herbert constantly searched but found no equipment, rigging, or models, not even scientific journals or technical books from which Meier might glean his knowledge of so many things. Meier never left the house unless it was to go on a contact, usually late at night, and no one came to the house to meet with him secretly.

"I saw Billy from morning to night," he later recalled, "and I never saw him making things like maybe speakers. I never saw him take pictures, I never saw a model. I never saw anything that looked like a model or balloon. I knew every room in his house, and I never saw anything. That's the reason I went there; I wanted to see him do something. But I never saw anything. Month after month I stayed in Hinwil, but he did nothing, no people came, nothing."

* * *

Herbert had known Meier for several months, when one night after Meier had had a contact, Herbert saw a dark red light rise above a secluded wood behind the Hinwil house. The light stopped. It moved to the left, then to the right. It changed color from dark red to pale blue and back to red again. Then it suddenly shot quickly into the sky and disappeared.

Another time, on a cool summer evening about seven or eight o'clock, Herbert and some others were working near the Hinwil house. When Herbert looked up he saw Meier suddenly smiling.

"What's happened?" he asked.

Meier replied, "I must go to a contact."

Then he ran quickly toward the woods, some distance from the house.

"Billy disappeared in seconds, running to the wood," Herbert said later, "and then all of us, the Schutzbachs and I, maybe one other person, heard the sound. It was coming from the wood."

The ethereal chords whined above the trees like no sound Herbert had ever heard. And he knew that Meier had nothing with him, nothing but a shirt and a pair of trousers. Nor, he was certain, could the sound have come from speakers wired in the trees; it seemed to emanate from no single source. "I am not crazy," said Herbert. "I listened to the sound."

And the contacts continued. Nearly every weekend when Herbert returned to Hinwil, Meier had added to the contact notes and shot more film of the beamships. He now had taken photographs of six variations of Pleiadian spacecraft, singly and in pairs, three, even as many as four, hovering over a valley or just above the tree line in bright sunlight. People who heard of Meier and, like Herbert and Harold, came to investigate for themselves, arrived filled with doubt and curiosity; but the photographs softened their skepticism and the contact notes seemed convincing because they were, in the words of Herbert, "absolutely logical." Then Meier began taking others to the actual contacts, and though none ever participated, each had stories to tell.

Two years had now passed, and contacts that once occurred during the day, affording Meier the opportunity to take his remarkable photographs, now came later and later at night. The weather often was inclement and Meier rarely rode his moped alone into the hills. Instead, Jakobus or one of the others present when the telepathic signal came through would drive him to the appointed place, wait in the dark, and then drive him home again. In that first year since coming to Hinwil, Herbert drove Meier to five contacts and saw him return from at least ten others.

Late one cold and foggy night, Herbert went with

Meier and Jakobus to a contact. Meier wore his boots and a medium gray leather coat, and Jakobus drove the three of them in his blue Volkswagen, Herbert sitting in the backseat. As always, Meier sat in the front seat, giving directions as he received telepathic instructions from the Pleiadians.

"It was always back and forth, back and forth," Herbert remembered. "I never knew this area well, but I did not feel we actually traveled a very long way. We always went around and around because he wanted to be sure that no people were following. After a short time, he said, 'We must stop here,' and then we stopped. And then he said, 'Oh, let's go back a little bit.' Then we went back about fifty or a hundred meters and he said, 'Okay, now you stop.'

"I remember the place that night," he continued. "It was a narrow dirt path, difficult for two cars to pass. At the left side was a little space, maybe for turning, and we stopped there. There were small trees on the left, and the main wood was on the right side. And he went to the right side over the path, and then a little bit down and into the woods. We sat in the car, then got out, walked, and looked up to the sky, but it was full of clouds and it was nighttime so you could not see anything. It was not raining, but it was wet and foggy. I stood outside with Jakobus a short time smoking a cigarette, and all my clothes became wet. We discussed nothing about the contact and nothing about Billy; we discussed cars, funny things about life, nothing special, nothing about the case.

"We were completely in the deepest night in the deepest woods. And we stayed with the car two hours waiting for him. I said, 'What is he doing?' Then he finally came back.

" 'You're crazy,' I said. 'You stayed a long time, it's too cold.'

"He said, 'I stay in the ship, I'm not cold.'

"I took his hand; it was quite warm. We were freezing. I said, 'Was it nice?'

"He said, 'Yes.'

"Then I saw he was dry. When it's so wet outside the

39

leather coat should have been wet first. But he was quite dry.

"And he was very happy," continued Herbert. "When he came back he was always happy. Sometimes he was mad, sometimes he was sad, like everybody else. But when he came back from a contact he was always happy, very quiet and peaceful. I think that's the word."

When Herbert and Harold returned from a contact with Meier they would all talk till five, maybe six, in the morning, Herbert and Harold drinking Pepsi, Meier drinking coffee with cream, and all of them smoking. They talked about space and the extraterrestrial societies that flourish there, the power they used to propel their ships, the weapons they employed, their social system and domestic concerns. They also discussed the problems of planet Earth, its true history, future wars, and prophecies.

"These were the most interesting nights I ever had in my life," Herbert recalled. "When I spoke with him I always had the feeling he knew many, many things that other people did not know. And he had an especially good way of explaining things. But I never saw him reading science books. He never did that. And he never said to me, 'You must believe this' or, 'If you do not do that you cannot have this.' He was able to do too many things we never understood."

Herbert found Meier's story to be "completely different" from what he had read in books about other so-called contactees. With the others, the writing was always from an earth perspective.

"Adamski, Howard Menger, and many women say they have contacts with other intelligences from Mars or Venus," explained Herbert. "I read those books, too, but I know that what's written inside is totally crazy. They say we have life on Venus, and if you go to the other side of the moon there are cows and sunshine. Or the whole Earth is watched by UFOs that control everything. Or the UFO people are in the government in different countries. That's crazy. In Billy's writings, especially the first seven hundred pages or so of the contact notes, you always have the feeling this is not the mind of an earth person. It's completely different. I have known Billy too long a time, and Billy is not crazy."

* * *

Harold traveled to Hinwil less frequently than Herbert, though still often. One afternoon in the winter of 1977, he stood in the attic of the old farmhouse helping Meier print the contact notes. Suddenly, Meier's forehead began to glisten and his eyes closed. After a few seconds, the color returned to his face and his eyes opened once again. When Harold asked him if he was all right, Meier said only that there would be a contact later that night.

In the kitchen after dark, Harold and Jakobus waited for Meier to receive another telepathic contact. About one o'clock Meier came into the kitchen, saying it was time to leave. They drove in Jakobus's old blue Volkswagen for almost an hour until they reached a narrow dirt road in the forest, where Meier told Jakobus to stop.

"It was pitch dark," Harold later remembered. "Billy said he would leave, and we had to wait there. Jakobus was so scared he trembled. I still remember that."

The night was bitter, ten to fifteen degrees below zero on the Celsius scale. While waiting for Meier to return, Jakobus stayed close to the car; but Harold, trying to keep warm, paced back and forth about a hundred feet away. The two men said little to each other. Meier had not been gone long when suddenly they heard the sound of the beamship. Months earlier, Harold had heard the original cassette of the sounds, the ones recorded the afternoon Hans Schutzbach had stood in a field with Meier and listened to the eerie resonance until the police came. Harold had noted immediately that there were other sounds as well on the tape—a car horn, a dog barking in the background. Now, as he stood in the dark and the cold listening to the strange warbling noise, he strained to hear the telltale bark of a dog or the honk of a horn, either of which would have proved to him that Meier was simply

41

rebroadcasting the same recording. Harold had served in the army for two years, where he had been trained to detect the origin of sounds in the forest at night. But that night, as he listened, he had no idea from where the sound came.

"I tried to find out whether it came from above, below, or the side," he recalled. "When you hear a sound it reflects from the sides. But you could not know where this came from." Nor did he hear any other sound, only the eerie pulsating of the beamship somewhere in the sky above their heads.

When the sound subsided, the walkie-talkie crackled with Meier's voice, directing them to a place about a mile away, where they found him at the side of a road waiting.

As a professional photographer, Harold was even more intrigued by Meier's photographs, convinced that if Meier had faked any of the photos he would be able to detect the forgery. He studied them constantly. In a darkroom, he himself had produced many photo montages, juxtaposing people and figures to make them appear real.

"I know how to do it," he said. "For a montage to look real you need a dark background." Almost all of Meier's hundreds of photos showed the beamships in a bright blue sky, sometimes occupied by white clouds.

Harold picked up one of Meier's photos as an example. "I would not know how to do this. I could make a model and pull it up, but there is somebody coming by for sure, a farmer, a hunter, tourists, and they would ask, 'What is this man doing?' "

Another photo, referred to as the sunlight scene, showed a beamship hovering next to a large leafless tree at the edge of a cliff. Light from the setting sun burnished the bare branches of the tree and highlighted the curved rise of the ship. "I have enlarged that picture," explained Harold. "I also put the slides in the projector and I made them small, not big, and then I looked at them with a magnifying glass. You can see more that way. You can see that the branches are in front of the ship, not behind. You must be blind not to see that." With the tree over thirty feet tall and obviously some distance from the camera, this would mean that the ship behind the branches of the tree was also a large object, as large as the twenty-one feet Meier had claimed.

Harold once sneaked into Meier's locked study and carefully went through every drawer, box, and shelf, searching for models, sketches, experimental film, anything to indicate that Meier had somehow fabricated the photos or any of the other evidence. He found nothing.

* * *

One of the most convincing things Herbert ever witnessed Meier do occurred not in the cold and damp forest, but in the Hinwil house kitchen with no one else around. Typically, Herbert had stayed up late, alone, sitting on a kitchen stool and leafing through a magazine with one hand. In his other hand he held a knife, carving thin slices of salami and feeding them to the Meier's St. Bernard, Anita.

About three o'clock in the morning, he heard someone coming down the stairs. Meier appeared in the doorway of the kitchen in his nightdress.

"What are you doing?" said Herbert. "You should be sleeping." He could tell by the lines on the man's face that Meier had been stirred from a deep sleep.

"I must go for a contact," said Meier.

"You're crazy," said Herbert.

But Meier said that he had been contacted and he had to go. After awakening Popi and asking her to fix him some coffee, he gathered up his clothes, boots, and leather coat, and walked out into the night. An hour later he returned, drank another cup of coffee to warm up while he took off his clothes, then went back to bed.

Why did he do that? Herbert asked himself. Nobody is here. Only me. He doesn't need to do it for me. It's crazy. When there are many people here maybe he would feel he must give a demonstration, maybe he would go for a pretend contact. But there is nobody. Nobody.

FOUR

In the early fall of 1964, Timothy Good toured India as a violinist with the London Symphony Orchestra. The son of a violinist, Good had begun playing the violin at age five and later trained at the Royal Academy of Music in London for four years. Now, at age twenty-two, he had been with the London Symphony Orchestra for a year, playing in the first violins. The tour of India, his first, was to last several weeks, taking Good to all of the country's major cities.

In New Delhi, the orchestra stayed at the Ashoka Hotel, and one afternoon between rehearsal and the concert Good took some time to browse through an artist's boutique that earlier had caught his eye in the lobby of the hotel. He had been struck by several paintings, especially a collection of oil portraits of Indian leaders including Gandhi and Nehru, surrounded in pale auras. As he looked through the glass at the paintings now, a woman in the shop approached him and invited him in.

Good introduced himself and learned that the woman was Elizabeth Brunner, the artist who had painted the unusual portraits. The two of them talked at length about the paintings and Brunner's inspiration; then the conversation led to things metaphysical, and finally to Good's hobby, the study of UFOs.

In the mid-1950s, while still in his teens, Good had become fascinated with the existence of flying objects no one seemed able to explain. Pilots observed them, radar confirmed the pilots' observations, yet the objects always outmaneuvered and outpaced the fastest jets. Good wondered, as did many people, if the governments of various countries knew more about these mysterious objects than they were telling the public. Now traveling all over the world with the orchestra, he had the opportunity on his own to investigate reports of strange sightings and claims of contact. As he explained more of his hobby to Brunner, he sensed in her someone who also believed in the existence of extraterrestrial societies and their probable visitation to the earth. After they had talked on the subject a short while, Brunner made a suggestion to Good that he found intriguing.

As Good remembered, "She said, 'You ought to meet a chap who's fallen in love with a spacewoman. He's just left India.'"

Unfortunately for Good, the man had been expelled from the country only a few days earlier, allegedly for having no money. Brunner surmised that the man was asked to leave the country for another reason, which she told to Good.

"She felt it was perhaps because he talked too much," he recalled. "It's a dumb thing to talk about UFOs in India. She advised me not to do so, publicly at any rate, while I was there."

Brunner then showed Good an article from the New Delhi *Statesman* dated a few days earlier, September 30, 1964: "The Flying Saucer Man Leaves Delhi—Swiss Claims He Has Visited Three Planets."

Good began reading. In the article, the writer gave the flying saucer man the pseudonym Edward Albert. He wrote that he found Albert "sitting bare-bodied in one of the cave-like monuments at Mehrauli near the Buddha Vihara." The man had been living in the cave for five months, ever since his arrival in India.

"Mr. Albert sounds rather weird," wrote the reporter. "But then he clearly is not eager to talk about his experiences which, to say the least, are remarkable. Indeed, the little that he has to say has to be pried out of him. He doesn't want publicity; he doesn't care if anyone believes him or not."

The man had revealed to the reporter, "I have not only seen the objects from outer space, but have taken photographs and even traveled in them." He showed the reporter about eighty photographs, "all taken with an old folding camera and neatly kept in an album." But when the reporter asked for two or three of the photos to illustrate his article, the man "politely" declined his request. He told the reporter, "I can't spare them." He said he had taken over four hundred such photos, but most of them had been stolen in Jordan and India.

Since the reporter could show none of the photos to his readers, he took notes on what he saw as he viewed the album and used his descriptions to give the readers a feel for what Albert had photographed. "The objects in the photographs vary in size and shape," he wrote. "One is a globular object with a round disc in the centre; another is funnel-shaped; a third is like a neon lamp; a fourth is a big, bright cross and others bright zigzag lines. Some of these have been taken on the ground and some flying in the sky." The man now sitting in the cave claimed he had taken the photographs in Greece, Jordan, and India.

Good read on. Besides having photographed the ships, Albert claimed to have been visited frequently by entities from elsewhere in the galaxy and to have traveled to at least one other inhabited planet. On this unusual planet, "All of the objects were white," he told the reporter. And the space people themselves looked very much like earth humans except they were taller, had a certain glow about them, and were spiritually more advanced. They expressed themselves through the transmission of thought patterns.

The reporter noted that the man's belongings consisted of only a few articles of clothing, his photo album, a folding camera, and two small bags. Traveling with him was a pet monkey named Emperor. At the conclusion of the interview Albert and Emperor were to pack up their few belongings and, with a new friend from Germany who had lent Albert a small amount of money, to begin hitchhiking back across the Middle East and eventually return to Switzerland.

Before they parted ways, he told the reporter, "I have a mission to fulfill," but he refused to say what it was. "I will disclose it when the time comes, positively before a year."

"The story of Mr. Albert is as incredible as it is startling," the reporter ended his article. "He proposes to relate to German scientists his experiences, show his photographs and the objects that he says he has collected from the planets he visited. Has Mr. Albert created history, or is he a mystic who has let his imagination run wild? Time alone will tell."

Many years after the article appeared in the New Delhi *Statesman,* the reporter, S. Venkatesh, responded to a letter inquiring about the mysterious Mr. Albert. He wrote: "I distinctly remember meeting the man and he seemed, on recollection, very serious about what he was saying. I for one would be eager to know what he did later on, whether he encountered any more space men and ships and whether he disclosed anything to anyone later, as he promised he would."

Timothy Good read the article twice and returned it to Elizabeth Brunner. She herself had met and spoken to Albert, but other than suggesting another friend who might be able to help Good locate the man, she could add little to what was in the article.

"She said he was obviously full of this girl," remembered Good, "in love with this girl from outer space." She added only that she felt he was "sincere, and very enthusiastic." Not certain of the man's name and having only the few clues with which Brunner and her friend could provide him, Good decided nevertheless that the story was sufficiently interesting for him to pursue.

"I don't like to make judgments on people until I've met

them myself," said Good later, "so in 1965 I eventually tracked him down. It was very difficult."

The man lived in eastern Switzerland in the foothills southeast of Zurich. His real name was Eduard Albert Meier. During a winter concert tour in 1965 the London Symphony Orchestra played in Zurich, and while there Good went looking for Meier and found that he was living with a sister in a small village not far from Hinwil.

"I actually went out there in the snow and got out to his house and he wasn't there," recalled Good, "so I just had brief words with his sister, who didn't speak any English. She gave me a number where I could contact him, and I spoke to him on the telephone afterwards. He told me that he had recently had an accident, the result of which he had lost an arm. I can't remember much more than that. He gave me the impression of sincerity at that time. Subsequent to that, I informed Lou Zinsstag about Meier; however, she didn't do anything about it for a long while. She had difficulty getting in touch with him, he was pretty elusive. But she tracked him down eventually and had lots of meetings with him."

* * *

Considered to be the grande dame of European ufology, Louise Zinsstag, now gray haired and in her early seventies, lived in Basle, Switzerland, along the northern border where the Rhine separates Germany from France. An articulate and cultured woman who wrote and spoke several languages, including Russian, Zinsstag was diminutive and energetic. Despite her religious convictions, a colleague once wrote of her, "A true 'bon-viveur,' Lou had a tremendous sense of humour and a healthy appreciation of good food and wine." In addition to her consuming interest in UFOs, Zinsstag pursued her passion for the theater, cinema, museums, and foreign travel.

Zinsstag's mother had fourteen brothers and sisters, nearly as many aunts and uncles, and scores of cousins, one of whom was the famous Swiss psychiatrist Carl Gustav

Jung. Though her second cousin was more than twenty years her senior, Zinsstag spoke and wrote to him often, especially in his later years. Perhaps their most common topic of conversation was one of Jung's lesser-known works, a lengthy essay published in 1958 entitled *Flying Saucers: A Modern Myth of Things Seen in the Sky*. Jung wrote in his introduction to the book:

> These [UFO] rumors, or the possible physical existence of such objects, seem to me so significant that I feel myself compelled to sound a note of warning. It is not presumption that drives me, but my conscience as a psychiatrist that bids me fulfil my duty and prepare those few who will hear me for coming events which are in accord with the end of an era.

Taking their cue from the word "myth" in the title, those who denied the existence of UFOs claimed that Jung's essay explained away UFO sightings as "psychic projections" and "mass hallucination." But though Jung did not know what UFOs were, he was certain they did not leap whole from the human imagination.

"We are dealing with an ostensibly physical phenomenon," he wrote, "distinguished on the one hand by its frequent appearances, and on the other by its strange, unknown, and indeed contradictory nature."

Jung himself had studied the subject for ten years before he published the book.

> So far as I know, it remains an established fact, supported by numerous observations, that Ufos have not only been seen visually but have also been picked up on the radar screen and have left traces on the photographic plate. . . . It boils down to nothing less than this: that either psychic projections throw back a radar echo, or else the appearance of real objects affords an opportunity for mythological projections.

By the time Jung died in 1961, his cousin Lou Zinsstag had amassed the largest collection of UFO case histories and photographs in Europe. Eventually she would publish the first UFO journal in central Europe and write two books on the subject. One of the books would be about the famed contactee George Adamski, with whom she began a correspondence in 1957 that lasted for seven years. So active and outspoken on the topic of UFOs was she that a senior official of the Swiss Security Services once summoned her to his office and ordered her to publish nothing more on the subject. On his desk lay a magazine open to the page on which her most recent article appeared.

Zinsstag had met Timothy Good in 1965, not long after Good had discovered "Mr. Albert" and tracked him down to a small village in eastern Switzerland. When Good related the story to her, she recalled having heard about the man even before that, but she could remember nothing of the circumstances, only that in 1956 or 1957, somebody had written an article about a Swiss boy named Eduard Meier who had had his first encounter in 1942, when he was only five years old. In the nearly ten years that had passed since then, she forgot completely about him.

But after Good passed along what little information he had on Meier, Zinsstag made no effort to contact him until the summer of 1976, when news of Meier's experiences made its way to Basle before the first article appeared in *Quick*. On June 28, 1976, Good received the first of a long series of letters from Zinsstag, as she pursued the Meier case and relayed to Good her impressions of the man and his story.

"I got in touch with Eduard Meier, having found out his address through a schoolboy from Bern who came to see me," she wrote in her first letter. "I wrote to Ed and received a very friendly letter with a dozen of his pictures, some of them quite extraordinarily good. I sent money for more. He said he has about 250 of them, all shot by himself. He also has got some films. I wrote him that I shall come to see him as soon as possible. He says that he is fulfilling a task given to him almost forty years ago, so I expect him to come as a high priest, but never mind when you see his photographs."

Less than two weeks later, Zinsstag became one of the many who began to travel to Hinwil to seek out and speak to Meier. When she returned from her visit, she again wrote to Good on July 10, 1976.

"Eduard is a young invalid, 38, who has lost his left arm in a car accident some ten years ago. He was a truck driver. He looks intelligent and fit and uses his right hand with astonishing dexterity. His wife is a Greek girl spiritually handicapped as far as we found out, but they have three little children. They live in a very neglected household in a very old farmhouse with poor furniture, guarded by an enormous dog who loved me. Eduard goes out very seldom and never alone, and never without his gun, so he told me. He has been shot at once or twice. . . . He's been in contact with ET since his fifth year. Together with his father he saw a ufo and met an ET back in 1942. Since then it happened with some regularity that every eleventh year he gets new visitors.

"For a hundred francs, I shall get 50 color photos, and the young man promised me to make a good representative choice. Besides the ufo pictures and a splendid film of twenty minutes, he showed us some other pictures which I have difficulty to describe. Eduard told me that he had been in outer space several times and he has seen some of our planets from a rather near viewpoint. First, I could not believe it and just made polite noises, but then he showed us those photos. Among them is one which would make a sensation. In their flying saucer he and his companions watched the latest Soyuz-Apollo coupling, and for a moment they were at a distance of three meters. In these pictures you see the back of a Russian cosmonaut, his helmet, and the three letters 'COI' on his outfit. On another one you can see the coupling maneuver in action, much better than on TV. Other pictures I will not describe in the letter. It's too difficult.

"I'm still at a loss how to judge the man. His education is even poorer than the one of George [Adamski], but I don't mind that. Yet I don't like his manner. . . . He is anti-religious, and as far as I can see from a pamphlet of his he defends the witches, attacking the Roman Church for ignoring them, etc. He might very well be a witch himself. His eyes gave me this impression from the beginning. But he's honest, frank, polite up to a certain point, and, I can understand this very well, very impatient and a bit tired of being interrogated all the time. While we were there he had several telephone calls, one from Budapest, others from Austria and Germany."

Before a few weeks had passed, Zinsstag had traveled again to see Meier and again, on August 6, 1976, she wrote to Good of the latest impressions she garnered during this second visit.

"I have seen Eduard Meier again, the most intriguing man I have ever met. He showed me other photographs of such a nature that I can hardly mention it. When he starts talking you can well imagine listening to a demented person, everything he says is so fantastic. But lo, there are his photos from outer space, which nobody has ever seen, not even at NASA I'm sure. . . . He sends his respects and love and looks forward to seeing you sometime in autumn. He still remembers your telephone call. He is so modest and sincere he even told me of his time in jail. His life story sounds so fantastic that I can hardly believe it. But one look at his photos reassures me every time."

* * *

For nearly a year, Zinsstag read about Meier in magazines, read his contact notes and teachings, and visited with him for hours in Hinwil. An intelligent woman who for twenty years had known and talked at length with numerous "contactees" besides Adamski, Zinsstag was neither naïve nor gullible, nor was she willing to dismiss all contactee claims as nonsense. Forces exist, she thought, for which we presently have no explanation. But she clearly did not know what to make of Meier. After each meeting and often between her interviews, she wrote to Good about the case. Another letter, postmarked October 24, 1976, closed: "More than ever I think that he is a good man, although Esther [a journalist and friend of Zinsstag's] is afraid that he could be under a magic spell or even a witch himself. I don't think so, but there's something very unusual about this man, as you will notice."

In the fall of 1976, Zinsstag, accompanied by Good, flew to the United States to speak to various people in ufology, to interview alleged contactees, and to gather more material for the book on Adamski that they would co-author. A few months after they had returned from the States and she had had time to visit Hinwil, Zinsstag wrote a letter to Good dated January 3, 1977.

"Re: Meier. I am now on such good terms with him that it won't be a problem to see him anytime I like. However, I am holding back, because I can't get rid of the idea that this woman Semjase does him no good. . . . I am sure that within a rather short time she will let him drop, because it is out of the question for him to fulfill her wishes. . . . What he misses is a name, a good one, and he will never get that because he was in prison as a youngster. And most of all he misses a real education, although I must say his technical knowledge is absolutely astonishing. He seems to have gotten a certain pre-education in his twenties while he traveled in Syria and Israel and Jordan, which serves him very well for understanding the difficult things Semjase talks through with him. . . ."

A month later Zinsstag wrote, "If Meier turns out to be a fake, I shall take my whole collection of photographs to the ferry boat and drown it in the old man river of Basle."

* * *

By the fall of 1976, Meier's contact notes had grown to over eight hundred pages, and the run of articles in European magazines had aroused the curiosity of hundreds of people who had traveled to see him. Witnesses later said they saw people lined up outside the Hinwil house as though waiting in line to buy tickets for a soccer match. Perhaps more difficult to know for certain, it seemed that others even followed Meier whenever he left his house, hoping to glimpse one of the silver beamships or the fair-haired Semjase, or catch Meier in the act of fabricating his photographs with models or somehow creating the strangely swirled landing tracks. Once, Meier and others swore, he was followed by a Volkswagen with rotating antennas mounted on the roof.

But the contacts continued, and Meier described to his visitors what would happen each time the Pleiadians directed him to a contact site in the hills: First, he said, the silver beamship would appear and wait for him silently a hundred or two hundred feet off the ground. Then with the magnetic force field temporarily reduced, Meier would walk beneath the hovering ship, and in a moment, untouched by any visible force, his body would begin rising toward the hold. During the five-second transfer from ground to sky, Meier could observe the landscape.

"If you have a channel that goes up with the wind, and you put in a feather, you have exactly the same thing," he said, describing the experience.

Those who heard his stories imagined a darkened, secluded site suddenly aglow, with the inner circle of trees seeming to undulate in a pure and gently pulsating light. Though Semjase sometimes landed the ship and met with Meier in the meadow, she now utilized the "anti-gravity" system more frequently. A third, even faster, method was potentially dangerous: Meier could be dematerialized.

Meier called this method the "teleportic," which worked only, he said, "if I am clear in my head and heart." Using it, the Pleiadians could break down Meier's molecular structure as he sat in his office, rematerialize him on board the ship, converse with him for an hour or two, then break him down a second time and reassemble him in an instant inside his office again, or at the edge of a road to be picked up by Herbert, Jakobus, or one of the others who might have driven him to the contact. When he was "upped" by this method, Meier could feel nothing; the danger lay in the return, for Meier would again have to be clear in head and heart. According to Meier, if the ship hovered high in the atmosphere ready to place him back on earth, and he jumped into the teleportic shaft without his head and heart being clear, he would "die for sure."

"You see," explained Meier, "they take me up in this way only when they have checked me over and over. And if there is only a very, very small point which isn't clear, they can't go to it. Then I have to go out on my bicycle or tractor or by car, and they take me up the other way."

The opening in the ship through which Meier entered with the "anti-gravity" method was round and located at the bottom. Meier had seen it either open or closed and did not know how it worked. The interior of the craft Meier described as looking like "a watching central," or security observation room with many small television screens. The windows around the perimeter appeared to be glass and metal at the same time. As the ship entered different atmospheres they changed color; in methane they would turn yellow, in other atmospheres a shade of green, blue, or red. As the ship traveled through interstellar space, a scanning device had to be used for navigation, for in space nothing could be seen through the windows.

Near the ship's controls were three chairs, "like normal chairs, but you can use them as very comfortable seats, or two of them as beds." The beds, however, were not like those on earth, not like "a feather bed" where you sleep on top. The beds in the beamship wrapped around you.

The extensive control panel was dominated by an array of "metallic blots" accommodating one to four fingers or the entire hand. The blots were in rows of different colors—silver, gold, red, blue, yellow—and were never touched; the hand or fingers were only placed lightly over them. Small wheels, switches, and rows of levers completed the instrument panels. "The driving of the ships is very, very easy," said Meier. "There is a red knob, with a small leg, and with it you can do every maneuvering thing you like."

* * *

At each rendezvous, Meier learned more about the Pleiadians, how they viewed themselves and the earth humans, their purpose in coming to the earth and in contacting him. During one of their meetings, Meier asked, "Why do you not appear in mass and show yourselves to the public, and why do you not contact governments?"

"The masses would merely revere us as gods, as in ages past," explained Semjase, "or go off in hysteria. That is why we regard it as prudent to make contact with individual persons only for the time being, to disseminate, through them, the knowledge concerning our existence and our coming to this planet.

"Furthermore, all earth governments are made up of human beings for whom power hunger and a thirst for profits are characteristic. They only want, under cover of peace and friendship, to occupy our rayships, to exercise absolute rule over the earth. But they would not stop there. They would try to capture the cosmos, because they do not know any limits. They, on the other hand, are not even able to create peace and friendship among the nations on earth, not even in their own countries. How then could they be capable of holding such might in their hands as our rayships? We have no interest in revealing ourselves to the general public. It is for the present advisable to maintain contact only with single earth humans, and by them slowly to allow the knowledge of our existence and mission to become known, and to prepare others for our coming.

"A further warning: It lies in the frame of evolution that earth man must develop himself spiritually before he will solve certain scientific secrets. Even then, the danger exists, that the barbarous earth man, exercising his technical knowledge, might use it for evil-minded and power-hungry motives. He must remember that when he attains the necessary techniques, he cannot fly to other planets in the hope that he would always be the victor. Other cosmic inhabitants are not helplessly exposed to attack from another race. There could follow deadly defeat for earth humankind and complete slavery, which would equal the falling back to primeval times. When earth man tries to carry his barbarous greed for power into the cosmos, he must consider his own complete destruction.

"This all must be told to the earth beings, for their spiritual reason is still poorly developed. This was the unfortunate experience of a second race of humans in your own solar system. Their planet was lost in a vast explosion, and nothing remained but the desolate asteroids whirling around your sun."

* * *

The community of Hinwil had plans to destroy the farmhouse at No. 10 Wihaldenstrasse to make way for more apartment buildings. Though the official reason for the Meiers's eviction had nothing to do with the constant presence of so many cars in their driveway, or the strange comings and goings of Meier himself, or his philosophy, the neighbors and town administrators felt relieved when they knew he would be gone soon. In truth, Meier, too, wanted to find a more secluded and private place to live. By Christmas of 1976, he had found a fifty-acre farm that straddled both Kanton Zurich and Kanton Thurgau, near the village of Schmidruti, thirty minutes from Hinwil.

Considerably higher and farther back in the hills, Schmidruti consisted of a primary school, gardening shop, shooting range (made compulsory by the Swiss military for even the tiniest of hamlets), the Gasthaus zum Freihof, a post office, log business, and Subaru dealership with a garage but no showroom. The latter four stood side by side along the cobblestone row bordering the only street winding through the village. Above the farm, at the top of a hill undercut by the road, sat a single military building, used as a barracks, and an underground rocket silo, which occasionally opened its doors and pushed into view a huge and conventionally armed missile. Seventy-five people, most of them farmers, lived in and immediately around Schmidruti.

The Herzog farm, which Meier wanted to purchase, sat behind Schmidruti, a few hundred yards down the cobblestone way, which quickly turned to a dirt and pebble path. Real estate in Switzerland is difficult to find at any price, and good farmland is even more rare. The price for the Herzog farm was 360,000 francs, approximately $240,000. Meier had no money, but visitors who were impressed by his teachings eventually raised or mortgaged that amount. One woman who had recently received an inheritance secured the loan on the farm.

When Meier moved his family in April 1977 from the Hinwil house to the farm at Schmidruti, Herbert Runkel and several others came to help. They moved everything out of the three-story house and put it into cars, trucks, and a borrowed trailer to haul it up to the farm. Herbert, always suspicious, took the opportunity to investigate even more closely the contents of the Meier home.

"We had a big trailer," he recalled, "and we went, I don't know, seven, ten times, up and down. We worked together several days to bring all the furniture, beds, and goods to the cars—all the things from his office, all the books, all the big printing machines. It was a lot of goods. At that time I looked at everything coming out of the house because some people said, 'Maybe he used models, maybe there is some equipment to make models, or there is an old model, a special kind of paper, a special kind of aluminum foil, something like that.' But there was nothing. He had no equipment to make anything. It was only a house for living and for writing."

In a letter to Timothy Good, Lou Zinsstag described the Herzog farm as "a large estate." But the reality hardly fit the description. The Herzog farm was an abandoned fifty acres of weeds, mud, and outbuildings falling down.

"You could compare it to a battlefield," Meier's friend Jakobus described it.

The house had no electricity and no running water. Beneath the three-foot flood in the cellar lay two feet of mud. Old and diseased trees on the land bore little or no fruit, and underbrush grew thick in the surrounding forest. Water that could have been used for irrigation flowed at will, eroding the land in some places while leaving other sections dry.

Meier, with more help from friends, immediately began to renovate the place. Electricity and plumbing would come later. First they removed the mud by shovel and replaced it with dry gravel and poured concrete. Then they put in vegetable gardens, dammed and directed the water, filled ponds with irrigation, shored sagging walls on the barns and farmhouse until they could be rebuilt, and reshingled the roofs. They cut down the old trees and planted new ones, provided pasture for cows, and sowed several acres in crops for the animals. They often worked at night, mixing cement, and they always worked on Sunday. Meier taught everyone how to do the work that needed to be done—how to irrigate, plant, shingle, mix and apply mortar, wire, and plumb. He always worked in a beige one-piece coverall and his black cowboy hat, and was often seen at the wheel of an old green tractor. From midnight to three or four in the morning, when it was quiet, he would work in his office. In the middle of the day he often would experience a cooling perspiration across his forehead, turn pale, and suddenly disappear.

One afternoon Engelbert Wachter and two other men climbed a ladder to the top of the old carriage house, whose rotted walls had been replaced one at a time and which now was being prepared for a roof. The ladder rose and intersected with the roof at a point about twelve feet off the ground. The roof itself, a smooth, open surface thirty feet long by eighteen feet high, angled upward at a pitch of nearly forty-five degrees. Nothing stood near the building. Before they began laying shingles, from bottom to top, Engelbert and the other two men nailed a temporary brace from one side of the roof to the other near the lower edge, a simple platform so they would not fall.

Engelbert, with his pile of shingles, stood next to the ladder, and the other two men were farther over on the roof.

As Engelbert lined up the wooden shingles and pounded them into place, he saw Meier climb the ladder just to his left and start to pass behind him.

"I looked back to see whether there was enough room for him," Engelbert recalled, "and as I turned around Billy was gone. Not even a second had passed. I presumed that he fell down. I called the others and we all went looking for him. We looked out on the road. Nothing. I would have heard it if he had jumped down. But he had disappeared."

Engelbert later said to Herbert, "I felt his fingers tap me on my shoulder. Then I turned and he was gone."

Herbert had been working down below and had seen Meier climb the ladder, then step onto the roof. He looked away for a few moments, then heard Engelbert asking, "Where's Billy?" Herbert yelled up, "He's on the roof."

"Nobody saw him go," remembered Herbert, "and nobody saw him come. And five or six people were always working around the barn. Always. I saw him go to the barn, I saw how he went up to the roof. But he never came down. Nobody saw him come down. Nobody saw him for four hours." Meier suddenly reappeared, sitting on a cement slab by the barn, smoking a cigarette and appearing peaceful as he always did when he returned from a contact.

Another time Meier had left on a contact earlier in the afternoon, simply walking down the dirt path that passed through the farm and continued into the tall woods. Several people had then heard the singing of the ship. No one had seen him since that moment. Now the sun was about to set, though daylight would remain for another two hours. Engaged in more roof repair, Engelbert sat on top of the chicken coop, a building on the other side of the farmhouse that looked out over the deep and partially wooded valley forming the eastern boundary of the farm. He stopped his pounding long enough to light a cigarette, then exhaled and looked down the valley to a large nearby meadow.

"I was looking around," he later said, "looking at the trees, but somehow my glance was pulled back on that meadow. And as soon as I looked back Billy stood in the middle. In the middle of the meadow there are no trees. I looked at that meadow and I could practically see Billy appear out of nothing."

For six months, from the spring of 1977 into the fall, Herbert lived at the farm with the Meier family, the only one outside the family who slept there. The rest came in campers and trailers while they worked on weekends, and Jakobus stayed at his parents' house forty minutes away. During the six months he lived at the farm, Herbert constantly looked for but found nothing suspicious, no pictures, models, or equipment. And Meier never left the farm unless it was to go on a contact. All day, day after day, Herbert would see him either supervising the renovation of the house, barn, and outbuildings or out in the field running the old green tractor.

* * *

In the fall of 1977, Lou Zinsstag, who had visited Meier again at the farm, wrote a final letter on the Meier case to Timothy Good and a few other close friends. She entitled the lengthy missive, "Personal View of Eduard Meier."

"I had heard about this extraordinary man long before I met him," she began. "In the sixties I refused to believe the rumors that Eduard Meier was a true contactee. I rather took him for one of those numerous transmediums pretending to be in contact with space beings and spaceships, getting messages through trance. But at last, in 1976, I met him at Hinwil in the Kanton Zurich. It was because he had sent me some extraordinarily good ufo photos. I now had a feeling that, at least in thought, I had wronged the man.

"Instead of meeting a sickly, soft-spoken invalid, as expected, we found him to be a person full of vigor and strength, very self-assured with a fantastic story to tell. Although we had read and heard many exciting stories of contacts with extraterrestrials, and although we knew well that truth is often more fantastic than imagination, to hear Eduard Meier talk was a real shock. His friend who drives a car took us at once to a set of fresh traces, three identical circles in high wet grass hidden behind a wood in the neighborhood. Later, we listened for more than an hour to his story, and heard him explain his approximately three hundred photographs, including some he said he himself had shot in space. It was breathtaking. Yet, within me, I missed the feeling of joy and sympathy which I really should have felt. Some funny instinct was giving me a kind of negative pulse, signals which concerned Meier's person rather than the things he said and showed us. . . .

"Observing the man more closely, I saw that his features were worn out and hard, and that he had cold and tired eyes. His forehead was deeply lined, and he looked older than his forty years. But his voice was good and strong and healthy, and so were his movements. He was very adept in using his right arm. His smile was sometimes disconcertingly friendly and pure, but the feeling of discomfort never left me. It is still with me.

"This exposé is written for a very few friends who know me well, and also know Meier's story, so I do not need to go into details. With frankness, he told us about his girlfriend Semjase from the Pleiades. At first I felt much sympathy with her for having contacted a poor handicapped man like Meier. She seemed to be giving him some extremely interesting information on space and astronomy and to take him for a ride occasionally. A few months after my visit, Ilse von Jacobi sent me part of his writings, fifteen conversations with Semjase. They proved to be rather disappointing to me and I did not like at all her manner of speech. It sounded often rather faulty and unfriendly, rather frightening. . . .

"In 1976, Meier started to attack in his magazine *Wassermannzeit* every religion in the world, all churches and sects, refuting the need for worship or belief in God. It sounded rather familiar, poison for the people, and so on. The articles were written in an offhand but spiteful, even vicious way, and they sounded so superficial I doubt that either Semjase or Meier knew the difference between religions and such in the established church institutions. . . .

"I liked him less and less, and I stopped writing to him. But I continued to bring interested friends to his place. He always liked meeting new people and was always polite, even friendly, with them. I never talked to him about my objections, mostly because we were never alone. His story and his films never failed to impress me. There was, in my eyes, no reason to doubt his veracity, and soon I found out that the man suffered from a deep inferiority complex, that he was haunted by bad childhood memories, by his experiences at school, in a children's home, in the Foreign Legion, in jail, in hospitals. I was ready to take this into account and stayed friendly.

"Due to his lack of diplomacy, prudence, and understanding, he lost some very good friends. As he said, they were replaced immediately by newcomers, but there were some among his former friends who betrayed him and did a lot of damage to his image without his being aware of it. A lot of them even faked some ufo photos, doing pictures on a windowpane, showing them around and telling everybody how easy this was. I've got two of those fakes. I fell for them for only a few seconds, but people without training might readily fall for the trick. I, for one, am sure that Meier's pictures are no fakes. There's too much variety in them. If indeed he would be able to produce such perfect film materials he would be under contract with the best-paying movie companies for science fiction films, and he would be paid in the hundred thousands for each movie to be sure.

"As an invalid Meier draws a state pension of about 700 francs a month. Nobody in this country can live on such an amount with a wife and three children. Reluctantly, he's now asking for money for his interviews and demonstrations, which he did not do earlier. I know that he does not make money with his photographs, since I bought them for either 1.50 or 2.00 francs apiece, which barely covers his costs. He can't do the copies himself. To fake such extraordinary films anybody would need a lot of money, but obviously, Eduard Meier is a very poor man. . . .

"It was clear to me from the beginning that in due time

Eduard Meier's pictures would come under heavy attack, because it has been the fashion for the last two years to declare all close-up shots, showing clear details, as fakes, by those ufo researchers who pretend to know most and to do their research in a purely scientific manner. . . . Some of those sophisticated ufo researchers, always ready to call other people hoaxers, fakers and liars, might be helpful in a conspiracy of defamation. Intending to unmask scoundrels, they are keeping back curiosity and interest and good photographic evidence from important people at universities and in government circles. . . ." Signed, Lou Zinsstag, Basle.

In October 1977 a man wearing a sweater and a light windbreaker walked the leaf-strewn gravel path from the Freihof in Schmidruti to the Meier farm a quarter mile away. A handsome man, short in stature, with deep blue eyes and silver hair, Wendelle C. Stevens had retired a lieutenant colonel in the United States Air Force. He now traveled the world investigating unusual UFO sightings and claims of contact.

FIVE

Wendelle Stevens had retired from the Air Force in 1963, after twenty-three years on active duty, over 4,000 hours of flying time, and top-secret clearance. Graduated from the Army Air Corps' first test pilot training school, Stevens at age twenty had been a project officer for the development of the P-47 fighter plane, and during World War II had commanded an aircraft maintenance squadron, seeing only limited combat in the Pacific.

After the war the Air Force assigned Stevens to the Air Technical Intelligence Center at Wright Field, where he screened thousands of documents and advanced aeronautical blueprints captured by the Americans when the Germans fled their factories and air design centers. Many of the documents had been seized from the Nazi drawing board, details of exotic flying machines and rockets. Subsequently, Stevens was reassigned to Alaska, briefing and debriefing air crews of the Ptarmigan Project, a weather reconnaissance program in which B-29 crews mapped and photographed the polar surface. Because of encounters with strange circular aircraft reported by these returning crews, UFOs had piqued Stevens's interest even before the term "flying saucer" was coined in June 1947.

Stevens's first involvement with a UFO came during a debriefing in which one of his crews claimed it had spotted a "bogey" flying at an altitude much higher than they were capable. Before long, Stevens's B-29 crews inside the Arctic Circle had reported dozens more such sightings involving speeds and aeronautical maneuvers unknown to our technology. Later, Stevens himself clocked one of these "bogeys" on radar. It was traveling 7,000 miles an hour.

"Based on my previous experience in the Air Intelligence Center," Stevens said, "I was convinced that there was no earth technology capable of producing air vehicles that could fly at thousands of miles per hour and make sharp angled turns at such high speeds, stop and even reverse instantly, stand still in the air, descend and ascend vertically at low and high speeds, land on the ice and water, and submerge underwater and emerge again and fly away."

The B-29s on the Ptarmigan Project came outfitted with still cameras and movie cameras, and many times the crews who reported witnessing such maneuverability also captured the exotic craft in photographs and on film. Stevens himself saw none of the physical evidence, because as soon as the exposed film arrived in its cannister with the crew back at his base, Stevens sent it with the crew chief directly to Andrews Air Force Base in Washington, where, according to Stevens, "the officer was met by Pentagon intelligence and taken someplace."

Hearing nothing further about any of the sightings, Stevens began collecting articles and books on the UFO phenomenon. In a short while he had acquired some of the first UFO photographs ever published, and he began to exchange copies of these photos for new ones taken by amateurs, as sightings became more prevalent. By 1976, Stevens's library on UFOs included 700 books and nearly 3,000 photographs, probably the largest private collection in the world, and one that was utilized extensively by documentary filmmakers. For nearly thirty years he had corresponded and exchanged evidence regularly with most of the world's UFO researchers and investigators, and had personally investigated over a hundred cases in Bolivia, Canada, China, Ecuador, Japan, Mexico, the Netherlands, Peru, Puerto Rico, Spain, Sweden, Switzerland, and the United States; he had walked the sites, handled the evidence, and "looked the people in the eye." Occasionally, he had been warned by governments not to pry.

"When I first encountered the phenomenon in the Air Force," Stevens said, "I thought it was very interesting to know and I wanted to find out more about it. But then I found out that the people I was passing information to were denying that it ever existed. And I was running into trouble trying to tell my stories to somebody else. That piqued my curiosity, because of all the energy used to suppress the information. Why were they covering it up? If there was nothing to it, why worry about it? Then when I got to investigating my own cases and found that witnesses had turned pictures over to authorities, and they never knew really who these authorities were, and nobody could ever find the pictures again, I began to worry. Where were they all going? Who the hell was doing this and how?

"The phenomenon itself seems to be interwoven in our society from its very beginning, and we don't even understand that. If you go back through the Old Testament with different eyes you'll find some sixty-eight passages that describe UFOs. Eliza was taken up by a wheel of fire, and Moses was spoken to out of a burning bush. That's no more than a green fireball that hovers in front of the sofa in somebody's house and talks to him, which I've run into at least twenty times in my investigations.

"I think part of the reason I chase UFOs is that I find realities there that are not realities to most other people. And I wonder why. It's too widespread to be nothing but a mental aberration. There are 70,000 cases per year reported worldwide. That's far too much for accidental story telling. It's too much for a bunch of liars to be creating their own stories for their own prestige or status or whatever they seek as individuals.

"If I hadn't spent thirty years doing this I wouldn't

believe it if you told me. But I have come to accept it, because I have seen so many cases and talked to so many different people who are not in touch with each other, who are sane, rational people with no ax to grind, and these things have happened to them."

* * *

Lou Zinsstag and Wendelle Stevens had never met, though they frequently had exchanged photographs and information on UFO cases. During his thirty years of collecting and investigating, Stevens had acquired a reputation for having a knowledgeable eye when it came to analyzing photographs. Zinsstag knew of that reputation, and in the summer of 1976 she had written to Stevens, telling him briefly about the Meier case and mentioning the photographs taken by this one-armed, unemployed security guard. Prior to her letter, Stevens had heard nothing of the Meier case, but he knew Zinsstag by reputation as well as through correspondence, and he doubted her fascination with the case was unfounded. Though she was vague about their content, Zinsstag had twelve photographs she wanted Stevens to see; and instead of sending them by mail as she had often done in the past, she wanted to bring them herself from Switzerland to Stevens's home in Tucson.

In early September 1976, Zinsstag flew to the United States, accompanied by Timothy Good, to meet with some of the more prominent figures in American ufology, and to conduct research on George Adamski. On the prearranged day, she called Stevens from the Greyhound bus station in Tucson, and Stevens picked them up, got them checked into a motel, then drove them out to his house. They first wanted to see Stevens's UFO library, which took up an entire wall of the living room, floor to ceiling, the same wall on the other side in the dining room, and another wall in his small study. In addition to the 700 volumes on UFOs collected from all over the world, thirty blue binders containing Stevens's collection of nearly 3,000 UFO photographs stood side by side in three tight rows.

Briefly, they discussed various cases, but Zinsstag cut short the small talk when she pulled a folder from her satchel. As Timothy Good remembered, "Lou brought a sort of 'dossier' on Meier." Inside the folder lay a large envelope, which she opened carefully, then slid out a small stack of 5×7 photos. As she began laying out each photograph neatly on Stevens's dining room table, Stevens took one look and whispered, "I have nothing in my collection that even comes near the quality of these prints."

When Stevens examined a UFO photograph he looked first for relative focus, then for distance graying. "Distance attenuation is what I call it," he explained. "The further away an object is the more moisture, smoke, and dust there will be in the atmosphere between it and the lens.

"Then I would look for evidence of rephotographing. If it's got a fingerprint or specks on it, I turn it at an angle in the light. If what I'm looking at is not on the surface then it's printed in the photograph, and that means that something preceded this picture. Also, the distance light travels has some relationship to the color that arrives at the lens. The closer the object is, the more red it appears; the further it is, the more blue. Another thing to look at is light scatter, because the curved surface on a larger object scatters light differently than the sharply curved surface on a nearer object. A model can be perfectly realistic, but it will cast light differently."

Stevens examined each print carefully, holding it up to the light and tilting it. In thirty years of collecting and analyzing photographs of UFOs, Meier's photos were the most spectacular he had ever seen. Rarely was a UFO photograph more than a single accidental shot taken with poor equipment by an amateur who had no time to make adjustments for proper lighting, speed, and focus. Extremely rare was the photo taken in daylight, or with the UFO below the horizon, or with multiple craft in the same picture. And no one had ever taken a continuing series of photographs of the same craft.

In the Meier photos, shiny silver disks, glinting from

the sun, hovered in a blue sky above nearby hills and trees. A distinct red band encircled the upper convex rise on many of the sleekly contoured disks. Others were adorned with equally spaced knobs around the perimeter and a rococo dome on top. In all, Meier had photographs of six variations of spacecraft, each taken in daylight, some below the horizon, and some with two, three, even four spacecraft in the same picture. And each of the photos was the sharpest and clearest Stevens had ever seen.

Timothy Good later remembered Stevens's reaction. "He became absolutely in seventh heaven when Lou showed him the photographs. He was thrilled. Absolutely. Words to the effect, 'Best pictures I've seen.' "

* * *

When Zinsstag and Good had called from the bus station late that morning, Stevens had been entertaining friends down from Phoenix, Lee and Brit Elders. Lee Elders had been a close friend of Stevens for five years and was aware of Stevens's reputation as a UFO investigator. He and Brit were mildly interested themselves, having been educated in the phenomenon by Stevens. No one could go to Stevens's house and see the fat three-ring binders filled with pictures of flying saucers and not have his curiosity piqued. That afternoon, though, the Meier photos that Lou Zinsstag spread across the dining table amazed the Elders as much as Stevens.

"Photographs of UFOs," said Brit, "are usually fuzzy little balls in the sky that have no definition. And they are so far away and so much out of focus they could be just about anything."

She laughed. "Sure, somebody has taken a little tiny miniature setting, put it together, and filmed it. That's what that is."

"Actually Lee used to laugh at my UFO hobby," recalled Stevens. "When he saw the photographs, his position was, 'Ah, they're fakes. Anybody could look at those and tell they're fakes.' They looked pretty good to me, but I had run across a lot of good pictures that were fakes, so I kind of half agreed. But I thought, Man, these are the best fakes I've ever seen. How did he do it?"

For the rest of the afternoon and into the evening, Stevens studied the photographs and listened to Zinsstag recount her experiences with Meier. She told him about Meier's living conditions in the Hinwil house, his wife and children, and the many people who came to see him. She explained her relationship with Meier and how she had acquired the photos. The man was poor, she said, had only one arm, and seemed sincere. How many pictures had he taken of the craft? Stevens wanted to know. Oh, replied Zinsstag, quite a few more. As he listened, Stevens perceived that Zinsstag was trying to relay a sense of the man and his experiences without telling the whole story, as though she were protecting Stevens from some sort of sensory overload. The pictures spoke for themselves, but it seemed that much of the story, perhaps most of it, remained untold. This perception intrigued Stevens.

The following morning Zinsstag and Good left for Los Angeles. For the next year, Stevens corresponded with Zinsstag until he made contact with Meier himself and began a correspondence with him. Slowly, he realized that Meier had had more than a few contacts, that details of these contacts had been recorded, that perhaps many more, even hundreds of photographs existed, and that Meier may not have been the only one to have seen and experienced strange things in the forests surrounding Hinwil and now in the hills outside Schmidruti. In October 1977, a little over a year after Lou Zinsstag and Timothy Good had come to Tucson, Stevens decided the case was worth an on-site investigation, and he made arrangements to fly to Switzerland to meet Billy Meier.

"I'm just going to go over real quick and take a look," he told the Elders. He hoped to get prints of some of the Meier photographs for his collection, and mainly "to look the man in the eye to see if he's telling the truth."

The Elders laughed. "Tell us what happens when you get there," they said.

* * *

Stevens flew to London, then took the train to Wiesbaden, Germany, where he delivered a UFO lecture. The next day, he took another train to Zurich, where he rented a car and began his drive to the Meier farm, as picturesque a drive as one could imagine. In October the green countryside lay dotted with the bright reds and yellows of turning leaves, and many tree trunks supported burlap sacks filled with fresh-picked apples and pears. On nearly every hillside roamed light gray dairy cows with the *Glocke* or the *Treichle* dangling from their necks, tinkling as they grazed. Already the farmers had stacked winter wood head high, the split logs forming a face as smooth as a puzzle.

The Meier farm stood not so picturesque. Meier and his family had been living at the farm now for only six months. Mud still lay everywhere, and Stevens saw outbuildings standing askew, their roofs sagging. The main house, which shared a common wall with the barn, had no upstairs, only open rafters, and the roof leaked. The only bathroom facilities sat behind the house, a lean-to built over a pit. In the kitchen a pressure pump now brought in cold water from a holding tank, and Meier had wired the kitchen and the main room of the house with electricity for only two bare light bulbs. Most of the floors were still of dirt.

When Stevens arrived at the farm, he saw two cars with people waiting to see Meier, one from Munich, one from Berlin. A few young Europeans, hitchhiking, or on bicycles or motorcycles, had pitched tents on the driest piece of ground they could find and lived there for a few days, working in the field or garden during the day, and talking to Meier in the evenings. Invited by the Meiers to stay at the farm if he liked, Stevens himself slept in a bedroll in the rafters above what used to be the barn. He felt that any case worth investigating deserved time, and it appeared that the Meier case deserved more than most. He wanted to get as close as he could.

A year earlier in Tucson, Zinsstag had told Stevens only that Meier had had more than one contact and that he had taken at least a dozen other photographs than the ones she had brought with her. In his first day at the farm, after meeting Meier and talking with a few other people, Stevens confirmed his earlier suspicion that Zinsstag had held back some of what she knew about the case to avoid overwhelming him at the outset.

Much to his surprise, Stevens found that Meier not only spoke passable English, but had a colorful way of expressing himself. When the two men met, Meier even offered him a challenge: He said he hoped the colonel would ask questions not asked by everyone else.

"He had so many different faces coming and going," said Stevens, "and he had answered the same questions so many times for so many different people, he got sick of it. He didn't want to talk about it at all to outsiders. Because he'd explained to somebody else yesterday and somebody else the day before, and another one the day before, and another one the day before, and he didn't care. If you didn't ask the right questions, you didn't get the answers."

During his four days in Switzerland, Stevens accompanied Meier on several long walks into the forest behind the farm, and when the weather turned bad he sat with Meier in the kitchen for hours poring over photo albums and talking. When Stevens asked about recent pictures of the beamships, Meier gave him 130 photographic prints, charging him only for the cost of printing. Through an interpreter, Stevens also interviewed Popi, the children, and half a dozen other witnesses, including Jakobus, Hans Schutzbach, and Herbert's friend Harold Proch, who was visiting with his sister. Each had his or her own stories to tell, and each was so convinced the contacts were taking place that when Stevens asked if they believed them, the common answer was, "I don't believe. I know."

* * *

With the weather socked in, cold and damp, and visibility at the sites poor, the Gasthaus zum Freihof in Schmidruti provided Stevens with a quiet place to get away from the farm and sit in a warm parlor heated by a large wood stove. One gray morning, he retired to a table by the French windows that overlooked the road spiraling through the village, and began to read the background on the contacts. Meier's alleged experiences appeared to be far more complicated than a simple meeting three years earlier.

Stevens thumbed through the voluminous pages of contact notes, beginning with Meier's account of his first contact with Semjase, a Tuesday afternoon, January 28, 1975, in a field not far from Hinwil.

According to the notes, that January had been unseasonably warm in eastern Switzerland, and the winter had been unusually dry; little snow clung to the lower elevations. Meier wrote that in the early afternoon he had been at his house in Hinwil when the twinkle of a thought had entered his consciousness, and then words and symbols had formed a message, one he had been expecting but not quite so soon: He was to leave his house and bring with him a device for taking pictures.

Responding to the message, Meier had departed on his moped, taking with him an old Olympus 35mm camera with a broken viewfinder and a focus that jammed just short of infinity. He used this camera because the film advanced with a simple thumbwheel he found easy to operate with his one hand.

On his motorbike, he had ridden aimlessly through the village, turning when the glimmer of a command directed him to. After an hour, he found himself far from the village, on a remote road bordering a nature conservancy where he received a final command to stop his motorbike and wait. After several minutes a sudden stillness descended upon the meadow, and then a large disk-shaped object shot soundlessly through light clouds, slowed in a wide graceful arc, and crossed the meadow four or five hundred feet from where Meier stood aiming his camera. But the moment he snapped a picture, the disk had vanished.

When the disk reappeared again it hovered above a truck parked at the edge of the meadow, only a hundred feet from where Meier stood. He watched the disk suspended quietly no more than three hundred feet off the ground.

Meier estimated the disk to be about twenty-one feet in diameter, with reddish rectangles, like windows, encircling its upper mound. Beneath the craft, the hull, exceedingly old in appearance, seemed to undulate "as if little waves ran continuously through the lower side of the ship." The waves radiated downward, creating an aura around the truck. Meier took a second picture, and again the spacecraft abruptly broke its hovering pattern, rushed toward the east, and disappeared into the clouds.

Climbing onto his moped, Meier had then headed out across the meadow in the direction he had last seen the disk. Only moments passed before he felt a stillness suddenly descend upon the meadow. Then the disk came streaking through the clouds again, faster than any jet Meier had ever seen. It dropped speed quickly, banked slowly over the forest, and began its descent toward the clearing. Meier took two more pictures as the craft, without a sound, dropped lower and lower, and then landed.

In the warm parlor of the Freihof, Stevens put down the notes and sipped his hot tea. The encounter Meier was about to describe in the notes, he now knew, was only the culmination of a series of phenomena in Meier's life that Meier claimed had been set in motion thirty-five years ago. Before he read further, Stevens wanted to question Meier about the earlier experiences.

* * *

Back in the kitchen at the farmhouse Meier did not hesitate to tell Stevens the long story of his involvement with the Pleiadians, a story that began in his childhood. He said his first sighting of an alien spacecraft occurred one morning when he was only five and a half years old.

"This was in 1942 together with my father," said Meier. "He was behind the house under a walnut tree, it was summertime. When I saw the ship flying, it didn't necessarily seem strange to me. It did *look* strange in our world, but somehow I had the feeling that it was something familiar. It fell down from the sky, to the tower of the church, and then it came to us and left westward. It was very, very fast. Altogether I watched it fall for maybe one and a half minutes, and then when it left westward there were seconds only."

The object had reminded Meier of a huge discus, shooting overhead only 600 feet off the ground, completely soundless, and disappearing over the Höragenwald.

He asked his father, "Daddy, what's happened here?"

But his father only replied, "It's a secret weapon of Adolf Hitler."

"I was thinking that can't be true," said Meier, "that's something else. I don't know if my father realized what he saw, because he didn't bother with it anymore. I started to watch the sky day and night."

Meier told Stevens that two months had passed before he again saw the silvery flying disk, this time descending slowly toward a field where he was playing alone. But as the disk neared the grassy surface, suddenly, without a sound, it had vanished. Within moments of the disk's vanishing, something "similar to a voice" arose inside Meier's head. Accompanied by the drawing of vivid pictures in his mind, the voice thereafter spoke to Meier once a day. It requested that he answer, and seek answers of his own.

"In the beginning I didn't receive entire words or sentences," he explained to Stevens. "It was more like pictures. As time went by these pictures became words and sentences. Later I received messages in symbols. Once I tried to draw one of these symbols, but I was not able to do it."

Troubled by the voice and the pictures in his head, Meier had told Parson Zimmermann, the Protestant minister in the village, of the great flying disk he had seen and of the voice that had come into his head soon afterward. Zimmermann had a reputation in the village as somewhat of a mystic, far more liberal in his thinking than the parochial outlook of his parishioners.

"I knew Parson Zimmermann," said Meier. "He was the family priest, and I used to play with his children. Another reason I probably went to see him was that even as a small child I heard talk that he occupied himself with mystical matters. I told him about the experience I had together with my father, and then the voices I heard inside of me, the telepathic calls. That's why I went to him, because I thought I was going crazy. I used to go after school, it was not far from the schoolhouse. He told me that he knew about these flying objects, back then they were not called UFOs, this was nothing new to him. The people who flew in them would come from another world, not from earth. He told me that he understood this, but that he could not talk about it. He was a priest and he would shock the people. He told me to try to learn telepathy, to try to give answers. So I tried as I was told. After a few weeks it worked, and I was able to answer. I remember very well that Father Zimmermann told me not to talk about it to anyone, otherwise everybody would say I was crazy."

Now, whenever he heard the voice speaking to him, the young Meier would try to direct his thoughts inward, and before long he felt as if those thoughts made contact with something.

"The first reaction from the other side," he recalled, "was like a gentle and fine laughter, which I heard deep inside of me and felt, pleasant and relaxing. I still hear that laughter, but I can't define it. It was a very lovely laughter." Then the contact faded away once more, and Meier neither heard a voice nor realized pictures. Suddenly, all was quiet again.

On February 3, 1944, Meier's seventh birthday, a new voice, low and clear, came into his conscious mind "and ordered me to learn and to collect knowledge transmitted to me." Meier feared that the clarity of this new voice meant he had finally succumbed to insanity.

"I was afraid, because as a small boy I hadn't any experience with the telepathic way. I again had to go to ask Parson Zimmermann what was happening, and he informed me, and I slowly understood."

The low, clear voice Meier now heard belonged to an entity named Sfath, whose thought-transmitted teachings continued frequently through the summer of 1944. Then one day in September, as Meier walked alone in a meadow, Sfath suddenly announced himself telepathically and told the boy he should wait there and not be afraid.

"This was some time later and far from our home," said Meier. "It was three or four miles away behind a very big forest, a lonely place. There I saw something falling down from the sky, very, very slow and it became bigger and bigger. It was something like a metallic pear. Then this ramp opened and it came out, going down like an elevator. I entered the ship and we went up very high above the earth. There was a very old man who looked to me like a patriarch. His name was Sfath. He was a human being, like each other one here on earth, only very old. We talked for hours, then he brought me back to the ground. The funny thing was, he knew my mother tongue better than I."

The venerable Sfath told Meier he would remain his spiritual mentor only through the early 1950s, when a much higher form of life would assume the responsibility for further teaching. Meier had been selected for a mission, but Sfath revealed only that decades would pass before the boy knew its nature. Until that time, Meier had to be prepared to meet with many things, some that would cause him again to question his sanity, others that might bring physical harm. At the end of four hours, Sfath returned Meier to the meadow then departed, never to be seen again by the young boy. For many years thereafter, though, he had continued transmitting thoughts to Meier, preparing him, Meier felt, for the next step in his spiritual evolution. Then on February 3, 1953, when Meier turned sixteen, Sfath's voice had ceased in his mind forever.

Several months passed before the silence was again filled with a new voice, at once present and talking to him. Unlike the soft and harmonic tone of Sfath, the new voice sounded young and fresh, full of force. She was named Asket.

* * *

Asket came from the DAL Universe. "To your universe it is unknown," she instructed Meier, "but our universe is parallel to yours. It lies reckoned in your time on an equal plane. Many of the universes lie in time planes and spaces completely unknown to you. Because of technological developments, the barrier has been opened from our universe to yours."

When Meier was twelve he spent eight months in a tuberculosis sanitorium, and at fourteen the local guardianship office sent him to the boys' home at Albisbrunn for being consistently truant. At Albisbrunn he ran away three times before authorities returned him to his parents, and then he quit school before completing the sixth grade. As a young man, he worked at many jobs, from laying sewer pipe to milking dairy cows. Once, with several other young men, he was picked up by police for stealing and sent to a detention center at Aarburg, from which he again ran away, this time to France, where he joined the Foreign Legion, went AWOL a few months after completing training, and returned to Switzerland and the detention center. He told Stevens that after his teenage years of reformatories and odd jobs, Asket had encouraged him to venture out into the world, to explore and to learn. Inspired by her telepathic teachings and her reassurance, Meier said he began his first travels into the Middle East in 1958.

"I was told to go over there myself and see what is really there," he said, "because there is a connection with previous lives. The most important places were Jerusalem, Bethlehem, and Jordan. Very important again were West Pakistan, the foot of the Himalaya Mountains, and then India, mainly New Delhi and Mehrauli. And I have to add Turkey to this. All this has a connection with Emmanuel; that was his route and where he lived. I was told to get in touch with certain people, some of whom expected me, they were informed. In Mehrauli I learned the teachings and philosophy of Buddha from a Buddhist monk."

Weeks, even months had passed between contacts with Asket. Then suddenly her voice would be inside his head again, indicating she desired to transmit information to him.

"Do you have time?" she would say.

Most often he would say yes, because her instruction was more important than anything else. And if he said yes she would say, "Would you go to this place tomorrow and meet with these people?" Or, "I want you to go here and look at this." Or, "I want you to go there and learn this."

"It is something very normal," he explained to Stevens. "It's as if you called me and asked, 'Billy, do you have time for this?' Same thing."

Meier viewed such wanderings as part of the mission he had been given as a young boy. It was "instructive." As he explained to Stevens, he was "to get to know man, the soul of man, life of man, the background of the teachings." He was also to learn about nature.

"You learn a lot from nature," he said. "You observe plants and animals, how everything exists, how it comes to life, how it dies, how it can live together. That's how I learned the laws and commands of nature. The laws and commands of nature are the same as the laws and commands of Creation. Creation is not a separate power, Creation is in everything."

Working his way from Greece to Turkey, down through Syria, Jordan, and Iraq, into Saudi Arabia and out again through Kuwait, into Iran, further east to Pakistan and finally into India, Meier had traveled "by land, in cars, by hitchhiking, by bus and by train and by ship." He found employment as a snake catcher and a gardener, drove a nitroglycerine truck, sang in the streets, waited tables, herded pigs, sailed an oceangoing tug, sold pots, pounded nails, supervised a youth hostel, prospected for rubies and gold, posed as a veterinarian, coached, worked as a male nurse, picked grapes, designed jewelry, performed puppet shows, raised chickens, and taught German—all, he told Stevens, under the tutelage of Asket. During his travels he acquired the nickname "Billy," a result of his infatuation with the American West and folk heroes Billy the Kid, Buffalo Bill, and Wild Bill Hickok.

As Meier wandered from country to country, job to job, Asket had continued the telepathic teachings begun by Sfath, imparting to him even greater spiritual awareness.

"You are selected as truth offerer," she had revealed to him, "like numerous others at very early times before you. You have to become greater in knowledge than every other earthly human being of your time. Because of this, you have come under the controlling guardianship of a certain form of life which had to protect, lead, guide, and educate you. This embodies a law of the Creation which cannot be acted against, even by will, for truth offerers are not called for their mission at a certain age; they are destined from the time of procreation. Such a life will be difficult, for the creature concerned has extraordinary things to perceive."

Near the coastal city of İskenderun, Turkey, on August 3, 1965, winding his way out of the Middle East, Meier was riding in an old bus when it collided with another bus, throwing him out of a window. The accident severed his left arm just above the elbow. Meier told Stevens he had been left for dead by the side of the road and lay unconscious for several hours before a doctor happened by, checked him for signs of life, and had him taken to a local hospital. He spent two weeks there, and when he felt well enough to travel again he continued on to Greece, where he settled into a hotel in Thessaloníki, selling shirts "with German, with my hand, my eyes, my mouth, with my feet, with a pencil and paper." At a party on Christmas Day of that year, he had met a seventeen-year-old Greek girl named Kaliope Zafireou.

While Meier was in India in 1964, Asket had allowed him to photograph her spacecraft high above the Ashoka Ashram on the outskirts of Mehrauli. In the photograph, the craft appeared distinctly disk-shaped, topped by the slight rise of a dome, but otherwise undetailed. Meier still had the photograph and showed it to Stevens.

That year, Asket, as Sfath before her, had left him. In her final contact, she had informed Meier that for his own benefit as well as that of his new contacts' he would be monitored for the next eleven years. At the end of that time, if assured that he had achieved the proper spiritual plane to allow face-to-face contact, the new beings would reveal their presence to him.

"Your forefathers came from the Constellation Lyra," Asket had told Meier. "And when you have become mature enough to hear the new explanations concerning these matters, you will have the answers from the descendants of your forefathers themselves. The eternal truth remains for all times the eternal truth."

And so ended Meier's story of his youthful encounters.

* * *

Early the next morning, Stevens returned to the warmth and quiet of the Freihof's small paneled dining room, where he drank more strong tea and waded through the awkward English translation of Meier's first contact with the new life-form, the Pleiadians. He had left off with the spacecraft finally alighting in the meadow. As Stevens began reading again, Meier's notes described the craft, which, now landed in the meadow, seemed to pulsate. Its nearly translucent, golden-silver skin glinted in the sun. Except for the portholes around the dome, the smooth, contoured surface remained unbroken by projections or seams and unmarked by symbols.

Meier had walked toward the craft for a closer look and

better pictures, but when he had come to within a hundred yards, something suddenly checked his progress, "as if I were running against the winds of a soundless storm," he wrote. "With all my power I fought against it to move forward. I even succeeded in this, but only for a few meters, then the counteracting force was simply too great, and I sat down on the ground, stared over at the object and waited for what was to come."

In less than a minute, a figure had appeared behind the craft. As the figure approached, Meier could see that it was human in form, walked upright on two legs, and had two arms at its side. It was covered up to its neck by a tight, thin one-piece suit, dull gray in color and rough—almost like the hide of an elephant, he thought. A hard ring collar encircled the base of the neck, and the suit ended in darker, ankle-high boots.

The being, of course, was the Pleiadian Semjase, a woman with eyes an unusually pale blue. Her amber hair was parted in the middle and fell to her waist, framing her small nose, delicate mouth, and exceedingly high cheekbones. Meier had noted at the time that only two of Semjase's features truly differed from that of an earth human: Her small ears joined her head in a straight line instead of a gentle curve; and her white skin was so pale and so perfect it approached luminescence.

Semjase had walked confidently and gracefully toward him, touching his arm and gently helping him to his feet; then the two of them walked to a tree near which Meier had left his motorbike. There in the grass, for an hour and a quarter, they had talked, Semjase speaking German so that Meier could understand.

Meier wrote in the notes that for a long while the Pleiadians had desired contact with an earth human who was sincere in assisting them with their mission. They had nurtured and observed him since he was five years old, and since he responded adequately to each of several levels of communication he had continued to be contacted. In January 1975 he finally was ready to learn of the Pleiadian presence and to understand the simple mission for which he had been selected.

Semjase first explained briefly that Pleiadian civilization originated many thousands of years ago, not in the Pleiades, a star system much younger than our own, but in the Constellation Lyra. When war ensued, before the planet was destroyed, much of the population migrated to other star systems, in the Pleiades, the Hyades, and to a planet orbiting a nearby star known as Vega. On one interstellar journey, the new Pleiadians discovered Earth and its early life evolving in an atmosphere hospitable to their own. Since that time, according to Semjase, Earth had been destroyed twice by its own inhabitants: first by a civilization evolved from early Pleiadians who remained behind and mated with primitive earth humans; and second when a later generation of Pleiadians colonized Earth and produced advanced technology until war again destroyed the planet. Semjase and the Pleiadians who had chosen to return again to Earth were descendants of a peaceful Lyrian faction that now felt responsible for guiding Earth in its spiritual evolution, so the earth humans could avoid the setbacks long ago experienced by their Pleiadian ancestors.

To help them in their mission, the Pleiadians had contacted many earth humans telepathically, but the chosen ones eventually proved to lack knowledge, willingness, or loyalty. The few who possessed these qualities feared exposure, and so remained silent about the contacts.

"In the past we have witnessed those who were unable to determine the truth and were frightened by it," Semjase told Meier. "They claimed they would be accused of insanity, and that others would plan conspiracies to prove they were lying. This serves no purpose for the earth human or ourselves. If such humans had been sincere, we would have offered them the chance to take clear photo proofs of our beamships. We have allowed you this already, and in the future will come even greater opportunities."

Taking photographs of the Pleiadian beamships was to

be part of Meier's mission; pictures provided proof that the Pleiadians existed, and this reality was a necessary step before earth humans would begin to accept the truth that they belonged to a network of galactic societies. The Pleiadians themselves were only one of many millions of cosmic races that traveled freely in space.

"The earth human calls us extraterrestrials or star people, or however he wants," Semjase had continued. "He attributes to us supernatural abilities, yet knows nothing about us. In truth, we are human beings like the earth human being, but our knowledge and our wisdom and our technical capabilities are very much superior to his.

"One of our concerns is aimed at your religions and the detrimental effect they have had on the development of the human spirit. One thing above all has power over the life and death of each creature. This is the Creation, laws which are irrefutable and eternally valid. The human being will recognize them in nature, if he troubles himself to look, for they show him the way to spiritual greatness. While the earth human indulges in religion, the real spirit dwindles.

"On Earth," she added, "charlatans have spread the lie that we come by order of the Creation as angels, to bring to the earth humans the long-hoped-for peace, the truth, the protection, and the order of your God. This is a lie, for we never have received such orders and we never will. The Creation never gives commands. It is a law unto itself, and every form of life must conform to it and become a part of it. Bring this truth to the light of the world."

Before they parted that afternoon, Semjase had promised Meier that many contacts would follow, and that she also would transmit thoughts to him telepathically.

"Do not worry that I will do this at an unsuitable time," she had said. "I know to regard your character and your will for independence; thus I will always take my directions from you. The time will come when we will meet together in my beamship, and you will be able to fly into space with me. I will inform you later about this."

Semjase had then walked back through the meadow to

her beamship. Once she was inside, waves again emanated from the craft, distorting the shapes and colors of everything around it. A blue-red corona radiated outward. Meier took several more pictures as the beamship rose slowly above the pine trees and drifted to the north. It was exactly four o'clock when he exposed the last frame on his film; an instant later the beamship shot straight up into the clouds and disappeared from Meier's view. And once again the stirring had returned to the meadow.

* * *

One afternoon, with a break in the weather, Stevens asked Meier to take him to one of the contact sites. On his moped, Meier guided Stevens and the interpreter to a grassy bluff near Hasenbol, about forty minutes from the farm. On that bluff Meier had taken a series of photographs in which a beamship approached in the distance.

"The pictures," recalled Stevens, "showed the object beginning as a speck, just a little dark speck, and getting bigger and bigger and bigger until it's the craft hovering behind a tree."

Driving up to Hasenbol, Stevens was impressed by the terrain and puzzled at how Meier could have rigged the photographs to make the beamship appear to fly toward the camera from a point out over a deep valley. But as they neared the site another problem arose that had never occurred to him. The only way to get to the top of that bluff was by climbing a dirt road barred by a locked gate. Beyond the gate the road narrowed and finally became two ruts separated by a wide swath of thick grass cutting through meadow, then traversing steeply up the side of the bluff.

At the gate Stevens stopped the car, located the farmer who owned the land, and had his interpreter ask for permission to pass through the gate and proceed across the meadow.

"When we went through there he looked at everything," remembered Stevens. "He didn't open it, but he came and looked on the back of the moped and at the car, and wanted to know what we were going to do. And I don't think that he would have allowed Meier across there with a moped loaded with disks and rigging equipment. He might have let him in there with all that rigging, but at least he would have known about it."

While the farmer looked over the contents of Stevens's rental car and Meier's motorbike, Stevens asked through the interpreter, "Do you remember Mr. Meier here?"

The man said, "Yes, he was here over a year ago."

"Did he have anything unusual with him at the time?" asked Stevens.

"What do you mean?" countered the farmer. "He had cameras and a roll pack strapped on his back, and a tripod on his moped."

"No," said Stevens, "did he have anything disk-shaped, like the hubcap of a car or anything like that?"

"No, I didn't see anything like that," replied the farmer.

Meier stood next to Stevens, as Stevens asked the questions. "He knew what I was after," Stevens said later, "but he never objected to me asking these questions of him or of anybody else."

Later, as they drove back to Schmidruti, Stevens mulled over three things about Hasenbol: the locked gate, the stern and inquisitive farmer, and most of all, the steep drop below the grassy bluff. "That and the fact that the object approached from a gray spot in the distance in the haze, getting bigger and bigger and bigger all the way, from over this valley. I don't see how he could do it."

By now, several witnesses had described to Stevens the strange landing tracks left by the beamships, and Stevens wanted to see a set for himself. Two weeks before his arrival in Switzerland, there had been a contact in a meadow and a set of three tracks had been left behind. If nothing had disturbed them, they would still be there in the short grass. With Meier directing, Stevens drove to the site, where they got out of the car and walked through the woods to a clearing. Stevens recognized the indentations immediately and understood why they had puzzled so many people before him.

"The tracks I looked at had stems bent over that weren't broken and they never stood up," he recalled. "And that's mysterious. How can that happen? All grass stands back up again if you haven't broken the stem. I have never been able to figure out what kind of equipment he could have used to produce those tracks in wet grass without leaving a track to and from, except the one Semjase walked out on. You could salt the ground, but the salt would not make the grass grow greener, and it probably wouldn't grow at all if you salted it too much. When I asked him he had a ready answer, didn't even stop to think about it.

"I said, 'How come the grass doesn't grow back up?'

"He said he asked the Pleiadians and they told him it was the magnetic vortices under the landing pads that produced a change in the magnetic orientation in the plant, and the plant grew horizontally in its induced field rather than vertically in a normal field. I could be misreading it, I could be seeing it all wrong. But how in hell was he going to do that a dozen times over and never get caught?"

Stevens had investigated over a hundred cases in a dozen countries. He had walked landing sites, handled evidence, and talked to witnesses. But the Meier case was different. In Stevens's mind what set it apart was the number of principal witnesses who had seen something for themselves. Too many seemingly honest people had too many stories about Meier that couldn't be explained— people who had watched him closely, had waited for him to slip, and who had never seen anything suspicious. One of the most common stories Stevens heard was about the time the Pleiadians had teleported Meier out of his office. The office had one window and one door, both locked from the inside with a key. One afternoon, at least two people saw Meier enter the office, but no one saw him leave. Yet later in the afternoon, when everyone thought he was working in his office, he suddenly showed up on the road in front of the farm briefly disoriented, and three men had to break down the office door to get back in.

After Stevens heard the story, the next time he and Meier sat down for a question-and-answer session, he asked Meier to define for him the precise moment he was tele-ported from earth to a beamship. Meier, in English, tried to explain, using the example of being in his office.

"I maybe sit by the typewriter at the window," he began, "and suddenly I feel a very, very strong force clear-ing up everything in my head, but still holding the position of my body by the table . . . because I am already going into the ship with Semjase. And in that same moment I know I am sitting in front of the typewriter by the table. But a very short moment only, because I forget everything that is happening here. And then, in this moment, I am there, and not here."

This led to another question. Stevens wanted to know "where" Meier was when he met with the Pleiadians.

"If I am now in the ship staying on the ground," said Meier, "or a little bit over the ground, or if we fly off in the atmosphere, or out of the earth into space, or if we are walking around the ship, it is exactly the same. You see, there is the force field, and you always are inside there."

But Stevens wondered if during the contacts Meier was somehow in another dimension, or if the experiences with the Pleiadians were similar to astral travel, "a state of ecstasy, exhilaration," he suggested. He was implying that perhaps Meier's contacts took place solely on a mental plane and not a physical one.

But Meier answered, "I know what this means, astral travel. It isn't anything like that. It's so real, like we are sitting here. You see," he said, "they are really material."

* * *

Stevens understood now why Lou Zinsstag had been reluctant to tell him everything she knew about the Meier case. The four days in Schmidruti had been crammed with reading, questioning, viewing, thinking, and wondering. For the first time in thirty years he felt overwhelmed. He returned to Tucson with 130 new color photographs, many of them far better than the original twelve he had seen Lou Zinsstag arrange across his dining room table. He had several hundred roughly translated pages of the contact notes, and many statements from witnesses who described seeing things unimaginable.

"Some of them told me they saw him return in the middle of three men standing in a group in a rainstorm. Looked like he just popped out of the ground, and he didn't have any raindrops on him. That's unique, that's a real trick. I never had people present where the witness was teleported.

"No, Meier's a smart man and he's got a good mind, but he has only one arm, and he's limited in equipment, and he's watched by a lot of people. I don't see how he can do all these things."

Stevens went back to Tucson and told his friends Lee and Brit Elders, "If this man is perpetrating a hoax on the world, he is also successfully fooling his wife and his closest friends, and has been doing so for two and a half years."

"Steve came back shaking his head," remembered Brit. "He didn't know what to do. He spent three days at our house saying, 'You're not going to believe it. You've got to go. You're not going to believe it.' "

"I was worried about him," added Lee, "because I had observed so many UFO cases he'd been on in the past. He's had a hundred field investigations. But this time he comes back saying, 'You've got to go over there. This is bigger than all of us!' "

SIX

In 1967 Lee Elders had gone to work for Capitol Detective Agency in Phoenix, a job that allowed him to work his own hours and afforded him several months off each year to travel, explore, and eventually lead expeditions into the Amazon Basin, primarily the El Oriente region of Ecuador. Born in Bowie, Arizona, Elders had been reared in the desert, a place of hard edges and little subtlety. The landscape had shaped his personality: He walked with a determined forward lean, shoulders hunched, lost in thought, caring little for diplomacy. Brit Nilsson had met him at the Phoenix airport in 1974, as he returned from an expedition, banging his way through customs carrying an armload of blowguns and spears. He hadn't bathed in two weeks.

"I wish you could have met Lee back when I met him," she said later. "I couldn't stand him. He was the most horrible, arrogant you-know-what . . . he was obnoxious, is the best word to describe Lee. And he thought he was perfect." Brit, calm and well-reasoned, is a tall, buxom woman with large brown eyes from the Indian side of her heritage and blond hair from her Scandinavian ancestors. She recently had divorced. Though she was fifteen years younger, Lee eventually won her over, and she agreed to marry him.

Years of exploration in South America had etched deep fissures into Elders's face. A friend who had known him in South America in 1974, "back when Ecuador represented the equivalent of an Egypt in the early 1900s," claimed that Elders was the first non-native to enter vast regions of the Amazon Basin and forge relationships with the territorial Jivaros and Shuaras. Estimates at the time were that no more than one in every ten artifacts surviving the Spanish conquest of the Inca civilization had been recovered. During the early 1970s, based on four hundred-year-old legend and recent tribal rumor, Elders had arranged the financing and equipment for archaeological expeditions into the jungle in search of the Inca *huacas*.

Back in the States working again for the Capitol agency in early 1976, Lee Elders, then thirty-eight, had been assigned to a large transportation company, to find, screen, and qualify ten individuals the company could place within its employee ranks to penetrate a theft ring. One afternoon, while Elders talked to the company's head of security about the theft problem, a phone call interrupted their conversation. Elders overheard the security man say, "What do you mean you lost it?" Sensitive company data sent from one computer in one building to another computer across the street somehow had never made it to the second computer. The security man hung up the phone and said to Elders, "Holy Christ! How could this happen?" Elders explained to him that the information could have been intercepted.

Tom Welch, a close friend of Elders, worked for the same detective agency. That evening, Elders told Welch about the conversation he had had with the security guard, and Welch began searching for a "countermeasure" firm. Though he turned up several other private investigation companies like Capitol, none of them specialized in telecommunications. He expanded his search beyond Phoenix to include the entire Southwest and still found no one capable of investigating computer theft.

"Tom and I started talking," Elders said later. " 'There's a tremendous need out here for a company that could protect against this; maybe we should start one.' Then we started researching it and found out there's a lot of theft going on. Then after another six months of searching we stumbled on a company in New York that had state-of-the-art telephone analyzers which you could hook up on-line and do your sweeps with."

With this level of sophistication, in less than an hour they could probe a huge communications system and determine the use of every wire out of thousands in the system.

"We're not talking about something like black boxes and wands," said Welch. "We're not talking about little RF bugs; we're talking about manipulating the wiring. That's where sophisticated data theft takes place. They can run it right in front of everybody's nose, out of the building and anywhere in the city, and in some cases across the country."

In the latter part of 1976 Tom Welch and Lee and Brit Elders purchased the $20,000 telephone analyzer and founded Intercep, a company of licensed investigators trained in the protection of corporate security. Corporate officers suspicious of sensitive information leaks quietly hired Intercep to discover the source of the leaks, either in the ranks of their employees or as taps within their telecommunications system. With most of their work consisting of non-crisis security checks, Intercep specialized in preventing computer theft and the bugging of executive phones and offices by competitors. After a year and a half, they had performed for three of the top ten Fortune 500 corporations, and business already had expanded overseas.

*   *   *

When Wendelle Stevens returned from Switzerland he realized he had become involved in a case potentially so big he would be incapable of investigating it. There were landing tracks he could not explain, witnesses who needed further interrogation, scores of photographs he did not know how to analyze definitively.

"I was convinced there was so much here," said Stevens, "that no UFO club could ever investigate it properly. It would take several people, well equipped, trained in proper investigative techniques. I'd spin my wheels forever trying to find out what they could turn up in two days."

The Elders had already seen some of the Meier photos the day Lou Zinsstag laid them out carefully on Stevens's dining room table. The photos had impressed them at first, but Lee Elders was certain they were fake and Meier and the witnesses crazy.

"I came back," recalled Stevens, "and told Lee I didn't think they were a bunch of kooks. As a cross section of people they probably were more intellectual than we were and as smart as any of us, probably smarter than most of our UFO researchers."

"Well then," said Elders, "they ought to be able to find out what's going on."

"The man himself is not smart enough to fool all of those people," said Stevens. "I sat down across from him and looked him in the eye. He's a simple man, he's very sincere, he doesn't have much of an education, he doesn't have any resources, he doesn't have anything going for him. Plus a lot of people are watching him, and I couldn't find anybody who had seen anything suspicious."

"Bullshit," countered Elders, "they're pulling your leg over there."

Stevens listed four reasons the Meier case appeared unique among many thousands of UFO cases. "One," he said, "there are more notes and more information, and more detailed descriptions of events provided by witnesses, than in any other UFO case recorded. Two, there are more photographs and many of the photographs are better than in any other UFO case ever. Three, there is more physical evidence to study and analyze in this case than in any other UFO case known. And four, there are more individual contact events in this case than any other in history, and the contact is still going on!"

During less reserved moments, Stevens called the Meier story "the hands-down greatest UFO case of all time," and "the biggest, most spectacular, longest-running, most productive case in the history of the phenomenon."

But the Elders were not interested. Not only was Lee Elders busy, but he was also concerned about the reputation of his fast-growing security firm. "I'm just getting big into Intercep," he said, "and this wild colonel, who's just lost all objectivity after thirty years, gets me out chasing UFOs. My career's right down the toilet."

"What if the story's real?" Stevens asked him. "It can't hurt it then."

"But you don't have any proof that it's real," replied Elders.

"That's what I'm trying to find out," said Stevens.

"I wouldn't worry about the case," Elders told him. "It's all a bunch of baloney anyway."

"No, it's not," argued Stevens. "Something's going on there. It's changed too many people's lives."

"Steve," said Lee, "we just can't get involved in stuff like that."

Brit Elders kept a diary. Every evening she recorded the highlights of daily occurrences and conversations with friends. On November 19, 1977, she wrote the following entry: "Steve arrived Phoenix p.m. Blown away. 'Meier for real.' Three hours of ranting and raving. Lee not paying much attention. Never seen Steve so up. Can't interest Lee. Who has time to chase UFOs? Didn't phase [sic] Steve, kept rambling. Pushed for Lee to throw Intercep into investigation. Lee and I talked rest of night. He doesn't want to commit the company name to such a weird subject. Steve will have to understand. . . ."

Stevens resorted to pleading. He said, "Look, I've got a problem. I can go to the UFO organizations with this; they all would jump at the chance to get control of it. But they'll investigate it with mail order investigators, and they'll surely fuck it up like they do all of the others. I need some real investigation on this. I need people who know how to look for information, I need somebody who's got staying power, I need somebody who isn't going to waste time, who knows what to do and how to document it."

One of Stevens's main concerns was the rate at which some of the photographs were disappearing. Whether the story of the contacts was true or not, the evidence might be gone before anyone had a chance to analyze it. As Intercep grew over the next few months, and the Elders and Welch became more involved in the business, Stevens continued his pleas. Once they met Meier, walked some of the sites, and talked to the witnesses, he felt certain they would agree with him that *something* was going on. Elders and Welch humored, even teased him about his sudden devotion to this one case. But they knew Stevens well enough to realize something must be different about the Meier story; though for thirty years Stevens had maintained that UFOs were of extraterrestrial origin and he had a mind open to even the most outlandish of stories, he did require proof, and until he saw that proof he gave no credence to unsupported claims. The photographs were proof, but only if they held up, and despite their looking almost too good to be valid, Stevens had found nothing during his trip that would indicate they somehow had been fabricated. Though none of them would admit it at the time, the Elders and Welch had their curiosities piqued ever so slightly by Stevens's failure to uncover Meier's "technique." He had unveiled so many in the past, often by simply studying a photo in his hand.

"It wasn't just a tall tale," Welch said later. "Either there was one hell of an intriguing story how somebody did all of this and pulled it off under the guise of being a naïve Swiss farmer, or there might be, for the first time, an incredibly historic event."

* * *

In April 1978 the Elders had to travel to London on business. When Stevens heard about the trip, he immediately suggested it was a perfect opportunity: After they had concluded work for their client he could meet them in London and the three of them could then take the night train to Zurich. It wouldn't cost much. Then they could rent a car and drive through the Swiss countryside . . . they would love Switzerland in the spring . . . and spend a couple of days in a quaint guesthouse. Meeting Meier and talking to some of the people at the farm might even change their minds.

The Elders had never been to Switzerland, and the client was to pick up the tab for the flight to London. A few days on a side trip with Stevens, who typically investigated his cases carrying a small backpack filled with notebooks and apples, would be inexpensive. The Elders finally decided that if it meant that much to Stevens to have them just look at the farm and talk for a while with Meier they could afford the time.

"I don't think I convinced Lee by telling him what I saw," said Stevens. "What convinced him, I think, more than anything else was my appeal as a friend to come help me take a look, because there was nobody else I could rely on to do it. He said, 'We'll come over there, but we're not coming over to investigate any of your kookie stuff.' "

With the Elders scheduled to be in London the first of April, Tom Welch remained in Phoenix for the Honeywell Corporation's fourth national Computer Security and Privacy Symposium. The two-day affair promised the latest information "by many of the nation's most prominent authorities on the subject of Systems Security and Privacy." Honeywell had asked Tom Welch to give the featured address on "Electronics Communications Protection."

"Since we were trying to learn and constantly develop our abilities in our business," recalled Welch, "it required us to be at the frontier edge of computers and electronics and communications. By then we had had a ton of experience in a number of small cases, and we were picking up major clients. Some of our cases involved rather elaborate cover stories, new employees as well as an electronic penetration, industrial espionage, a variety of things. And it was here that we were developing a knack for bursting the bubble."

Their growing knowledge and experience provided Welch with the material for his presentation. He assumed it also would serve the Elders well in Switzerland. "There was a lot of potentially complicated detail involved with Meier," he said, "and if it was a hoaxing effort, it was on a grand scale. But we were very confident that by the end of a week, if there was a hoax going on, Lee and Brit would probably have gotten to the bottom of it. Our confidence stemmed from having this knack for penetrating the problems of our clients quickly. We had no expectation whatsoever of spending a lot of time on it."

* * *

At the end of March, Stevens flew to London with the Elders, and after a two-day sweep of the client's offices, the three of them reserved berths on the night train from London to Zurich, and departed the evening of April 1. After renting a tiny bright orange Renault in Zurich, they drove northeast on the autobahn to Winterthur, left the main highway, turned south, and continued through the countryside. The terrain was open and rolling, and speckled in the distance with three-story farmhouses under orange roofs, goats in the pen, and dairy cows with their heads bent into the green of the hillsides. Soon they passed through Turbenthal, then Wila, then took the unmarked turnoff to Schmidruti, and began climbing into the hills, where grayed patches of snow still clung to the ground in areas shaded from the sun. The last series of tight switchbacks finally straightened and the road leveled out just as they reached the short cobblestone row that comprised Schmidruti. They swerved off the main road, passed the

Gasthaus zum Freihof, and headed down the dirt and gravel path, now overhung by gray leafless trees. When they arrived at the farm, they saw Meier outside washing his face in the horse trough.

Since Stevens's first visit six months earlier, just before the snow and cold, little had changed around the farm. Spring rains and melting snow had turned the driveway back to mud, the roof still leaked, there was no plumbing, and the only heat came from a wood stove or the fireplace. To wash dishes, Popi had to collect water from the cold pump and boil it on the stove.

"It was a disaster," Lee remembered. "I mean you talk about poverty, it was there."

Brit recorded in her diary, "First impression—disaster area. Snow on the ground, bitter wind. Tiny white flowers coming through the snow. House looks like an old dilapidated barn, needs paint. Shutter on upstairs window hangs cockeyed. Big apple trees along hillside in front of house. Dirt, or rather mud, road to house. Raining, pouring."

Despite the wind and dampness, a small band of young people from various European countries had again migrated to the farm, the first of spring arrivals. Clustered in tents near the first barn, they were helping Meier dig trenches for a sewer line.

Lee Elders had formed little opinion of Billy Meier, though he expected to dislike the man for having perpetrated a hoax and for having been responsible for his detour to Switzerland. Furthermore, if he was to begin snooping around, looking for evidence that Meier was a fraud, he had to consider Meier as his adversary, someone to be watched closely. But when he met the man he found himself totally disarmed.

Meier dried his hand and face, and walked over to where Stevens and the Elders had pulled in with the car. Stevens introduced the Elders as his friends from Phoenix. "I met Meier," Lee said later, "and his eyes . . . that's the first thing I remember, because it was like I had known the man before, like he had known me before. It was an intriguing déjà vu experience."

Stevens and the Elders stayed at a guesthouse in Dussnang, a small village over the hill and fifteen minutes from the farm, where every half hour bells pealed from the steeples of two old churches. Because of Stevens's prior visit and continuing long-distance relationship with Meier, the man and his family accepted the Elders immediately. During the day Meier accompanied them on drives away from the farm to give them a feel for the countryside. Though early spring had arrived, the ground at the higher elevations where Meier had taken most of his photographs remained either too soft for driving or still covered with snow. At a few of the sites they drove and walked close enough to see from a distance the openness of the terrain, the angular pitch of the hills. At night they ate with the family at the farmhouse and listened to Meier's stories of the contacts. They had been taking place now for over three years. In all, Meier claimed to have met face-to-face with Semjase or one of the other Pleiadians over one hundred times. The notes had grown to nearly 3,000 pages of conversation on interstellar travel, life on Erra, universal law, advanced physics, archaeology, astronomy, Creation, the fate of other human races, the destiny of planet Earth, and spiritual societies obscuring even the Pleiadians'. Only fourteen days earlier, Meier had had another contact.

The man seemed open and honest, a fact, Brit noted in her diary, that intrigued Lee. "Not hiding anything," she wrote. "Eyes sincere. Does not look away when answering questions, extremely direct. Kids cute like all kids, love chocolate drinks. Kaliope very quiet, haunting."

"I tried to focus on Meier," Elders said later. "Steve had his area of expertise, Tom had his. I felt more comfortable in focusing on the man, trying to get close to him. That wasn't hard to do, really wasn't much of a challenge. I've read many books on psychology, and I watched his body language to see if it might tell something about him, see if he was defensive in answering questions, moved his arm, crossed his legs, that type of thing. I checked eye blink rate to see if it increased when I asked certain questions. But I never really detected anything of a nervous nature with him. He was very stable, very calm. Someone once remarked that the eyes are the mirror to one's soul, and if this were true then Meier had nothing to hide, because he didn't back down from you, he wasn't shifty eyed, he didn't look at the ground, he looked you directly in the eye."

Meier offered the Elders albums full of photographs to peruse, told them to read whatever they pleased in the translated portions of the contact notes, and answered their questions with a tired patience. One evening he showed them several films he had taken of the beamships with an old 8mm camera. In one of the films, a black-and-white segment shot on a cloudy day, a ship darts back and forth near a large pine tree. Suddenly it cuts in front of the tree and as it does so the upper branches sway as if in a backwash. Lee Elders had Meier run the short clip over and over, watching closely for the blast as the ship seemed suddenly to swing in front of the tree.

In another sequence, a ship flies into the scene at Hasenbol and comes to a perfect stop. It doesn't move or swing, but hovers until it takes off again. And there are other objects in the scene: snowcapped peaks in the distance, wind blowing through the branches of a pine tree to the right. Elders and Stevens imagined helicopters and long cables, but they still couldn't figure out how Meier made the ship come to a complete stop without swinging.

The extremes that took place each day began to bother Lee Elders. In the mornings and afternoons, he might embark on one of his inquisitive tours of the farm and surrounding forests and turn up nothing; or he would be out viewing sites from a distance, increasingly curious at how Meier was able to fake the photographs; then at night he would sit around the kitchen table listening to Meier's casual recollections (he sounded almost bored) of being teleported into a Pleiadian beamship or of traveling to other planets. Elders could not accept most of what Meier

101

said simply because it could not be true. But the next day he would go back out and view another site, talk to more witnesses, and perhaps see something new, like photos of the landing tracks, and he would get to wondering how he himself would manufacture something so convincing, and his mind would go blank.

Elders and Stevens took Meier's photos with them as close as they could get to the sites, and, using them for comparison and orientation, brainstormed on ways that Meier could have rigged a scene and photographed a hanging model. Or, far more complicated, how he could have set a model in motion and captured it on film.

"We matched them up," recalled Stevens, "that the pictures had to be taken right there, that that was the point where the photographer stood, and there was no way he could have rigged anything, because there are no trees around, no poles, nothing there, and the ground fell away downhill, at a steep angle, and the next one was four miles away coming up the hill, and the objects were out in between. We thought of rigging a pole with wires running out, but we couldn't find anything we could run the wires to because the trees were all a hundred feet away, and there was nothing else there. Plus there was no way he could have run a string of wires like that alone, getting up and down poles and trees with one arm. Have you ever tried to climb a tree with one arm? We thought if there were confederates, in three, three and a half years they would have found one, because we weren't the only ones looking for confederates; everybody there was looking for confederates."

The Elders had expected to find a commune filled with brainwashed teenagers trying to sell newcomers on the righteous message from the Pleiadians and the Prophet Billy Meier. But the only young people at the farm were the ones camped in tents who left after a few days of working and talking, and were replaced by new arrivals. Most of the people who came often to the farm, some to work on weekends, others to help Meier with his small publication *Wassermannzeit,* were at least in their late twenties, many of them older than Meier himself. One was a school principal, two were schoolteachers, one worked as a graphic artist, and another as a computer programmer. And nobody tried to sell anything, ideas or artifacts.

Originally prepared to dislike Meier, and still not trusting him, Elders nevertheless found himself enjoying the man's company. "It was fun talking and listening to him," he recalled. "We all had our shots of rum or coffee kirsch, and that took the edge off. I guess he was using alcohol on me as much as I wanted to use it on him, to see where I was coming from. But we'd have a couple belts and everybody'd loosen up. Meier led a fascinating life. His life reminded me so much of my years of exploration in South America. We had something in common to talk about. I was fascinated by his Middle East stories; he was fascinated by my expeditions into South America. We got along well."

One evening the Elders sat in the Meier kitchen, the only place they could get warm. Dinner that night consisted of hot chunks of a heavy bread that Popi had baked over the fireplace and a white cheese that Meier himself made from the milk of his two dairy cows kept in a stall beneath the house. Meier, in a reflective mood, sipped coffee from a white china demitasse adorned by a bright enamel rose. He told the Elders that every time he had contact with the Pleiadians he found it difficult to return to his normal life on Earth.

"If I go there," he said, "if I talk with them, if I am in the ship together with them, I never like to return to the earth. Every time I have trouble coming back. You see, if I am shouting there, really shouting, pounding my fist on the table, it's something else than if I am shouting here on the earth. I'm shouting there in peace and in love. Sometimes I have to make myself very, very angry to come back home. It's so peaceful and restful and loving there, speaking together with them. You see what *can* happen, and everything in the world is okay. There I am much more clear in my head, in my thinking and feeling, than here. Then I have to return to a world which is full of turmoil and shouting and everything. There is fighting, day after day, hour after hour, second after second. With them it is not so. If you are shouting there, it is with peace and love, too."

The Elders wanted to know the answer to a question that probably was the one most asked of Meier: Why had the Pleiadians specifically selected him for the contacts? Matter-of-factly Meier explained that he had been groomed for the contacts since he was a small boy, and before that, in a previous incarnation, he had had contacts with the Pleiadians. According to Meier, the Pleiadians' desire to reveal their presence slowly and without ceremony arose from events that occurred long ago, when early earth humans believed that visitors from elsewhere in the universe were gods or the angels of God.

"The Pleiadians distance themselves every time from such things," he explained. "There is one way around this problem. To tell the people, to tell them again, again and again, what's really happening, what the Pleiadians are really, that they are humans like the humans from this earth, that they are no more. What I have to do practically every day, I have to shout. I have to beat my fist on the table to tell the people what is real. And they have the same problem. But there is one way of teaching. Tell the people day after day, hour after hour, they are really not gods."

"But can they be accepted as people like ourselves?" asked Lee.

"Impossible to connect them," said Meier. "It's exactly the same thing if you have a motor that works with regular gasoline, and you go and put pitch into the gasoline, it blows up."

"They're not like us," said Lee. "They may look like us, they may talk like us—"

"But the vibrations," interrupted Meier, "the waves and everything, that's much higher."

The Elders, of course, had no way of testing Meier's story of what the Pleiadians looked like, how he came to be their contact, or what knowledge and information the Pleiadians, if they existed, had imparted to him. They tried to avoid dealing with such claims, which seemed too outlandish to believe, yet could not be disproved.

"Unless it happens to you," Brit said later, "you're always going to have that little doubt anyhow, 'Is it or isn't it real?' How do you explain it, and how do you rationalize it?"

They wanted to see more of Meier's tangible evidence, what he could offer to establish the Pleiadians' presence. Without this, Meier's stories meant nothing to them.

The next day they were out again, looking at a small meadow tightly surrounded by forest, where two sets of landing tracks had once appeared. At the site they studied the photographs of the tracks. The grass was not broken, just mashed down; according to witnesses it stayed that way for weeks; a single set of footprints led to and from each grouping of three six-foot pod marks. The Elders viewed everything from a perspective of simple logistics; how could it be accomplished: tools, time, expense, expertise? With the landing tracks, no vehicle could be driven to within 250 feet of the site. Whatever was used to make the tracks would have to be light and compact enough to carry through the woods at least that distance. It would have to be heavy enough to mash tall thick grass perfectly flat, yet light enough for one person to twirl without using a center pivot, for the tracks were smooth all the way across. However the swirling was accomplished, it would have to be carried out from a single point at the edge of one of the circles, for no footprints existed elsewhere. How could such an apparatus be made? How could it be transported? And how do you crush grass so it will never rise again, yet remain alive?

That night the Elders were back in the warm kitchen, listening to Meier talk more about earth humans being a younger stage of the Pleiadians' own evolution. "That is one of the reasons they study us," said Meier. "We represent an earlier part of their society."

"What does it feel like to be dematerialized?" asked Brit.

"It is a condition of being well-balanced," said Meier.

"Explain that, please," said Brit.

"As if you would find yourself in eternity," replied Meier. "It starts the moment the dematerialization begins."

"Does it end when you rematerialize?"

"No," explained Meier, "it does not end like that. That condition stays, depending on your own thinking and feeling. You see," he continued, "when I leave the ship, I jump into the hole, and into the hole they, what we call, 'arrange' the material. If you leave the ship and lose your material body, you will not realize it in that moment until the body touches some other material thing, like the ground or a tree."

"When they come out of the ship," asked Brit, "are they dematerialized and do they materialize when they touch the ground?"

"You can't see them," answered Meier. "But if they touch the ground, they will materialize. See, here in this hole [he points to one of the photographs], I don't know exactly if it is this one or one of these other two. But it is open here, and when they jump into the hole they will dematerialize."

"So when they jump out," said Lee, "you don't see them come down, you only see them in here?"

"Yes."

"Now, when their body forms, is there a whiteness . . . ?"

"No."

"It's just solid. It's just, 'They're here,' and then, 'They're gone.' "

"Yes."

"There are no stages of development."

Meier shook his head.

"Colonel Stevens once told me that sometimes when you came back you were out of breath," said Lee. "Is that true?"

"It's because of the atmosphere we have here," explained Meier, "and the atmosphere they have there. They have thirty-two percent oxygen. It is better and lighter breathing."

"The air on board the ship?"

"Yes. Just imagine you are somewhere out in the countryside and then you have to go to the city. And this is very fast, practically a split second from one place to the other."

"Is there anything you've been told not to discuss?" asked Lee.

"Mainly things that concern the future," said Meier. "Also not to talk too much about the teachings, because man has to think for himself to find out the truth."

* * *

"A lot of what he said had to be taken with a grain of salt," Elders said later. "It was hard to conceive of. But yet everything made such logical sense. I think what I focused on was the delivery of what he was saying. Was he emotional? Was he blasé? He was just sitting there as if he were talking about going down to the corner to get a loaf of bread—which made it all appear real; made it very believable.

"Basically he made you stop and think, Why shouldn't they be like us? Why should they be any different as far as family life or education? And if they're two or three thousand years more technologically advanced than us, then sure it would make sense that they carried little devices on their belts that could translate languages instantly. I had to go back to that one phrase he kept saying. 'They're no different than we are.' "

Meier talked on about civilizations that lived in har-

mony in the universe and traveled faster than light, about
life on Erra and the androids and the spiritual leaders
there, about his childhood experiences with Sfath. People
came from all over Europe to hear him speak of these
things. Lee Elders listened closely to everything Meier
said, searching for inconsistency. Not once did Meier con-
tradict himself, nor did he preach or try to sell them
merchandise. Though they offered nothing in the way of
objective proof, Meier's answers to their questions came
patiently and logically.

Unobtrusively, in their comings and goings, in their
conversations with witnesses, the Elders and Stevens explored the farm, the main house and barn, the outbuildings, and the nearby woods, searching for a darkroom, a
machine shop, or unusual rigging or equipment. Everything about the farm seemed old and crude, a cover perhaps, but basic necessities for pulling off such a sophisticated show would require at least electricity, and other
than the thin wire lighting a few bulbs in the kitchen and
living areas, no power lines came to the house or anywhere
else on the farm. But Lee Elders kept looking, finally
narrowing his search to four closed rooms.

"One was under the old carriage house where Jakobus
slept; there's a room down there. That intrigued me. Another was a storage place to the side of the carriage house.
The third area that intrigued me was the basement to the
house itself. And the fourth area was Meier's office. I kept
wondering, What's in there?"

One afternoon, under the pretense of an urgent need to
speak with Jakobus, Elders engineered a stunt Stevens
would never have tried on his own. He dragged Stevens
down the steps leading to Jakobus's room beneath the
carriage house. "We knocked on the door and sort of invited
ourselves in," recalled Elders. Immediately, before Jakobus
could rise, they combed the room and started babbling in
English about farming and the weather and whatever else
came to their minds, none of which Jakobus understood.
Before he could respond, they had satisfied themselves that

Jakobus and his room were clean. Then they started laughing and shook his hand. *"Danke, danke schön!"*

"Very Spartan conditions," said Elders, "nothing abnormal.

"The second area I got into was the equipment room. This was the side of the carriage house facing the farmhouse, and there was nothing in there except saws and hoes and grass cutters and things like this, a lot of equipment they used around the farm.

"And then finally we got into the basement under the house itself. We just went down one day. It was very easy; you come out the back stairs there, down the concrete steps, and turn to your right and come down the other steps. The door was unlocked. We didn't make it obvious that we were skulking or anything like that; we just walked to the door and opened it. 'Ah, wonder what's in here, let's see how they store their food,' or whatever, walked in, and checked it out. They used it for storing their cabbage and carrots and things like that. There was nothing down there. So except for his office we had totally explored everything that we could see which might be a hiding place for something."

Brit found herself in the office and the room adjacent when Elsi Moser, an English-speaking schoolteacher, took her back to show her some contact notes and 11 × 14 blowups of the photographs. But there was little to see—a few books, an old typewriter, an old desk with no drawers, two lamps, and a small cactus garden. "Nothing odd," wrote Brit in her diary. She even had the Meier children show her parts of the farm, including their rooms.

"We've seen nothing strange," Brit recorded after a few days at the farm. "Lee is in a quandary. It's hard not to like Billy and the others. We must remain objective. After all the evidence that's been presented—not analyzed, presented—Lee still questions all. Steve has no objectivity left, just wants more and more and more. I'm on overload."

Stevens and Elders also got into Meier's office after Stevens asked Meier about the sound made by the beamships. Stevens had overheard someone at the farm talking about the sounds, but neither he nor Elders knew a tape existed. Meier surprised them by offering to take them back to his study and play the recording for them. Elders turned on his own tape recorder to capture the eerie, warbling, at times piercing sound that, as far as he knew, could have been produced with a synthesizer. But the tape was nothing they could have analyzed back in the States.

"We were in one of those little crannies there next to his office," said Elders, "and there were chickens all through the damned place, and he was playing the sound and we were recording chickens clucking, roosters squawking, and the beamship purring. And it was a total disaster. When we got back it sounded like we were in a henhouse. So we had to retape them later."

After a few days of circulating around the farm and finding nothing suspicious, the only discovery that shocked Lee Elders was how Meier had his evidence organized.

"He kept everything in the closet and stuffed under drawers, in between mattresses. It was unbelievable. And that first year at the farm there were no doors to close off, just a little curtain between the living area and the area they slept in. People walked through there all the time. He used to keep these beautiful photographs in shoe boxes under his bed!" Several hundred photographs had disappeared.

*　*　*

Among the witnesses with whom the Elders spoke was Herbert Runkel, who told them of the first time he went on a contact with Meier, not the night of the dense fog, but an earlier night. Jakobus drove that night too. When Meier disappeared into the woods, it had been raining, there were puddles on the road, and the trees swayed in the wind. An hour passed as the two men sat in the car at the edge of the forest and talked, or walked back and forth to keep warm. They never saw any lights.

"Nothing," Herbert said to the Elders. "No animal, no

light, no car, nothing. No sounds, no house, no nothing. Only the wind blowing."

After an hour and twenty minutes, Meier had returned.

"I remember when Billy came back," said Herbert. "I put my hand on his shoulder, 'Hello, you are back,' and I saw his clothes were completely dry. I shook his hand. He was warm."

Lee Elders was certain this was merely a trick of some sort. He questioned Herbert. Could Meier have had a shelter in the woods, a small fire going, turned his coat inside out?

"No," said Herbert, "that's impossible because we were always looking around. We looked up at the sky and listened carefully because we wanted to see something or hear something, maybe when the ship rose up."

One thing that struck the Elders about Herbert was the confusion on his face when he recounted his experiences with Meier. The man obviously was intelligent and well read, yet he seemed totally perplexed by what he had seen. Often he would end a story by saying, "I am not crazy. I saw that with my own eyes."

Elsi Moser taught school in a nearby canton. A warm and intelligent woman of fifty who had lived for two years in England and spoke excellent English, Elsi told the Elders, "If Billy really had contact every time he said he did, I don't know. But he has had contact with extraterrestrials. I am certain of this."

One of the little things that had convinced Elsi that the contacts were taking place was a film Meier had shot with his movie camera on a tripod. In the clip, what appears to be a beamship hovers at some distance. Meier himself suddenly comes into the film from the right, the left sleeve of his old green sweater dangling as he walks away from the camera down a path. Then he stops and, with his right hand, beckons the ship to come closer. But the ship remains in the distance. Meier squats on his haunches, waiting for a minute or two watching the sky. Once, he looks at the camera and points to the ship, which still moves no closer. Finally, he shrugs, and with a look of disappointment walks back toward the tripod, as the ship still hovers high in the distance. Elsi told the Elders they would have to know German and the Swiss-German people to understand this, because the disappointment on Meier's face when the ship does not come closer is genuine.

Many witnesses had seen strange lights in the sky, perfectly silent lights, sometimes white, sometimes red and yellow and orange, often in twos, and flying crazy patterns. Even more of the witnesses had seen Meier himself do unexplainable things. Harold Proch told the Elders about New Year's Eve 1977, a night when Meier and about ten other people had been sitting around the kitchen table talking. Harold had asked Meier a question about parapsychology, but Meier did not answer directly.

"He asked if I had a two-franc piece," recalled Harold. "I didn't have one, so Elsi gave one to me. Billy took it and told me to hold his hand. I sat on the opposite side from him."

Meier wrapped his fingers around the two-franc piece, a coin the size of an American half-dollar. Harold cupped his hands around Meier's fist. Meier looked at the fist and suddenly his whole body began to tremble. The table shook, as did Meier's chair. Several people found themselves suddenly fearing the power that had been unleashed. Harold held on to the shaking fist, but when he looked up at Meier's eyes, what he saw there startled him.

"This is hard to describe," he said later. "It was as if you were looking into space through his eyes."

For fifteen seconds Meier shook violently as though the coin in his fist controlled him. His eyes grew larger and larger, deeper and deeper, his face now contorted and drained of all blood.

"Then he collapsed at the table," said Harold, "his hand opened and the coin fell out. It was black. All the people stood up, Billy was gasping, as if he were dead. It was phenomenal. And I sat face-to-face with him. I could see the reaction on his face. I have never seen anything like it. You can't describe this with words."

The hot coin had singed the palm of Meier's hand, causing a blister. When Harold had the coin analyzed, a metallurgist told him that to scorch such metal would require a heat of 1,500 degrees.

* * *

Another evening the Elders and Stevens sat again in the kitchen listening to similar stories from people who had seen Meier do things no one could explain. Meier had done so many things no one could explain that the stories had begun to sound the same to the Elders. Some people had seen him hold a twenty-centime piece between his thumb and index finger, and etch his fingerprints into the metal. Elsi had once seen him take a nail two to three inches long, stand it on its head on the kitchen table, then cup his hand on the table about eight inches away. In a moment, as though drawn by some irresistible force, the nail had started to dance across the table and vibrated upright all the way into Meier's motionless hand.

"When did you realize you had this power?" Brit asked Meier.

"When I was a small boy," said Meier. "I started to learn new thinking."

"For this power of the mind," suggested Lee, "could you use the word 'magic'?"

"You see," said Meier, "magic is a word that means only '*using* the power.' Nothing else. Only 'power using.' "

"And when did you discover you had magic in your life?" Lee repeated Brit's question.

"When I was a small boy."

"What did you do?"

"I was taught by Sfath," said Meier. "He told me how to use everything, how to study to learn."

"Could you make things move," asked Lee, "or put out a candle by thinking about it?"

"I was never testing," answered Meier. "I don't know."

And then he told them a brief story. When he was six years old and weighed only fifty-five pounds, his father was constructing a small addition to their house and had asked the young boy to wheel a cart filled with dirt out of a deep hole he had dug under a portion of the house. The cart weighed two or three times as much as Meier at that young age. But by "using the power," he told the Elders, he was able to lift the cart with his thoughts and transport it out of the hole.

Among the favorite stories told by witnesses who had seen Meier do unexplainable things was the time during a discussion he had melted a thick metal spoon in his bare hand. Meier had been stirring his coffee when, to emphasize a point, he raised the spoon out of the coffee and shook it. The raised spoon suddenly had turned to a silver liquid in his hand and dripped onto the table. Several people had seen this.

As he listened to this story, Stevens said, "Man, why didn't you save the liquid?" Nobody had thought to do that. With the liquid in small puddles on the table, someone had simply wiped it up with a damp cloth. But the story got Stevens thinking out loud. "God," he said, "what we could do with a piece of metal."

When Stevens said that, Meier stood up from the table and said, "Just a minute."

He walked out of the kitchen and they heard his footsteps heading out to the barn.

"He came back with this dilapidated, dirty, filthy cardboard box," remembered Lee. "And he put it on the kitchen table. Inside he had brown wrapping paper, and he started opening it. All of us were just hanging over his shoulder."

"I asked them to give me a piece of the beamship," said Meier, "but all they brought me were some metal samples."

Lee Elders stood quickly and took two pictures, one of Brit helping Meier open the box, and another of Brit and Stevens peering into the box. Inside lay several small packages of brown wrapping paper, and in each package, carefully wrapped, was a sample that Meier claimed had been given to him by the Pleiadians.

"We were in the kitchen there," remembered Elders, "and Meier had just shown us the metal. Bashenko was running amuck, slamming things against the wall, yelling, trying to get attention. On top of that, a chimney sweep was there cleaning the chimney. But we had the microphone close to Meier, you can hear what he's saying, and it was real interesting because he said one thing and that was that this metal is used to make the ship."

Meier started to unwrap the little packages, and one after another out came a small rock specimen, or a crystal, or a shiny fragment of metal.

"They told me that the metal is in four states," said Meier. "Here are the notes I made."

In each cubicle, brown and somewhat faded, lay small pieces of paper, Meier's handwritten notes on each of the specimens, describing briefly what each was and from where it came. According to the notes, one of the samples he unwrapped represented the next-to-the-final stage in a seven-step process the Pleiadians used to make the metal substance that comprised the hull of the beamships. On the table glistened a half-inch triangle appearing to be an alloy containing silver and gold.

Stevens had always told the Elders that pictures could be faked, but one thing that could never be faked was a piece of metal exhibiting unusual, possibly unearthly properties. However, this solid kind of evidence rarely accompanied UFO cases. In all of Stevens's experience such an intriguing piece of evidence had arisen perhaps twice. Yet Meier had been sitting on these specimens for over three years, and he had made no attempt whatsoever to use them to sell his story to Stevens, to "prove" he was telling the truth. Stevens had to ask about them specifically. And this was his second trip to see Meier. Again, Stevens learned that with Meier he had to ask the question or he would never get an answer.

Meier gave several metal and crystal samples to

Stevens and the Elders to have them analyzed back in the United States if they desired. Now nearing the end of their five days in Switzerland, they had many signed witness statements and several items that could be tested in a laboratory by a scientist—photographs, metal samples, sound recordings, and movie footage.

"It's overkill for us by this time," remembered Elders. "We've just heard sounds, we've heard all these stories, now he's showing us metal. It's just flat overkill. Steve had been there the year before and he had no idea . . . none of us had any idea . . . that Meier had metal specimens, or sounds, or the numerous photographs he had."

At the conclusion of their stay, Stevens seemed even more overwhelmed than he had upon completing his first trip to the farm.

"It just got to the point where one man couldn't have done so much so well to fool so many people for so long," he said. "Just too much for one person to accomplish. Having tried to do a number of these things myself I realized what was involved in faking a simple picture of a suspended object in the sky. To fake all of the types and kinds of pictures successfully and not be caught, with no confederates, no resources, no equipment, no money, no lab, and a broken camera and one arm, makes it a little bit difficult to believe that the whole thing is a fabrication and a fraud perpetrated by somebody for some reason when there wasn't even an apparent reason."

Because of his obvious intelligence and sincerity, the great deal of time he had spent observing Meier, and the resulting confusion in his mind, perhaps the most convincing witness had been Herbert Runkel. Herbert warned the Elders and Stevens that people who had seen only a few of Meier's pictures and then concluded that the object had to be a model and that the case therefore had to be a hoax, just did not understand the reality of the setting in which the story was taking place.

"These thoughts always come from people who know nothing about the case," said Herbert. "They hear about the case, or they see only one or two pictures. They never go to the place where the pictures were taken. Because people who have seen the places always say, 'That is not possible.' "

Though a shallow crust of snow remained in large patches on the ground, the Elders finally walked one of the sites, the high green bluff at Hasenbol. As he stood on top of the bluff Lee Elders thought about what Herbert had said. "My moment of truth did not come until I walked that site," he said later. "I went up to that hilltop where he shot, I'd say, thirty percent of the best photographs of his collection plus that film, and I knew right then and there something was going on—because of the distance involved, because of the terrain, everything about it. We marked fifty-two yards from where Meier stood to the tree the ship was hovering behind. That's a long distance. You're not going to use small models on that."

"And there's a drop right behind that tree," added Brit. "It just goes straight down."

"And it's always cold there," continued Lee, "wind's always blowing, cold and miserable. Yet he got movie footage on that site and photographs on that site. So that's when I started thinking, Okay, so he didn't take them with models, and they are not pasteups. So what are they?"

PART II

THE INVESTIGATION

SEVEN

On the clear blue afternoon of June 24, 1947, along the high, snow-covered ridges of Mount Rainier, Washington, a bolt of bright light hit a small mountain plane flown by Kenneth Arnold so suddenly that Arnold thought he was about to collide with another plane. Instead, he spied a formation of nine luminescent objects, bright enough to be seen a hundred miles away, skimming the mountaintops at extraordinary speed. Arnold thought he was watching a test flight of new and secret jet planes, but as they came closer he could see no tails on any of the craft.

The strange objects closed at right angles to Arnold's plane, flying like nothing he had ever seen: The echelon formed a pinnacle with the lead craft at the top, the others trailing behind and below, the reverse of military air formations. And their flight was erratic. As Arnold wrote later in his book, *The Coming of the Saucers,* "It was like speed boats on rough water or similar to the tail of a Chinese kite that I once saw blowing in the wind." The craft fascinated him with the way they "fluttered and sailed, tipping their wings alternately and emitting those very bright blue-white flashes from their surfaces."*

When Arnold landed in Pendleton, Oregon, he attempted to locate a representative of the Federal Bureau of Investigation, but was unsuccessful. Instead, he talked to other pilots at the airport about what he had seen; then local reporters heard of the sighting, and within two days Arnold's story had hit 150 newspapers. He told the press the craft flew "like a saucer would if you skipped it across the water," prompting one reporter to coin the term "flying saucer."

In the midst of a cold war with the Soviet Union, intelligence analysts in the United States suspected the Communists of conceiving ingenious and extravagant plots to spread their propaganda, even among the American populace. When the story of Arnold's sighting appeared in print, his politics, finances, business, and reputation in the community were investigated by Military Intelligence, the FBI, the Central Intelligence Agency, and the Internal Revenue Service, each hoping to discover that Arnold was unstable, publicity-conscious, given to exaggeration, or linked to the Communist Party. But not only was Arnold considered an excellent mountain pilot with a cool head, calm hand, and 20/15 vision, his general reputation in the community and as a family man was impeccable.

Then other reputable citizens, many of them pilots, reported strange aircraft penetrating hundreds of miles inland from the West Coast, aircraft that appeared super-

---

* Arnold timed the lead craft from the southern edge of Mount Rainier all the way to Mount Adams, a distance of 39.8 miles, which the disk flew in one minute and forty-two seconds. In the summer of 1947, the fastest experimental aircraft on earth was thought to be the U.S. Army's X-1, developed by Bell Aircraft Corporation. A bullet-shaped fuselage with a rocket engine, the X-1 was powered to exceed the speed of sound, 760 miles an hour, but no pilot had yet been able to fly it that fast. Chuck Yeager would not break the sound barrier in the X-1 for another four months. Yet Arnold's figures, trimmed conservatively, had the shiny metallic disks traveling almost Mach 2, or twice the speed of sound.

sonic, sophisticated, and unconventionally designed. Newspapers reported each of the new sightings, and the public wanted to know what they were.

Hallucination, said the Air Force. There was no need for an investigation into the presence of these flying saucers because all of the sightings were due to hallucination. Secretly, they wondered if perhaps Communist sympathizers, attempting to frighten the American public, had reported bogus sightings to increase cold war jitters. Or was the intention to get the Air Force so soft on responding to myriad reports of lights in the night sky that waves of Soviet bombers could penetrate our air defenses unchallenged?

But then their own pilots, navigators, generals, and advanced radar detectors began reporting strange flying craft that could stop on a dime, hover, ascend and descend in a straight line, turn at right angles, make no noise, and then take off at speeds into the thousands of miles an hour. If it was the Soviets, why had no bombs been dropped, no missiles been deployed, or overt strategic action taken by these craft? They would simply appear at all times of the day and night, in all parts of the country, dazzle their onlookers with their incredible speed and maneuverability, and then disappear. No one considered what later came to be known as the extraterrestrial hypothesis, the possibility that such technology might originate on worlds trillions of miles into our galaxy or even beyond.

* * *

During World War II, American and British pilots had reported seeing strange objects that flew at fantastic speeds and glowed from orange to red and white, and back to orange again. They named them "foo fighters." One pilot saw fifteen of them during the day, describing them as five-foot golden spheres that shone with a metallic glitter. Near Truk Lagoon in Japan, B-29 bomber crews reported the balls came up from below their cockpits, hovered over their tails, winked their lights from red to orange, then back to red, then to white. One pilot said they glowed with an eerie red phosphorescence and had no wings, fins, or fuselage. Allied fighter pilots thought they were secret German experimental devices designed to cause fear and confusion. Intelligence officers figured they were radio-controlled objects launched to baffle radar. The Germans and Japanese thought they were secret weapons launched by the Allies. Scientists in New York surmised everyone had been seeing "Saint Elmo's lights," small balls of luminescence often connected with metal during electrical storms. The Army Air Forces dismissed the whole episode as a result of "war nerves" and "mass hallucination."

The summer before Arnold's sighting, hundreds of people in Scandinavia had watched flights of "ghost rockets" in the night sky, speeding balls of light that resembled meteors but behaved in what was described as "unmeteorlike fashion." American intelligence suspected the source might be Russian experiments at the captured German missile center at Peenemünde, but no evidence existed, and eventually the ghost rockets ceased flying without offering a clue as to what they were or from where they came.

But in 1947, Arnold's sighting captured the world's imagination. Only three months later, such sightings had become so frequent that General Nathan Twining, head of Air Materiel Command, wrote a letter to the commanding general of the Air Force that concluded: "The phenomenon reported is something real and not visionary or fictitious. . . . The reported operating characteristics such as extreme rates of climb, maneuverability (particularly in roll), and action which must be considered evasive when sighted or contacted by friendly aircraft and radar, lend belief to the possibility that some of the objects are controlled either manually, automatically or remotely."

Quickly and quietly, the Air Force established Project Sign, which began officially two weeks after an F-51 fighter pilot, Thomas Mantell, died chasing a UFO near Louisville, Kentucky. Mantell's last words were: "It's metallic and it's tremendous in size. Now it's starting to climb." A few seconds later: "It's above me and I'm gaining on it. I'm going to 20,000 feet." It was not yet three o'clock in the afternoon. Mantell was not heard from again; an hour later the tower lost sight of the UFO and learned that Mantell's F-51 had crashed.

Before the wreckage had cooled, the Air Force offered a solution that seemed to satisfy press and public alike— Venus. For thirty minutes, Mantell had chased the planet, even climbing without oxygen beyond the point of blackout, to get a better look at Venus. He had died in pursuit of a planet millions of miles away. Though Venus indeed would become the solution to many of the sightings, on that day, at three o'clock in the afternoon over the state of Kentucky, Venus was a pinpoint of light so faint it could not be seen by the human eye. Even the secret report filed by Project Sign investigators concluded: "The mysterious object which the flyer chased to his death was first identified as the Planet Venus. However, further probing showed the elevation and azimuth readings of Venus and that object at specified time intervals did not coincide. It is still considered 'Unidentified.'"

Project Sign drew only high-level intelligence specialists, and period correspondence reveals that amid a great deal of confusion bordering on panic, they developed two categories of theory: earthly and non-earthly. In the earthly category, the Russians outdistanced our own Navy, which earlier had been conducting secret experiments with the XF-5-U-1, a circular craft nicknamed the Flying Flapjack. In the non-earthly, "space animals" placed second behind interplanetary craft.

Since the second theory was impossible to test, intelligence analysts sought initially to determine if captured German rocket and missile testing centers, now in Soviet hands, had produced these sophisticated aircraft. German aeronautical engineers had been developing several radical designs, and an intelligence rumor held that the Russians were continuing the experiments. Intelligence analysts studied every intelligence report dealing with German aeronautical research and computed the maximum performance that could be expected from the German designs. They even contacted the German engineers themselves. "Could the Russians develop a flying saucer from these designs?" they asked. The answer was that no aircraft could perform the reported maneuvers of the flying saucers. Such maneuvers and fantastic speeds would either tear apart or melt all aerodynamic materials known on earth. Even if such an aircraft could be built, the human body would not survive at the controls.

One strange sighting after another continued to baffle the Air Force. From 1948 into 1951 "green fireballs" flew over the supersensitive Atomic Energy Commission installation at Los Alamos, traveling an estimated maximum speed of 27,000 miles an hour. Dozens of scientists, Air Force special agents, airline pilots, military pilots, and Los Alamos security inspectors submitted over two hundred reports of seeing the objects—huge half moons, circles, and disks flying at extreme velocities and emitting a green light so bright it caused the contours of surrounding mountains to glow momentarily at night. Some of the witnesses reported watching flat, disk-shaped objects traveling at equally high speeds and varying in color from brilliant white to amber, red, and green.

A private pilot flying one night north of Santa Fe encountered one of the fireballs and described it this way: "Take a softball and paint it with some kind of fluorescent paint that will glow a bright green in the dark. Then have someone take the ball out about a hundred feet in front of you and about ten feet above you. Have him throw the ball right at your face, as hard as he can throw it. That's what a green fireball looks like."

The Air Force hired Dr. Lincoln LaPaz, an expert on meteors, to solve the mystery, but LaPaz concluded the phenomena were not of meteoric origin. He thought the fireballs were guided missiles being secretly tested nearby. But the military and the FBI knew that no such secret experiments were under way in this country, and they had now been assured that the Russians were also incapable of conducting such experiments.

In January 1949 a cable sent from the San Antonio field office to FBI Director J. Edgar Hoover noted that at weekly conferences involving military intelligence the main topic was "the matter of 'Unidentified Aircraft' or 'Unidentified Aerial Phenomena,' otherwise known as 'Flying Discs,' 'Flying Saucers,' and 'Balls of Fire.' *This matter is considered top secret by Intelligence Officers of both the Army and the Air Forces* [emphasis in original]."

Publicly, the Air Force maintained that flying saucers were nothing more than the sun reflecting off low-hanging clouds, or crystals from shattered meteors glinting in the sun's rays, or gigantic hailstones gliding through the atmosphere. But their intelligence analysts began to focus seriously on the possibility of extraterrestrial origin.

In 1951 several reputable scientists speculated that the green fireballs over Los Alamos were unmanned test vehicles projected into our atmosphere from a "spaceship" several hundred miles above earth. About this time, three White Sands scientists with a telescope, stopwatch, and clipboard tracked a flat, oval-shaped object a hundred feet in length and whitish silver in color flying at an altitude of 296,000 feet and a speed of 25,200 miles an hour. One of the scientists, a naval commander, later wrote in an article cleared by the Navy, "I am convinced that it was a flying saucer, and further, that these disks are spaceships from another planet, operated by animate, intelligent beings."

When an airline captain and his co-pilot sighted "a deep blue glow" along the underside of what looked like a wingless B-29 fuselage that came within 700 feet of their DC-3, intelligence analysts at Project Sign decided it was time to write an "Estimate of the Situation." The top-secret "Estimate" concluded that from all evidence collected, the presence of the mysterious flying objects could best be explained by visitations from advanced extraterrestrial societies. And this hypothesis might have formed the basis for all future UFO research if Air Force Chief of Staff

General Hoyt S. Vandenberg hadn't adamantly refused to accept it. Instead, he fired the document back to Air Intelligence, where it was quickly declassified and burned, encouraging Sign personnel still bucking for promotion to drop their original hypothesis for an official new one: UFOs don't exist.

* * *

Performing most of their security work late at night when corporate offices lay deserted, the Elders and Welch had become night people who functioned best in the early hours of the morning; Stevens could go either way, as long as he had a breakfast of sausage, eggs, and pancakes after midnight. When the Elders returned from Switzerland, the four of them spent hours in all-night coffee shops, eating breakfast or pie, drinking coffee or iced tea, and collectively scratching their heads over Meier. At 1 or 2 a.m. they might drive to Good's on Camelback Road or Carrow's on Thomas, tell the waitress, "We'll have iced tea, and leave us alone," then retire to a corner booth in the back of the restaurant to argue over Meier for the next two hours. "We became connoisseurs of iced tea," said Welch.

Between bites of breakfast and sips of coffee, Stevens would shake his head. Sometimes he would even jump up and pace excitedly back and forth next to the booth, admitting openly he had lost all objectivity in the case. "I don't understand a lot of things about this," he would tell the others. "But I am convinced that something strange happened, and I am convinced that Meier could not fake the pictures, and I don't think there's anybody around him that could."

After one of the late-night sessions, Brit wrote in her diary, "Steve excited about stuff from Billy. Thinks we've got a 'real one.' Lee still skeptical, calling in favors, hopes to find good qualified people for analysis. Initial budget $10,000 set aside. Plan trip to L.A., try to dig into universities there, maybe turn in interesting stone."

Later Brit admitted she pushed Lee hard to get involved in the Meier investigation. "He was reluctant. Deep down inside he liked Meier, they hit it off. But with Intercep and everything that was happening, it was hard to let go and start off in a new direction. But Lee's a very curious person, and this had too much to offer. He sat down and said, 'How did he create this hoax?' Steve was already committed, Lee was the balance."

Stevens's only concern was that Meier might have almost too much evidence. And the number of contacts Meier claimed, like the clarity of his photographs, made his story seem even more suspect.

"The conventional idea of a contact is a quick happenstance, a onetime experience that passes, doesn't come back," Stevens explained to the others. "When the second contact occurs it reduces in the minds of UFO buffs the credibility factor. It's kind of a 'lightning doesn't strike twice in the same place' syndrome. When it happens a third time, credibility is reduced even further. This happened over a hundred times."

Lee Elders retained his skepticism, challenging Stevens again and again, for no matter what the witnesses had said, he had difficulty understanding certain things, like Meier's sudden disappearances and just as sudden reappearances. He thought the man had somehow merely persuaded the others to imagine he had vanished: "I can't buy that somebody can be standing in his office and have all his molecules broken down into a beam of light or whatever and transferred two miles away to another locale. I just cannot conceive of this."

Then he would argue with himself in front of the others, as if he were alone. "But we have so much supportive evidence documenting other things that we can't say, 'Well, if they say this crazy thing is happening, then the whole thing has to be a hoax.'

"But, my God," he would argue again, "if this thing *is* legitimate, how do we logically explain Meier being dematerialized?"

Then they would spend two and a half hours trying to comprehend how he disappeared.

"Did he really disappear?" they wondered.

"Our comfort level," said Elders, "was dealing with solid, tangible evidence. But there's another level here that just taxes the imagination. You can't say that the case is a hoax because it contains this level, any more than you can leave it out and say the case is real. But it's unexplainable."

The arguments over Meier got longer and became more frequent, involved more restaurants, more sausage, eggs, and hot pie, more coffee and iced tea. As Stevens had predicted, Meier and his story had gone right to the core of the Elders's curiosity, challenging their considerable investigative skills. Once recalling the many late-night conversations, Lee Elders said, "It wasn't so much, 'Do you think Meier is telling the truth?' We were way beyond that. It was the mystery that was driving us crazy, these little things that didn't make sense."

The brief side trip they had taken to Switzerland reluctantly, and only as a favor to a friend, had piqued their interest and at the same time failed to yield an explanation for the bizarre story. But in addition to their own impressions, they now held several items of hard evidence. They could argue forever over imponderables, but proper analysis of the evidence would give them answers.

"So we went directly for the hard stuff," remembered Brit. "We worked with the photographs, the metals, the sounds, everything like that. We went in looking for how he did it, because we didn't believe it was real."

* * *

At the Elders's apartment in Phoenix and on Stevens's dining room table in Tucson sat several stacks of paper, film, and other evidence waiting to be examined—rough notes taken at a few of the sites, the interviews and signed statements of many witnesses, hundreds of translated pages of the contact notes, taped interviews with Meier, over two hundred photographs, pictures of landing tracks, metal and crystal samples, and seven 8mm films. The Elders and Stevens labeled every piece, catalogued it, then combed through it all, searching for clues and inconsistencies. In thirty-two years of studying UFOs, there was little about them Stevens did not know, and he had never heard of a case with so much evidence.

"It's a lot of work," said Welch. "You have to sit down and analyze it. Not study, not read—analyze. Do we have any correlations here? Find them all and list them, potential or otherwise. Do we have any contradictions? Find them all and list them. Everything. We had to develop an attack plan. So on a daily basis we were jamming on our notes, getting together on the things that Lee and Brit had learned from their first trip, and that Steve had brought back, correlating data, and planning our next trip in July, which was to be my first trip there."

With computer theft occurring more and more frequently, and the reputation of Intercep growing apace, the Phoenix-based security firm continued to expand. But the Elders and Welch also spent more and more time on the Meier case. Between conducting communications sweeps for various corporate clients, they met frequently with Stevens to analyze the data they had collected and to plot a course on how to proceed. At the beginning they had initiated a rapidly expanding list of questions to be answered; the next step was to pin down a precise, acceptable method for determining the authenticity of photographs.

"The photographs in a sense were too real," remembered Welch. "They were so clear and so stark, it was as if a craft was in the air over your driveway and you walked outside and took a picture of it. They were that vivid."

Stevens already had examined the photogrpahs closely, looking for missing or misplaced shadows. The only additional test they could think to perform was to blow up a photo into the largest format possible, then search it carefully with a microscope for inconsistencies in the grain. Such inconsistencies would indicate that Meier had placed the craft in a scene either by exposing the same piece of film twice or by superimposing two separate pieces of film to create a single picture. Either way the grain would appear thickened around the craft. But when they blew up the film and examined the grain, they found nothing.

Stevens continued his work, begun a year earlier, of cataloguing the photographs according to site. In the process he discovered that, as with the Hasenbol series, nearly every picture Meier had taken was part of a *sequence,* with the flight path uniform from picture to picture as the object moved low over the hills or flew directly at the camera. On his first trip to Switzerland Stevens had noted that the numbers at the edge of each slide in Meier's collection were in proper order with no interruptions. Stevens also discovered that Meier's camera had a "signature," a tiny speck of dirt or lint just to the right of center near the top of each slide. The signature itself remained constant in every picture.

In Switzerland, Stevens had taken about twelve of what he thought were original Meier slides to a photo shop in the city of Winterthur. At his instruction the shop had made clean internegatives of each slide, first-generation copies that Stevens brought back to the States to have tested. But so much of the evidence in Switzerland had been through so many hands that he could not be certain of the generation of the slides he had taken to Winterthur. As he would discover later, many of the people who had come to Meier in the early days of the contacts had been permitted to borrow Meier's negatives to make copies of the photographs. They had returned the copies to Meier and kept the originals.

* * *

For several weeks the Elders, Welch, and Stevens had been sifting through the data and designing procedures for testing the evidence when an acquaintance heard about their efforts and contacted a friend of his, documentary filmmaker John Stefanelli. As an independent producer, the thirty-six-year-old Stefanelli had made two theatrical features, five documentaries, and many educational films. Before that he had worked at Disney for seven years, including two years in production budgeting on such films as *The Love Bug* and *The Jungle Book*. He knew how special effects experts transferred images on to film and how much it cost to stage such special effects.

"If this Meier thing was a fraud," he said, "it was done with some sort of special effects technique. And a lot of those techniques were used by Disney Studios and I was very familiar with them because of my experience there. I knew what it cost."

Stefanelli's friend had told him the Elders were investigating a rare UFO case, one that for the first time presented a significant amount of evidence for scientists to study; the thought of documenting on film the testing of that evidence intrigued him. But Lee Elders hesitated to show the evidence to anyone. Not until the acquaintance assured him that Stefanelli was a knowledgeable producer with a good track record did Elders confirm the investigation and offer to show some of the evidence to Stefanelli. They agreed to meet at B. B. Singer's, a mid-Phoenix cocktail lounge.

When Stefanelli arrived there he found Lee Elders and Tom Welch sitting in a corner half-circle booth. Elders had nothing with him but a thin manila folder lying in front of him on the table. After introducing themselves the three men talked for a while, about Stefanelli's background and experience in film, including his years with Disney, and about the Elders's trip to see Meier and what they had brought back with them. Once he felt satisfied that not only was Stefanelli legitimate, but he also wanted to produce a credible film, Elders opened the folder and spread before the filmmaker a dozen high-gloss 8 × 10 photographs. Stefanelli nearly came out of his seat.

"The pictures just knocked my socks off," he said. "I was very impressed. My first reaction was, 'Wow!' My second reaction was, 'Oh, come on, this is really hard to believe.' "

"You could tell he was having problems with a lot of it,"

Elders said later. "We must have had the same look on our faces when Meier was telling us about the Pleiadians coming to Earth in seven hours, and how they have gardens back on Erra."

Stefanelli sat there in a quandary. In his mind the crazy things Elders told him about Meier could not possibly coexist with the reality of the pictures. So either the crazy story was, in fact, true or the beautiful photographs had somehow been faked. And he couldn't believe they had been faked.

"If someone was doing this fraudulently," he said, "they were doing a hell of a job. I was fascianted by it. And the more I got into it, the more I found it really intriguing."

Stefanelli met often with the Intercep group and Stevens in his own office and Lee Elders's apartment, monitoring the progress of their investigation, and on his own, arranging for some preliminary testing of the evidence. He put together a prospectus, persuaded two screenwriters to pen a treatment, and began talking to investors. His idea was to follow the Elders's investigation, document all of the testing, even arrange a science outlay in the film budget for assuring quality scientific analysis, and then produce a two-hour docudrama.

"It's an absolutely fascinating story," he said later. "Whether it's a fraud or whether it's true, it's incredible. And my approach was not to try to prove it or disprove it; it was just to go after all the evidence and analyze it to its fullest extent."

But finding scientists willing even to look at the photographs, examine the metal, or listen to the sounds proved to be far more difficult than Stefanelli had anticipated. He knew the public still laughed at people who saw flying saucers, but with hard evidence in his hands he expected scientists to be at least intrigued. When he took a sample of the metal to UCLA for preliminary analysis, he returned with the sample and the discovery that the stigma of UFOs still existed.

"When I went in," he recalled, "I expected to be greeted

with open arms, and I wasn't at all. I was just another kook coming in off the street. I explained the project, I told them what evidence there was and what the story was, and they just didn't want to be bothered. They finally turned me over to a graduate student who had some interest in it. He did some testing, kept the sample for a couple of days, and came back and said the testing had been inconclusive. He did say it was unusual, it could be from another planet, but it was certainly possible that you could find it on this planet."

* * *

With General Vandenberg's refusal to accept the extraterrestrial hypothesis, Project Sign became Project Grudge in early 1949. Grudge personnel evaluated reports on the premise that UFOs *couldn't* exist. They explained every sighting as a weather balloon, a meteor, or the planet Venus. What came to be known as the Grudge Report concluded that unidentified flying objects were no direct threat to national security, and that reports of such objects resulted from a mild form of mass hysteria or the misidentification of conventional objects, or were hoaxes fabricated by psychopaths and publicity seekers. But Dr. Allen Hynek, Ohio State University astronomer and consultant to Projects Sign and Grudge, had studied 237 of the best sightings and attributed only 32 percent of them to various astronomical bodies. Another 12 percent had been discarded as being weather balloons; and hoaxes, incomplete reports, and airplanes made up exactly one-third. No one could explain the remaining 23 percent, not Hynek, not the Air Force Weather Service, and not even the subcontracted Rand Corporation. The Grudge Report dismissed them with this sentence: "There are sufficient psychological explanations for the reports of unidentified flying objects to provide plausible explanations for reports not otherwise explainable." From the beginning of 1950 to the middle of 1951, Grudge remained a project in name only.

Not until 3:04 on the afternoon of September 12, 1951, did Air Force Intelligence have reason to resuscitate Proj-

135

ect Grudge. On that day the teletype at Air Technical Intelligence Command spit out three feet of tiny print on a sighting at Fort Monmouth, New Jersey, that had occurred two days earlier. At eleven o'clock in the morning, a technician at the Monmouth radar school had been demonstrating the latest tracking equipment to a group of military VIPs. Capable of automatically "painting" a target, the new device could track the fastest jets. But when it locked on a low-flying object two and a half miles east of the radar station, the set immediately kicked back into manual operation. The operator again switched the set to automatic, and again the set kicked back to manual. For three minutes the target remained in range as the radar operator frantically tried to force the set to track it automatically and the set refused to respond. Finally, the embarrassed technician turned to the VIPs gathered around the scope and said, "It's going too fast for the set."

In the vicinity less than a half hour later, the pilot of a T-33 jet trainer, with an Air Force major on board, saw flying below him a disk thirty to fifty feet in diameter and silver in color. As he rolled the T-33 and dived toward the disk, the silvery object stopped, hovered for a few moments, then accelerated heading south, and without slowing made a 120-degree turn and disappeared out over the ocean.

Immediately, the Director of Air Force Intelligence ordered a new UFO project and assigned Captain Edward Ruppelt as its head. Later in his book, *The Report on Unidentified Flying Objects,* Ruppelt wrote that when he arrived at Air Technical Intelligence Command he was told, "The powers that be are anti–flying saucer, and to stay in favor, it behooves one to follow suit," a carryover from the mind-set of Grudge personnel. Ruppelt described them as "schizophrenic," officially laughing at the UFO reports coming in, and individually, in private, defending the phenomenon. Grudge became Project Blue Book in early 1952, and the reports trickling in each month increased to about twenty. In April they jumped to ninety-nine. The following month, the Secretary of the Air Force said in a press statement, "No concrete evidence has yet reached us either to prove or disprove the existence of the so-called flying saucers. There remain, however, a number of sightings that the Air Force investigators have been unable to explain." Then at 11:40 on the night of July 19, 1952, seven objects suddenly appeared on the radar screen at Washington National Airport, three miles south of the nation's capital.

* * *

The seven green blips cruised through forbidden air corridors, moving slowly across the radar screen at 100 to 130 miles an hour. Suddenly, two of the objects accelerated to tremendous speed and almost instantaneously flew beyond the range of the radar, a distance of 100 miles. Four radar controllers agreed that nothing like an airplane could cause the blips on the scope. Then two other radar centers, one at nearby Andrews Air Force Base, called in. Painted on their scopes, they had the same targets performing the same speed bursts; and now the targets had moved into every quadrant on the scope and were flying in prohibited airways over the White House and the Capitol. One of the targets had been clocked at 7,000 miles an hour.

As airline pilots in the vicinity radioed that they were being followed by unknown aircraft, or that the aircraft suddenly seemed to be leaving, the luminescent blips on ground radar would appear or trail away. In the early hours after midnight, the most powerful of the radar installations, located at Washington National Airport, radioed the operators at Andrews that one target appeared to be hovering directly above them. When the operators rushed out and looked up they saw "a huge fiery-orange sphere." And then all of the objects disappeared.

One week later the same radar controllers locked again on the mysterious objects. This time the objects formed a wide arc around Washington, and the controllers called in two F-94 interceptors, which arrived just after midnight. But when the jets appeared on the radar screens, the targets suddenly disappeared. The jets returned to base. As soon as the jets departed, the targets appeared once again. In the interim, Langley Air Force Base in Virginia had received calls of bright lights in the sky, "rotating and giving off alternating colors." The Air Force scrambled another F-94 from Langley and the pilot made visual contact with one of the lights, but as he closed on it, it suddenly disappeared, "like somebody turning off a light bulb." The radar operator in the F-94 made contact three more times, but each time contact was broken as the strange object apparently accelerated out of range within seconds.

A few minutes after the object broke radar contact for the last time, the green blips appeared again en masse on the radar screens at Washington National Airport. The Air Force scrambled two more jets and this time the targets remained stationary, so the radar controllers could monitor both their movements and those of the jets as they came on to the screen. But when the pilots themselves closed in for visual contact, the objects sped away. Finally, one of the pilots saw a light hovering in exactly the position radioed in by one of the radar controllers. He flew closer and the light remained motionless. Then he cut in the after-burner and rapidly closed, but moments before he would have overtaken the light, the light suddenly blinked off, and the pilot found himself traveling at Mach 1 speed into a black sky.

Three days later the Air Force held a press conference at the Pentagon, the largest and the longest since World War II. Before taking questions from the press, Major General John A. Samford, director of intelligence, pointed out that of the one to two thousand reports investigated by the Air Force to date, the bulk could be attributed to "either friendly aircraft erroneously recognized or reported, hoaxes, quite a few of those, electronic and meteorological phenomena of one sort or another, light aberrations, and many other things.

"However," he continued, "there have remained a percentage of this total, in the order of twenty percent of the reports, that have come from credible observers of relatively incredible things. We keep on being concerned about them."

One of the press corps asked how the radar controllers on the previous two Saturday nights had interpreted the blips on the radar screen.

Samford replied, "They said they saw 'good returns.'"

But, he pointed out, this did not necessarily mean the objects had to be solid body aircraft. Birds could give off good returns. Radar could even bounce off invisible temperature inversions, hit a ground target, and show up as a blip on the screen. But Samford's aide, an expert on radar, was not sure how that theory accounted for the sudden disappearances and reappearances of the targets, or the incredible speeds at which they seemed to travel. Nor did it explain the visual corroboration of several airline pilots in the air at the time.

When another reporter asked Samford his opinion of the "temperature inversion" theory, he responded, "My own mind is satisfied with that explanation." But he also felt they should continue their research, that the objects were probably some sort of phenomenon that science would someday be able to explain. Personally, because of their apparent ability to change direction and speed instantaneously, Samford felt the objects were not "material."

Late in the press conference a reporter asked Samford if he could state unequivocally that none of the strange flying craft observed during the previous five years had actually been ultra-secret military weapons. Samford replied it was always possible that an observer had mistaken a jet fighter for a flying saucer.

"What I was aiming at," said the reporter, "was this popular feeling. . . ."

"Of mystery?" interjected Samford.

"Of mystery," said the reporter. "Of something. That it's some very highly secret new weapon that we're working on that's causing all this."

Samford chortled. "We have nothing that has no mass and unlimited power!"

And everyone laughed.

By the end of 1952, 1,501, or nearly twice as many sightings as each of the previous five years combined, had been reported, and over three hundred of these remained unexplained.

* * *

While exploring every angle of the Meier case they could think to explore, the Elders and Welch began a search through campus libraries at the University of Arizona and Arizona State for information on the star cluster Meier claimed to be the home of his extraterrestrial visitors—the Pleiades.

"In an investigation like this," said Welch, "nine out of ten times you're presupposing it's a hoax because that's the way you're testing, that's the way you're interrogating. But let's suppose for a moment that it's real. Then we ask, 'If this is true, were there other Billy Meiers in the past?' We began at that point, and what popped up in a couple of weeks is what I call the Pleiadian Connection."

With the help of Lee Elders's sister and several friends in California and the East, they searched through libraries and secondhand bookstores for hundreds of books, magazine articles, trade journals, and doctoral theses at various universities.

"What was startling was a consistency," said Welch. "From an astronomical point of view you're talking about an extremely young, extremely insignificant system of stars. Yet at different parts of the globe, many times simultaneously, many times a thousand years apart, history and mythology mention the Pleiades and their importance. They're noted as being the source of knowledge in the rice culture in Asia, and in the potato culture in Europe and South America. These societies attributed their knowledge to a series of events in mythological form involving messengers from the Pleiades. Why in so many times, in so many parts of the world, are the references similar? Why all this energy toward the Pleiades? They're revered, they're looked at as the center of heaven, and they're looked at as a source of ancestry and wisdom and guidance."

Though other stars and star groups are mentioned in history, to the surprise of Welch and the Elders, the frequency of reference to the Pleiades seemed to exceed that of its closest rival, Orion, by nearly ten times. When they had collected every mention of the seven stars they could find, Welch and the Elders had scores of references to the Pleiades and their importance in cultures all over the world and from all periods of history, including three from the Bible. The Book of Job spoke of their "sweet influences."

But Welch wondered if perhaps Meier himself had conducted the same research in Swiss and German libraries.

"My first thought was, What are the odds of him doing that very thing? But a lot of these connections were not readily available; you had to be looking for them. So if you picked a star system and said, 'Let me see if I can find something on that,' you're talking about quite a bit of research before you come across the Pleiades.

"At one point, I remember us all sitting down kind of tired, Wendelle was up from Tucson at the time, it was late at night, and we were talking about some of the connections that each of us had separately discovered. And we're sitting there with, oh, it must have been about seven or eight legal-sized pages front and back of noted connections we'd come across. And somebody said, 'God, we've spent over a thousand hours on this already and it seems like we've just begun.' "

*   *   *

A tight cluster of several thousand stars, the Pleiades lie in the constellation Taurus, nearly five hundred light years from earth. The principal stars shine bluish-white and radiate intensely, illuminating surrounding clouds of gas. The Pleiades are young, too young for intelligent life to have evolved. But Meier had repeated specifically that the Pleiadians had not originated there, only that they had migrated to the Pleiades after engineering a planet to their liking.

Early civilizations recorded that the seven brightest stars were once visible to the naked eye, though today only six can be seen. Aligned with nearby Orion's Belt, the Pleiades are often mistaken for the Little Dipper, but their configuration is far more compact and appears to be enshrouded in a gossamer haze, one that inspired Tennyson to describe them as looking "like a swarm of fire-flies tangled in a silver braid." Of all the stars in this beautiful swarm, Alcyone is the brightest, shining with a brilliance one thousand times greater than our sun.

In *Star Lore of All Ages,* published in 1911, William Olcott wrote:

> No group of stars known to astronomy has excited such universal attention as the little cluster of faint stars we know as 'the Pleiades.' In all ages of the world's history they have been admired and critically observed. Great temples have been reared in their honour. Mighty nations have worshipped them, and people far removed from each other have been guided in their agricultural and commercial affairs by the rising and setting of these six close-set stars. . . . This little group, twinkling so timidly in the nights of autumn in the eastern heavens, links the races of mankind in closer relationship than any bond save nature's. No wonder that they have inspired universal awe and admiration, that within this group of suns man has sought to find the very centre of the universe.

Legends from pre-Inca peoples living in Peru speak of inhabited stars and "gods" who visited them from the Pleiades. The astronomical writings of China mention the Pleiades as early as 2357 B.C., worshipped by young women as the Seven Sisters of Industry. The Greeks aligned temples with their rising and setting. In Egypt, on the first day of spring, the south passageway of the Great Pyramid perfectly framed the Pleiades; some scholars even maintained that the seven chambers of this enormous monument were inspired by the cluster's seven visible stars. May Day and the Japanese Feast of Lanterns are remnants of ancient rites in honor of the Pleiades. The Hopi call the star cluster Choo-ho-kan, Home of Our Ancestors. And Navajo legend holds that men arrived on earth from the stars, particularly the Pleiades, and that we continue to be visited by our celestial relatives.

Attempting to explain the seeming coincidences between customs of ancient cultures and those of more modern societies, R. G. Haliburton wrote in *Nature Magazine* in 1881 of the universal reverence for the Pleiades. He noted that the Samoans of the South Pacific called their sacred bird the Bird of the Pleiades, and that the Berbers of Morocco claimed that paradise lay in the heavens circumscribed by the cluster. Haliburton concluded his article, "Even if the theory of prehistoric astronomers and of some modern men of science, that the Pleiades are the center of the universe, should prove to be unfounded, I am persuaded that the day is coming when the learned will admit that those stars are the 'central sun' of the religions, calendars, myths, traditions, and symbolism of early ages."

Agnes Clerke, in *The System of the Stars,* written in 1907, called the Pleiades "the meeting place in the skies of mythology and science. The vivid and picturesque aspect of these stars riveted, from the earliest ages, the attention of mankind; a peculiar sacredness attached to them, and their concern with human destinies was believed to be intimate and direct."

Though the Pleiades form little more than a speck in the visible night sky, no other star group has been mentioned as frequently in the literature and mythology of world cultures for the past two and a half millennia. And in every instance, the tiny cluster of seven was portrayed as female: the sisters, the virgins, the maidens, the goddesses.

* * *

Puzzled over how to analyze the Meier evidence and how to capture the scientists and their work on film, John

Stefanelli had looked for a consultant. In Phoenix he located a sound and light technician, Jim Dilettoso. Short, gaunt, and mercurial, the twenty-eight-year-old Dilettoso was involved in myriad projects in the entertainment industry staging sound and light shows with lasers, computers, and sound digitizers. A friend had recommended him because the young technician had been a part-time consultant for a documentary film on the testing of the Shroud of Turin, the 2,000-year-old funeral sheet that purportedly had covered the body of the crucified Christ; Stefanelli wanted to subject the Meier photos to the same computerized image analysis as that performed on the shroud.

At their first meeting, Stefanelli showed Dilettoso six of the photographs of extraterrestrial spacecraft allegedly taken by Meier.

"Good special effects," thought Dilettoso. "I was trying to figure out how I would make them. Couldn't be models because of the properties of the edges and the reflective surface. No, I'd build a rigid structure out of aluminum or titanium, shaped like a flying saucer, actual size twenty feet, and fill it with helium like a Goodyear Blimp. That was just my initial reaction. Later I came to find out that the cost is tremendous, or it doesn't look real.

"But the first thing Stefanelli wanted to know was, 'Well, can we test these pictures?' and, 'What labs can we get into?' I'm looking at the guy, thinking, Does he have any idea what he's asking? That's not equipment you go out and rent by the hour."

Using contacts from his film days in Hollywood, Stefanelli already had begun his search for scientists; at the same time he had launched his campaign to attract investors. He later estimated he traveled to Los Angeles between thirty and forty times, trying to interest someone in backing the film, someone who at least could finance the cost of properly analyzing the evidence.

"There were a lot of things we wanted to do," he said. "And I had a fair amount of success at finding people to tell

me what sort of tests should be performed. The problem
was getting the people who would do them without having
to spend a small fortune. Everyone I did uncover wanted a
lot of dollars—we're talking maybe tens of thousands—to
do testing. But I didn't have the money to do that."

Stefanelli found himself in a catch-22: Without sufficient testing having already been completed yielding positive results, it was nearly impossible to interest anyone in
funding the project; and without funding he could not hope
to have the evidence tested by qualified scientists.

"Once I found out that there were substantial costs
involved," Stefanelli admitted, "I really didn't push it so
hard."

The Elders, Welch, and Stevens saw less and less of
Stefanelli, but at the same time they began seeing more
and more of Jim Dilettoso. With Stefanelli's project on the
wane, Dilettoso, now thoroughly intrigued with the Meier
story, offered to help direct Intercep's efforts in the scientific areas to interest scientists in government and university laboratories without having to pay enormous fees. To
the group, Dilettoso looked and spoke like a former child
prodigy who simply had become bored with school. He had
attended several universities but never earned a degree,
though he seemed to understand computers and had a
knack for ferreting out information. Despite his Einstein
hairdo and dizzy ways, they liked him; he could talk faster
and better, and seemed to know more about a variety of
subjects than anyone they had ever known.

"My first impression of Jim," said Welch, "was that he
seemed to have an extremely detailed mind. He was involved in creating the support behind entertainment-ori-
ented events, the science behind it, computers, electronics,
sound systems. I could tell by the way he spoke that he was
very familiar with certain kinds of technical equipment,
particularly in the computer field. And he was unique in
one sense: He could sit down and carry on an intelligent
conversation with people having different areas of exper-

tise and hold his own in each one technically. So I thought he might be what we needed to further the investigation."

* * *

After the wave of sightings around Washington, D.C., in 1952, the National Security Council ordered the Central Intelligence Agency to determine if the existence of UFOs created a danger to national security. One CIA memorandum, written August 1, stated that "so long as a series of reports remains 'unexplainable' (interplanetary aspects and alien origin not being thoroughly excluded from consideration), caution requires that intelligence continue coverage of the subject. . . . It is strongly urged, however, that no indication of CIA interest or concern reach the press or public, in view of their probable alarmist tendencies."

With influential people in Washington wanting answers, the CIA appointed a team of five eminent scientists to study the UFO problem: Dr. H. P. Robertson, from the Office of the Secretary of Defense; Dr. Luis Alvarez, a physicist who fifteen years later would receive the Nobel Prize for physics; Dr. Samuel Goudsmit, an associate of Einstein from the Brookhaven National Laboratories; Dr. Thornton Page, deputy director of the Johns Hopkins Operations Research Office; and Dr. Lloyd Berkner, also of Brookhaven. Dr. Allen Hynek, the Ohio State astronomer and special consultant to Blue Book, attended selected meetings as an associate member, but was not asked to sign the final report.

The group, known as the Robertson Panel, secretly convened on January 14, 1953. The first morning they watched two color films, one taken at Tremonton, Utah, the other at Great Falls, Montana. The films represented what Air Force Blue Book personnel considered the best evidence of extraterrestrial visitation.

The Navy Photograph Interpretation Laboratory had analyzed the Tremonton film for a thousand hours and concluded that the twelve objects flying in loose formation could not be birds, balloons, aircraft, or reflections; and whatever they were, they were "self-luminous." But despite the Navy's findings, the panel *assumed* that the cinematographer, a naval commander, was probably mistaken in his estimate of how far away the objects were, that they probably were considerably closer, and that therefore the formation of flying objects was probably nothing more than sea gulls or some other kind of bird "reflecting the strong desert sunlight but being just too far and too luminous to see their shape." Similarly, they dismissed the two objects in the Great Falls film as probably jet airplanes that had been seen in the area a short while before, though the man who took the footage testified he knew the difference between jets and the two objects he filmed.

After reviewing only six cases in detail, and fifteen cases generally, the panel concluded that nothing they had seen or heard offered scientific data of any value. The reports, while great in number, were poor in quality, and any attempt to "solve" them would be a tremendous waste of resources. They stated that most sightings could be reasonably explained, and that "by deduction and scientific method" they probably could explain all other cases as well.

An aeronautical engineer, who for fifteen months had served as the Air Force project officer for UFOs in Washington, reviewed several of the better sightings from Blue Book files for the panel and concluded that he saw only one explanation for the presence of the unusual flying objects— extraterrestrial visitation. But the panel would accept none of the cases cited by the engineer because they were "raw, unevaluated reports."

After a total review of approximately twelve hours, the panel concluded: "We firmly believe that there is no residuum of cases which indicates phenomena which are attributable to foreign artifacts capable of hostile acts." However, "the continued emphasis on the reporting of these phenomena does, in these parlous times, result in a threat to the orderly functioning of the protective organs of the body politic." The panel was concerned that if the reports continued, the American population might be vulnerable to "possible enemy psychological warfare" through "the cultivation of a morbid national psychology in which skillful hostile propaganda could induce hysterical behavior and harmful distrust of duly constituted authority."

Among other things, the panel recommended that the two major UFO research groups—Aerial Phenomena Research Organization (APRO) in Sturgeon Bay, Wisconsin, and Civilian Saucer Intelligence (CSI) in New York—"be watched because of their potentially great influence on mass thinking if widespread sightings should occur. The apparent irresponsibility and the possible use of such groups for subversive purposes should be kept in mind." The panel also recommended that national security agencies "take immediate steps to strip the Unidentified Flying Objects of the special status they have been given and the aura of mystery they have unfortunately acquired."

Last, the panel outlined a program to educate the public to identify known objects in the sky, and to "debunk" the phenomenon and therefore reduce interest. The program would consult psychologists versed in mass psychology, utilize an army training film company and Walt Disney Productions, and employ famous personalities selected for their believability. The panel specifically suggested Arthur Godfrey.

Twelve years after he sat on the panel, Goudsmit wrote in a letter (to David Michael Jacobs, author of the definitive treatise, *The Controversy Over Unidentified Flying Objects in America: 1896–1973)* that the subject was "a complete waste of time and should be investigated by psychiatrists rather than physicists." To Goudsmit the extraterrestrial theory was "almost as dangerous to the general welfare of our unstable society as drug addiction and some other mental disorders."

Dr. Hynek, the Air Force special advisor to Blue Book who in time would evolve from a skeptic to the recognized dean of UFO study, disagreed with the panel's conclusions. They had rendered judgment in just four days on a phenomenon he had been studying for four years and still could not explain. And the more he studied, the more perplexed he became.

* * *

Before Dilettoso had joined their group, Stevens located a physicist in San Diego, Neil Davis, who was part owner of Design Technology, a photo optics laboratory under contract with General Dynamics and the U.S. Navy. Though Davis could not perform the ultra-sophisticated computer image processing possible at some of the government-sponsored labs, he could quickly eliminate several possibilities of hoaxing technique or tell Stevens he was wasting his time with the photographs.

Davis consented to test one color print, three by four and a half inches. His conclusions, he told Stevens, would have to be preliminary because a complete and proper scientific analysis could only be conducted on an original negative; Stevens could not be sure the internegative he gave to Davis was even first generation.

The photograph Stevens selected to be analyzed by Davis was of a silvery beamship hovering approximately 150 feet off the ground near two long piles of cut and debarked pine. Emerald grass and a dark green tree line, a bluish sky, and smoky hills in the distance filled the rest of the picture.

Davis first examined the print under a microscope to compare the sharpness of the object with the sharpness of the scene. "There is no discernible difference in image sharpness," he wrote in his report. Next he magnified the photograph ten times, made color separation black-and-white negatives, and scanned them with a microdensitometer for uniform density. "Examination did not reveal any details which would cast doubt upon the authenticity of the photograph."

Then Davis carefully examined the print and his freshly made negatives for evidence of double exposure, superimposure, photo pasteup, or a model at short range suspended on a string. He wrote, "Nothing was found to indicate a hoax." Furthermore, "Examination of the location of the shadows and highlights in the photograph verifies that the object and the scene were apparently taken under the same conditions of illumination."

After conducting all tests on the photo, Davis concluded, "Nothing was found in the examination of the print which could cause me to believe that the object in the photo is anything other than a large object photographed a distance from the camera."

Davis's findings encouraged Stevens, but Elders, still cynical, punched holes in his enthusiasm. The results gave them a green light on the photographs for now, he admitted, but much more sophisticated analysis would have to be performed. And Elders reminded Stevens that a metallurgist at the University of Arizona had already examined one of Meier's metal specimens and labeled it "potmetal," a low-grade casting alloy used to make such things as tin soldiers.

"These were the initial steps in the analysis," recalled Welch. "Compared to what ultimately occurred, they were very, very, very basic."

Welch suggested that before they ran more tests on any of the evidence, they needed additional information from Switzerland. No one yet had stood on the sites with the Meier photos in hand, determined where Meier had stood, and then measured distances to objects in the pictures. Such comparisons might give them clues as to how Meier could have staged the scenes. Welch, too, wanted to roam about the farm with both eyes open. As the son of an ex-FBI agent, he knew he might see things the others had missed.

EIGHT

As a boy Tom Welch remembered watching his father circle tough FBI cases, some of them involving attempted Communist infiltration of unions in Chicago and Tucson. His father had probed and thought, gathered his information, and assessed it. Welch's fascination with his father's work influenced his own curiosity about how things are, as opposed to how they seem to be. "My interests have always run along the lines of investigation," said Welch, "of digging behind mysteries. Even when I was young I remember distinctly a number of cases of my dad's where things so elaborately obvious turned out to be so different in reality. And how that was dug up just fascinated me."

Ten years younger than Lee Elders, Welch was six feet tall and thin, with a narrow brown beard and mustache outlining his jaw and upper lip. A Roman Catholic, Welch had been educated by priests of the Jesuit Order, which perhaps explained his demeanor. Whereas Elders visibly simmered, quick to exude charm or release a formidable temper, the soft-spoken and articulate Welch remained detached, composed, and analytical. The two men greatly complemented one another.

Welch was the only one in the group who had yet to visit the Meier farm, to speak with Meier and the wit-

151

nesses, to observe at least the countryside where Meier had taken his photographs and shot his movie footage. Welch knew Lee Elders well, and through him had spent time with Wendelle Stevens. He respected their opinions, but until he experienced for himself the feel of the place, the demeanor of the people, and had the opportunity to test some of his own hypotheses, he reserved judgment on the case.

The Honeywell Symposium in Phoenix had been an international conference attended by representatives of government agencies, the banking industry, and the military of various countries; and Honeywell had presented Tom Welch as an expert in electronics communications protection. Already, another international client had called from outside London, requesting the services of Intercep. Elders and Welch continued to sweep corporate offices and search for leaks in corporate telecommunications systems. But their curiosity over Meier and his story was growing, and as it did, Intercep slowly received less and less attention. Welch ceased making his frequent speeches at service club luncheons, and the firm no longer solicited business through private contacts.

"We were still doing a lot of work for Intercep," said Elders. "Steve was working on Meier. But we reached a point where we finally had to just put Intercep on the shelf because we didn't have time for it."

At the end of July, a large financial institution eighty miles outside London contacted Intercept through the Honeywell Corporation. Fearing that a competitor had tapped into their telephone system, the directors of the company wanted an immediate sweep of the entire office building. Elders and Welch blocked out a full two weeks on their slowly shrinking Intercep schedule and told Stevens to meet them in Switzerland after they had concluded their work in London. Now warm and dry in the hills southeast of Zurich, they finally could walk and measure the sites where Meier had taken his photographs.

Elders and Welch flew to London and after several long

days of work solved their client's problem. Then they boarded the train for Zurich, where Stevens was to pick them up in a rental car and drive them to the farm. With better than a week to investigate Meier, the people, and the sites, and to pursue the theories they had formulated back in Phoenix, Welch figured they would leave Switzerland with answers. But by now Elders had seen and heard much with his own eyes and ears, and he was beginning to sense the difficulty of Meier's having fabricated the entire story and all of the evidence. No education, no accomplices, no resources. It was becoming easier to believe that perhaps part of Meier's story was true.

Still, some things seemed not to fit, others simply were too outlandish to believe, and nothing definitive had yet been done with the photographs. It even appeared that the metal sample was anything but extraordinary. Though Elders admitted confusion, Meier's evidence had to pass several more tests before he would concede there might be some degree of truth in what the man claimed.

As planned, Stevens met them at the train station in Zurich and drove through Winterthur to the small village of Dussnang, over the hills and about fifteen minutes by car east of the farm. They checked in at the Gasthaus Brücken-waage, where the Elders had stayed the previous spring, a three-story guesthouse with green shutters bordering many windows, each sill now bursting with bright red geraniums.

Though they had had little sleep on the night train to Zurich, it was a sunny morning in Switzerland, and Elders and Welch wanted to get to the farm as soon as possible. After they had unloaded the car and carried their things up to the room, the three of them drove over the hills, through the farms and pear orchards, to Schmidruti. Welch sat in the backseat, observing the countryside and thinking about the information he wanted to collect at the sites, from the configuration of the forests surrounding the landing track sites to the distances between objects in the photos. But he kept reminding himself not to overlook the less obvious.

"I wanted to get a feeling as much as I wanted to get facts," he said. "I wanted to get an insight into the people there as much as I wanted to get measurements and other things that we had scheduled out."

As when Stevens had arrived at the farm late the previous fall, and again when the Elders had been there in early spring, young people from all over Europe had come on motorcycles and by foot to Hinterschmidruti, and pitched their tents in various places around the farm, some in the large grassy field below the duck pond. As it was midsummer, the weather had turned mild and warm, and the number of those camped there had greatly increased. Others, many of them older, had driven there, and of these many slept in the tiny, simple rooms at the Freihof along the cobblestone row in Schmidruti. Verena Furrer, the Freihof's cherub-faced proprietress, said that in summer the people who came to see Meier accounted for 25 percent of her business. "A few French," she explained, "but most are German, some are Austrian, Americans, a lot of Swedes, some Dutch."

Meier was waiting for them in front of the farmhouse when they arrived. He now had a full beard, reddish in spots and beginning to curl. As they shook hands, Welch looked into his eyes as Elders had done before, but he saw and felt nothing familiar, no magnetism, no déjà vu. Welch saw only an "earthy man wishing for a simpler life."

"He looked to be in the middle of something not under his control," said Welch, "something he was learning from."

Welch noted immediately that Meier was not an "eager" man. Although he acted cordially toward Welch, he seemed at the same time almost indifferent to his presence. Welch soon discovered this indifference pervaded the farm.

"I expected either to have a story laid on me—in other words, people making an effort to explain things out of enthusiasm or some ulterior motive—or the reverse, people trying to hide something. Instead, it was as though we weren't even there. They would answer any questions that

Called "the sunlight scene," this photograph, taken March 29, 1976, at Hasenbol, was the last in a sequence of nine that Meier took as the beamship approached from the west. The Hasenbol site, with its radical weather and steep drop behind the tree, impressed the investigators more than any other.

Mount Auruti stands in the background to the south of Hasen-bol. In Meier's 8mm film of this same scene a Japanese production crew noticed the sudden brightening of a red light on the ship's flange just above the two red lights that appear here on the bottom of the ship.

Kaliope and Eduard Meier.

A jet fighter on maneuvers with the Swiss Air Force flew into the scene as Meier took this photograph near Schmarduel April 14, 1976.

From left to right: Lee Elders, Wendelle Stevens, Eduard Meier, and Tom Welch on a hill overlooking the Meier farm.

Brit Elders interviews schoolteacher Elsi Moser at the farm in Schmidruti.

Physicist Neil Davis of Design Technology in Poway, California, examined this photograph taken August 3, 1975. Three years later, just beyond the stacks of debarked pine, Meier recorded the beamship sounds analyzed by Los Angeles sound engineers Nils Rognerud and Steve Ambrose.

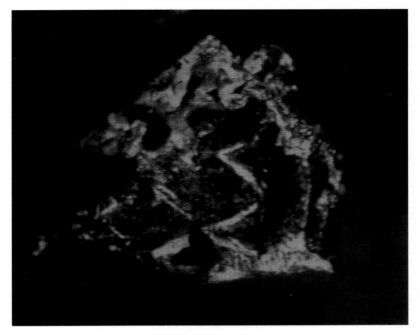

The metal fragment, which represented one of the final stages in the manufacture of the material for the beamship hull, glistens under Marcel Vogel's electron microscope at IBM. The unique sample disappeared while in Vogel's lab.

The photograph taken by Austrian schoolteacher Guido Moosbrugger one night while on a contact with Meier June 13, 1976.

Taken March 3, 1975, this is the first in a sequence of photographs of a beamship and an accompanying remote-controlled craft; one of the photos in this series appeared on the cover of Europe's newsweekly *Der Spiegel* November 17, 1978.

From outside a chicken wire cordon Meier views landing tracks that appeared below the farm in 1980. In these and other tracks with the same counterclockwise swirls, the crushed grass never turned brown and died, yet it never rose again.

we had, and they related to us one to one, but they had no reaction one way or the other to what we were doing."

Though Welch had many questions for Meier, he had already decided that little of substance could be learned from the man himself; the story lay in the eyes of the witnesses and the terrain of the contact sites. Meier served only as a focus for the story; not someone to question, but someone to question others about. Welch was more interested in walking the sites and talking to the Swiss weather bureau than in chatting with Meier.

The procedure they had devised for assessing the contact sites was to take each 3×5 print in the series photographed at the site, locate the exact point from which the photographs had to be taken, and begin measuring. "Measure distances, measure heights, measure the width of trees, even the height of blades of grass," said Welch. "Looking for that kind of detail is the way we walked onto each site."

Beginning that afternoon and continuing for the next several days, they visited four of the alleged contact sites, accompanied by Meier. Just driving to the sites, Welch perceived problems with the theories they had formulated back in Phoenix: some of the sites were up steep grades, passable in summer, but a strain for the car to climb. Yet Meier had taken many of his photos on these sites in late winter or very early spring, when snow covered the paths or melted and turned them to mud.

Welch remembered, "That's where the theories started disappearing."

They had been at the first site only briefly when Welch noticed another similar problem, one of many experiences he soon labeled "gross consistencies." A gross consistency was usually a simple observation that in some small way corroborated Meier's story. Singly each added little weight; collectively they made a curious story seem even more mysterious.

What Welch noted at the first site and every one

thereafter was that from the time they got out of the car, looked over the site, and began taking measurements, no more than twenty minutes would pass before someone came up and asked them who they were, or what they were doing, or why they were there. Or they would simply stand and watch. Once, Welch walked onto a site, expecting it to be secluded, only to find a farmhouse not more than a hundred yards from where Meier had taken his photographs.

Driving to the site near that farmhouse along a side road, Elders, Welch, and Stevens had encountered another car traveling in the opposite direction. Moments later, when Meier directed Stevens to pull off onto a narrow path leading to the site, the other car had turned around, followed them, and parked. Then the occupants had watched them walk around the area measuring trees and distances for most of the time they were on the site.

"Essentially we thought we were dealing with remote sites," Welch said later, "where you could fairly well do anything you wanted unseen and uninterrupted for a lengthy period of time. And that you could get to that site without being observed. This was another factor just blown out the window."

Welch obtained weather reports, thinking he could use them to confirm or invalidate the background of the pictures taken at each site. For example, he offered, August 8, 1975. Was that actually a cloudy day? "Wouldn't it be funny," he said, "to learn that the shot here with the deep ruffled clouds in the background, storm clouds, could not have been shot in 1975 in August." Although he found no inconsistencies, Welch discovered that often the weather reports themselves could be misleading. The sites lay mostly in the foothills where the weather could change in minutes. And having experienced these radical changes at the sites, Welch could then listen to the nearest weather source reporting mild temperatures and consistent skies during that same period.

"The weather impressed me to no end," said Welch. "Particularly Hasenbol. You can stand there for an hour, and in some cases nothing will happen; it'll be a beautiful sunny day. At other times you'll go from beautiful sunny to deep clouds and a little mist and rain and fog to what seems like it's definitely going to snow and get cool and then hefty breezes pop up all of a sudden. It was like standing in one place and going to three or four different climates, and not moving an inch. And that presented another angle we hadn't thought about—the further difficulty of faking anything on those sites because of the weather. And you can't just visit those sites for five minutes to learn this; you have to spend some time at them."

One thing Welch had starred in his notes was to view the drop behind the tree in the Hasenbol photos. He had formulated various theories on how Meier could have rigged these photos of a beamship that appears to be almost in the branches of the tall leafless tree. Late on a sunny afternoon they climbed the steep, rutted path to the site, where Welch found a grassy bluff facing into the setting sun and in the distance a succession of jagged peaks as far as he could see. When he walked to the tree at the edge of the bluff and saw the land drop sharply away, roll down and down across a wide valley, his theories simply "dissipated in the wind."

The tree was fifty-two yards from where Meier had taken the picture. By measuring the trunk of the tree as it stood, and as it appeared in the photo, basic triangulation gave him the size of the beamship.

"That's often a simple mistake people make when they're hoaxing," explained Welch. "The ship they film just couldn't be the size they say it is when compared to the other known objects in the photograph."

According to their measurements, the beamship at the edge of the tree over Hasenbol had to be approximately twenty-one feet in diameter, as Meier had always said.

"We had developed some possible theories by that time that we wanted to apply to the circumstances," said Welch, "taking a real strong look at the sites and doing some measuring. But you go to one of those sites, and you compare the photographs right there, and you see the perspective for yourself. Just eyeballing it you know you're not dealing with something that is easily rigged by amateurs, because of the nature of the terrain, the topography, the wind, and even the laws and regulations of Switzerland. The country is so small and jets run down those valleys sometimes no higher than two, three hundred feet, and you'll see them doing barrel rolls, loops, and dogfights at that height. So there were a lot of little technical things that kind of blew out the perception of this being an easily explained circumstance.

"Now . . . here's the conditions under which these photographs were taken at Hasenbol. You have severe cold, you have high winds, you have a good amount of snow on the ground. We were there in summer and you could barely get up the hill because it was too muddy and slippery. What we're talking about here is passing that farmer's house on a very wintry late afternoon. Anybody out in that kind of weather is a little unusual and the people there are nosy as hell. Now here comes a man on a moped, all right, and he's going to go up through this farmer's land, up this bluff, in this weather . . . and it's not snowplowed up there . . . he's going to go up there in the wind and the weather, and he's going to deal with all the technical factors in the midst of all that."

Always present, yet far more subtle than the difficult terrain or the curiosity of strangers, one thing that would have made the hoaxing of the photographs virtually impossible occurred to Welch only slowly as he stood at site after site. Finally, he focused on what he had been feeling in the air—moisture—heavy, constantly changing, and invisible, except to a camera lens. For all its beauty, perhaps largely responsible for that beauty, Switzerland is a damp country. A large object posing independently could be photographed several times in a matter of seconds and the atmosphere would remain constant throughout the series. A model of any size would require setting up and repositioning, a procedure that could consume an hour or more. In that time the background might change.

"You have weather so inconsistent," remembered Welch, "that in fifteen minutes you can go from literally zip, clear sharp air to very thick air, actual mist. That alone would drive a technician crazy trying to fake photos. It would cause too much bluing.

"Also," said Welch, "you need time. Because if it's a model, you've got to throw it five times before you get your shot, or hang it and run it and play with it a bit. This would drive you crazy with the wind, the moisture, there are probably a dozen factors. If you're going to fake this you need time. The one thing you can see that Meier did not have a lot of at any of these sites, whether he's faking them or taking them, is time."

* * *

By the mid-1950s, a coterie of men claimed not only to have seen remarkable spacecraft, but to have flown in them and to have talked at length with the occupants. They were known as contactees, and their stories so captured the public imagination that they completely thwarted Air Force efforts to downplay flying saucers. They also undermined the work of private UFO organizations searching seriously for answers.

The contactees, most notably George Adamski, Truman Bethurum, Orfeo Angelucci, Daniel Fry, and Howard Menger, each claimed to have been contacted by "space brothers" who gave him a "mission" to save the world from greed, corruption, and the atomic bomb. The space brothers took them aboard a Venusian, Saturnian, Jupiterian, or Martian spaceship, where they saw beautiful women and received further instruction from Orthon, Aura, A-lan, or Neptune, and heard of idyllic conditions on their home planets, a situation to which the people of Earth could aspire. National interest in the contactees was so great that over a hundred fifty flying saucer clubs sprang up dedicated just to them. In 1954 contactee George Van Tassel sponsored the first Giant Rock Convention in Yucca Valley, California, a carnival affair with contactees giving lectures on their experiences and selling souvenirs from booths. Over five thousand people came.

In the fall of 1956 the thirty-four-year-old Menger, a pipe-smoking sign painter with black wavy hair and a long thin neck, appeared with his story on the *Tonight* show with Steve Allen. Journalist Jules B. St. Germain described the scene in the November 1957 *Argosy:* "The audience's original reaction, which ranged from snickering to outright laughter when it learned that Menger claimed to have ridden on a 'flying saucer,' changed to a mood of perplexed wonderment and keen interest shortly after he started speaking. Amusement soon became interested silence." Menger told the audience that earlier that year the space beings had taught him to communicate through telepathy, and had flown him to Venus where he saw "beautiful domed buildings."

"I rode through space in a Venusian scout ship," he said. "It is a difficult feeling to describe, a feeling of no motion, of suspension in space. I was shown, through some means of tele-projection, a view of life in a city on Venus. It was not too different from ours. More orderly, quiet, much more beautiful."

He also had traveled to the Moon, where he could breathe the air with little difficulty.

"Most of the people who have contacted me," he said, "have been from the planet Venus, although I have seen others from Mars and Saturn. Some live on our Earth among us."

After Menger's radio and television appearances, so many thousands of people came to his home in Highgate, New Jersey, that at one point the police had to be called in to unravel a traffic jam in front of the house. St. Germain, visiting in late fall 1956, found three hundred people there on a single afternoon.

The public demanded little proof, seemingly content

with a contactee's "sincerity." As evidence of his contacts, the father of contacteeism, Adamski, showed skeptics eighteen photographs, some of spots and shadows, and some of a murky, bell-shaped object with what appeared to be wheels on the bottom. He also had one Venusian footprint cast in plaster of paris and containing a coded message. Other contactees had less to show. Bethurum offered a note written in French. A contactee named Buck Nelson sold $5 packets of hair from a Venusian St. Bernard he said weighed 385 pounds. Angelucci and Fry had only their word.

Like Adamski, Menger had photographs, five of them, one of a black mummy shape standing before a glaring rounded object—a Venusian in front of his scout ship, said Menger. Menger also cut a commercial record called "The Song From Saturn," "actual music that came from another planet." He once wrote to one of the UFO organizations, "We are tired of mysteries, hearsay, and ugly rumors circulating about saucer researchers and contactees. Incidentally," he added, "we have a scientist who is working on the qualitative analysis of the vegetables brought back from the Moon."

* * *

In January 1957, Major Donald Keyhoe, a graduate of Annapolis, retired Marine Corps pilot, and former aide to Charles Lindbergh, became head of a privately organized group called the National Investigations Committee on Aerial Phenomena. Formed only several months earlier, NICAP eventually boasted a membership of 12,000, including many politicians, scientists, and high-ranking military officers. Keyhoe established NICAP headquarters in Washington, D.C., and appointed prominent people to its board of governors, one of whom was Vice Admiral Roscoe Hillenkoetter, a Naval Academy classmate of Keyhoe's and the first director of the CIA in 1947. Intent on pushing UFOs into the political arena, Keyhoe and other NICAP members appeared on television and radio nine hundred times from 1957 to 1966.

Because of close and reliable contacts within the military, Keyhoe had been privy to much of the early (and secret) information concerning the Air Force's confusion over flying saucers. He knew that many sightings had been made by impeccable witnesses who had reported fantastic things, and that lacking feasible alternatives many intelligence analysts had leaned toward "interplanetary" as an explanation. Based on this information, Keyhoe had written many of the early articles and books on the subject. In 1950 he had concluded that the Air Force knew the origin of these splendid and mysterious craft, and that official statements, "contradictory as they appear," were simply "part of an intricate program to prepare America—and the world—for the secret of the disks." Seven years later, if the Air Force had a secret, they still were keeping it.

As head of NICAP, Keyhoe opened war on two fronts: one with the Air Force for keeping UFOs classified, and the other with the "lunatic fringe" for tainting the study of UFOs by legitimate investigators. Too many people constantly confused NICAP with the crazies who had flown to Venus and eaten "space potatoes." Though he was convinced UFOs were of extraterrestrial origin, he refused membership to anyone who claimed contact with the occupants.

One of many letters he wrote to contactees went to Howard Menger. "We have been informed," he said, "that during your lectures and upon other occasions you have stated that this Committee endorses your claims and views, including your claims to have met and talked with space people and to have visited the moon. This is to inform you that this Committee does not in any way endorse such claims by you or anyone else."

While battling to avoid the stigma of the contactees, Keyhoe also fought the military on Capitol Hill by pushing for congressional hearings on UFOs. He wrote letters, made speeches, and provided current information to congressmen, impressing many with the quality and quantity of the facts he presented. But each time his lobbying efforts persuaded a House or Senate subcommittee to consider an open hearing on UFOs, the Air Force would somehow convince one or two of the members that the whole matter of UFOs perpetuated itself only because the public had an insatiable appetite for the fantastic. Congressional hearings, they said, "would merely give dignity to the subject out of all proportion to which it is entitled." Whatever they were, said the Air Force, UFOs were harmless, at the most perhaps curious. The country was safe.

Keyhoe, however, felt he had abundant proof that something indeed was happening, and that the Air Force not only had been inept in its efforts to solve the problem, but had made "contradictory, misleading and untrue statements" to congressmen and the public. So strongly did Keyhoe believe the Air Force *was* concealing what his editor had called "the biggest story since the birth of Christ," that he proposed a showdown: Before the House Subcommittee on Space Problems and Life Sciences, NICAP and the Air Force would present evidence on the existence of "superior" craft piloted or otherwise controlled by extraterrestrial beings. Then NICAP would answer Air Force questions, and the Air Force would answer NICAP questions. If the subcommittee agreed with NICAP, Keyhoe wanted an end to the secrecy. If Keyhoe's proof failed to convince the subcommittee, he would dismantle the entire NICAP organization.

But before the scheduled pre-hearing, one member of the subcommittee spoke with Blue Book personnel privately and concluded there was no need even to consider the hearings. The head of the subcommittee then attacked Keyhoe for his "malicious intent toward a great branch of the military." He called Keyhoe's proposal "a cheap scheme to discredit the Air Force."

But the Air Force's own special advisor to Project Blue Book, Dr. Allen Hynek, had secretly and consistently suggested that the Air Force delve deeper into the UFO phe-

163

nomenon. Although he could explain most of the 15,000 sightings that had come to his attention, he wrote in *The Saturday Evening Post* in 1966 that "several hundred are puzzling, and some of the puzzling incidents, perhaps one in 25, are bewildering."

As Keyhoe waged his war in the halls of Congress during the late fifties and early sixties, the public sighted fewer and fewer mysterious objects flying in the sky. Constituents lessened the pressure on congressmen for answers, and reports coming into Blue Book decreased so markedly that Hynek himself thought the phenomenon might go away. Then one night in March 1966 eighty-seven coeds at Hillsdale College in Michigan watched a glow of red, yellow, and green lights rise from a swamp only a few hundred yards from their dormitory.

Roughly "football-shaped," the glow seemed suddenly to fly at the dormitory. Then it stopped. Then it flew back to the swamp where it hovered. The county civil defense director watched the glowing object through binoculars for three hours. The following night, sixty-three miles away, a dozen people in Dexter, Michigan, several of them police officers, watched another glowing object rise from a marshy area on a farm. At about a thousand feet the object stopped, hovered for a few minutes, and then flew away. A farmer and his son had approached to within five hundred yards of the object and heard it take off with the sound of a ricocheting bullet.

The two sightings sent reporters into a frenzy, and the Air Force dispatched Hynek to investigate. But when he arrived at the Hillsdale campus, he could hardly get to the witnesses. Journalists looking for answers had swarmed the campus and the farm, and emotions ran so high that even the police now saw flying saucers everywhere. The head of Blue Book called Hynek in Michigan and told him to stand up before a crowd of reporters in this near hysterical community and issue a statement on the cause of the sightings. But Hynek had nothing to say. He had no idea what could have caused the lights.

"Searching for a justifiable explanation of the sightings," he wrote in the 1966 *Saturday Evening Post* article, "I remembered a phone call from a botanist at the University of Michigan, who called to my attention the phenomenon of burning 'swamp gas.'"

Three days after he began his investigation, in the midst of being pulled in one direction by TV cameramen and in another by news reporters at the largest press conference in the history of the Detroit Press Club, Hynek uttered the words "swamp gas." He had only meant to say that this rare gas, known to burst into tiny flames that sometimes floated above the ground, was a "possible" cause of the sightings; but no sooner had the words slipped out of his mouth than the press conference erupted in a clamor of reporters rushing to the phone.

The Air Force and Hynek both looked foolish. Not one of the hundred-plus people who had witnessed the lights accepted the explanation. The civil defense director said that the pulsating lights he had watched through binoculars for three hours that night unquestionably came "from some kind of vehicle."

House minority leader Gerald R. Ford castigated the Air Force for their "flippant answer" to the Michigan sightings and called for a "full-blown" congressional investigation into UFOs. Two and a half weeks later, for the first time in the nineteen-year history of the phenomenon, the House Armed Services Committee held open hearings on UFOs.

"At that point," said Hynek in an *OMNI* magazine interview in 1985, "I had to ask myself when I would become scientifically honest and say that I just didn't know what the sightings were and that they deserved further investigation."

* * *

During the congressional hearings of April 5, 1966, Secretary of the Air Force Harold D. Brown revealed that an ad hoc group of scientists called the O'Brien Panel had secretly convened only six months earlier to review the UFO problem. The panel had concluded that UFO sightings had potential scientific value and recommended that the Air Force supplement Blue Book with science teams from selected universities who could mobilize quickly, gather data while fresh, and evaluate that data thoroughly. But with few sightings being reported and public interest on the wane, the Air Force had felt no pressure to implement the panel's recommendations, so it had done nothing. Now, with press coverage of the recent Michigan sightings firing public interest, and Congress pressuring the Air Force to find answers, Secretary Brown told the House Armed Services Committee that the Air Force would immediately begin a search outside the military for teams of scientists to study the UFO problem. The subject embodied so much misunderstanding and sensation, however, that several universities, including Harvard, MIT, University of North Carolina, and University of California, refused to participate. After months of searching, the Air Force Office of Scientific Research finally offered a $313,000 grant to Dr. Edward Uhler Condon at the University of Colorado to conduct the entire study with the help of special consultants and a staff of twelve, half of whom were scientists or psychologists. What became known as the Condon Committee remains the most controversial episode in forty years of UFO history.

Condon, sixty-four, a noted physicist and former president of the American Association for the Advancement of Science, had once served as deputy director of the highly secret Manhattan Project at Los Alamos, where he provided several pieces to the A-bomb puzzle. He also had been instrumental in the development of radar. His stature as a scientist satisfied both the Air Force and the science community, and his reputation for bucking governmental authority (he was one of the few to checkmate young Richard Nixon and the House Un-American Activities Committee) seemed to assure that UFOs would receive a fair hearing.

But in September 1966, two weeks prior to the first meeting of the committee, Hynek had dinner with Condon. Later, in the *OMNI* interview, Hynek recalled that the renowned scientist was "quite clearly negative" toward the subject of UFOs. When Hynek then visited the project offices, he found the project coordinator, Bob Low, already writing on a blackboard the chapter headings and *conclusions* for a report that as yet had not been researched and would not be complete for another two years. Hynek's early experiences with the two men running the project would prove prophetic.

Though the Air Force at the behest of Congress had established the Condon Committee to settle the UFO controversy, within months the committee itself was adding to the confusion. In January 1967, Condon addressed an honorary scientific fraternity, telling them, "It is my inclination right now to recommend that the Government get out of this business. My attitude right now is that there's nothing to it." Then, according to the *Star-Gazette* in Elmira, New York, he smiled and added, "But I'm not supposed to reach a conclusion for another year."

A mesmerizing storyteller, Condon loved to spin a good yarn and kept many audiences in near hysterics with material provided him by the lunatic fringe with which he came in contact during his tenure as head of the committee. For instance, a well-dressed gentleman in his fifties arrived at committee headquarters one day in a chauffeured Cadillac, announced himself as "Sir Salvador," agent of the Third Universe (the Second Universe was populated by bears), and demanded three billion dollars to build a spaceport to accommodate ships from the Third Universe trying to land on earth. According to *UFOs? YES!*, a book published in 1969 by Condon Committee psychologist Dr. David Saunders, Condon actually researched the "case" and found that Sir Salvador had recently been released from a mental institution. Nevertheless, Condon soberly reported his findings to Washington. When an Ontario, California, man gave a specific date and time for an imminent landing on

the Bonneville Salt Flats, Condon notified the Governor of
Utah and dispatched an investigator who waited for two
hours in vain next to members of the Utah Highway Patrol
and a brass band. In September 1967, the *Rocky Mountain
News* in Denver quoted Condon as saying, "The 21st cen-
tury may die laughing when it looks back on many things
we have done. This [the UFO study] may be one."

Condon himself investigated few if any of the truly
perplexing cases and rarely discussed the progress of serious research with his staff. In fact, his staff saw little of
him. And Low, who ran the project in Condon's absence,
refused to investigate potentially important cases suggested by the staff; at the same time he occupied himself
with what other members considered irrelevant research.
On one trip to Europe, ostensibly to research UFOs, Low
spent much of his time in Scotland studying the mystery of
the Loch Ness Monster. According to Saunders's book, Low
"explained later that this was relevant to UFOs because
neither one exists and it was important to see how they
were studying something that does not exist."

Because of his own experiences as a scientist, Hynek
anticipated that the committee would find UFOs "of importance to the national interest," and that the committee
would recommend that Congress establish a commission for
studying "the many truly scientifically challenging cases."
In a letter to Condon in January 1967, he wrote, "There are
so many scientists who have now expressed a 'subterra-
nean' interest in UFO's that I am moved to organize as
loosely as possible, an 'Invisible College of Interested Scientists.' "

But as months passed, Hynek and others who addressed the committee noticed both Condon's and Low's
disturbing preoccupation with the obviously explainable
reports. Condon continued to make jokes in public about
contactees, giving the impression that such stories formed
the bulk of UFO facts. And Low was too quick to point out
how easily most cases proved to be some sort of astronomical phenomena or a misidentification of a known object.

UFO researchers had known this for years; they wanted an explanation for the difficult cases.

Then in the summer of 1967, one of the scientists on the staff discovered a memorandum written by Low in August 1966, just before the university signed the contract with the Air Force. Low had titled the memo "Some Thoughts on the UFO Project," and addressed it to university officials. In the memo he noted that several of the scientists at the university wanted to avoid the project because the study would have to be objective, and that meant admitting the possibility that UFOs exist. Low capsulized their feelings by saying, "It is not respectable to give serious consideration to such a possibility." But Low had an answer. He wrote, "The trick would be, I think, to describe the project so that, to the public, it would appear a totally objective study but, to the scientific community, would present the image of a group of nonbelievers trying their best to be objective, but having an almost zero expectation of finding a saucer." One way to achieve this, he suggested, would be to stress the investigation of the psychological makeup of people who claimed to see UFOs, and to downplay the physical evidence.

Low's memo so offended Saunders and Dr. Norman Levine, an electrical engineer on the staff, that they sent it to Donald Keyhoe, who turned it over to a prominent scientist outside the committee. Condon countered by firing Saunders and Levine for "incompetence." Two weeks later, February 15, 1968, Mary Louise Armstrong, Low's administrative assistant, resigned, stating in her letter of resignation that there was "an almost unanimous lack of confidence" in Low, and that Low "had indicated little interest in talking to those who carried out the investigations or in reading their reports." She could not understand how most of the scientists had "arrived at such radically different conclusions" from Low's and noted there was "a fairly good consensus among the team members that there is enough data in the UFO question to warrant further study. . . .

"To say in our final report," she continued, "as I believe

Bob would like to, that although we can't prove 'ETI' does not exist, we can say that there isn't much evidence to suggest it does, would not be correct. I do not understand how he can make such a statement when those who have done the work of digging into the sighting information do not think this is true. . . . I do not think it is an unfair conclusion on our part to say that Bob is misrepresenting us."

Other staff members quit, too, and an article in *Look,* May 14, 1968, publicly exposed the problems within the Condon Committee, promoting a new congressional investigation. On July 29, 1968, as the Condon Committee began winding down its operation and writing its final report, Hynek, Dr. Carl Sagan, and four other scientists, including Dr. James McDonald, testified before the House Committee on Space and Astronautics.

In only a few years, Jim McDonald had become the most articulate proponent of UFO study. Tall, lean, dynamic, with a photographic memory, he was far more vocal than Hynek. David Michael Jacobs, in *The Controversy over Unidentified Flying Objects in America,* reported that at the first meeting between McDonald and Hynek in 1967 McDonald had walked into Hynek's office, pounded on his desk, and exclaimed, "How could you sit on this information for so many years without alerting the scientific community!"

Holder of a master's degree from MIT and a doctor of philosophy from Iowa State University, McDonald headed the Institute of Atmospheric Sciences at the University of Arizona. Highly respected, he had done extensive research on cloud seeding, hurricane reduction, and ozone problems caused by SST emissions. Though he had discovered UFOs much later than Hynek, he called the study of UFOs "the most important scientific problem of our time," adding that "we do not know what they are because we have laughed them out of court."

"My own present opinion, based on two years of careful

study," he told the House Committee on Space and Aeronautics, "is that UFOs are probably extraterrestrial devices engaged in something that might be very tentatively termed 'surveillance.' Indeed," he added, "I have to state, for the record, that I believe no other problem within your jurisdiction is of comparable scientific and national importance. These are strong words, and I intend them to be."

Hynek told the committee that only two things kept scientists away from UFOs: One was lack of hard data (the Air Force, interested only in national security, had failed to collect sufficient scientific data); the other was the sensationalizing of UFOs by contactees and pulp magazines. Between the two, said Hynek, the science community's misconception of UFO information was "powerful and all-encompassing."

Each of the experts to testify before the committee recommended the subject be given further scientific study. Then the committee adjourned and everyone awaited the Condon Committee's final report.

On November 15, 1968, the Condon Committee released a document 1,485 pages long. The committee had examined ninety-one cases, each listed in one of five categories: astronaut sightings, optical and radar sightings, old cases, new cases, and photographic evidence.

Astronomer and professor of astrogeophysics Dr. Franklin Roach wrote the chapter entitled "Visual Observations Made by U.S. Astronauts." A consultant to NASA, Roach had briefed and debriefed the astronauts on their experiences in space aboard Mercury and Gemini flights. After examining ten of the more intriguing sightings, Roach could explain only seven of them. He wrote that, "The three unexplained sightings which have been gleaned from a great mass of reports are a challenge to the analyst. Especially puzzling is the first one of the list, the daytime sighting of an object showing details such as arms (antennas?) protruding from a body having a noticeable angular extension. If the NORAD listing of objects near the GT-4 spacecraft at the time of the sighting is complete as it presumably is, we shall have to find a rational explanation, or alternatively, keep it on our list of unidentifieds."

Physicist Gordon Thayer wrote the chapter "Optical and Radar Sightings" and concluded that one case, which occurred in Lakenheath, England, in August 1965, was "the most puzzling and unusual case in the radar-visual files. The apparently rational, intelligent behavior of the UFO suggests a mechanical device of unknown origin as the most probable explanation of this sighting."

One of the photographic cases examined by astronomer and photoanalyst Dr. William K. Hartmann involved two photographs taken by a farmer in McMinnville, Oregon, in 1950. Hartmann and his staff not only analyzed the original negatives, but found and interviewed the farmer. Hartmann concluded: "This is one of the few UFO reports in which all factors investigated . . . appear to be consistent with the assertion that an extraordinary flying object, silvery, metallic, disk-shaped, tens of meters in diameter, and evidently artificial, flew within sight of two witnesses.

"It cannot be said that the evidence positively rules out a fabrication," he added, "although there are some physical factors such as the accuracy of certain photometric measures of the original negatives which argue against a fabrication."

Hartmann noted that about two percent of cases involving photographic evidence "appear to represent well recorded but unidentified or unidentifiable objects that are airborne—i.e. UFOs." This, wrote Hartmann, "is not inconsistent with the hypothesis that unknown and extraordinary aircraft have penetrated the airspace of the United States."

Many of the case reports contained conclusions like this: "If the report is accurate [it was made by six Air Force officers and confirmed by ground and airborne radar] it describes an unusual, intriguing, and puzzling phenomenon, which, in the absence of additional information, must be listed as unidentified." And this: "Taking into consideration the high credibility of information and the cohesiveness and continuity of accounts, combined with a high degree of 'strangeness,' it is also certainly one of the most disturbing UFO incidents known today." Or: "In conclusion, although conventional or natural explanations certainly cannot be ruled out, the probability of such seems low in this case and the probability that at least one genuine UFO was involved appears to be fairly high."

Condon, who investigated few if any of the cases and talked rarely with his staff about their research, wrote the conclusion for the report.

"No direct evidence whatever of a convincing nature now exists for the claim that any UFOs represent spacecraft visiting Earth from another civilization," he claimed. Furthermore, "nothing has come from the study of UFOs in the last twenty years that has added to scientific knowledge." And finally, "Careful consideration of the record as it is available to us leads us to conclude that further extensive study of UFOs probably cannot be justified in the expectation that science will be advanced thereby."

In the *OMNI* interview eighteen years later, Hynek said, "It almost seemed to me as if Dr. Condon had not read his own report. The report itself presented real mysteries."

An eleven-member panel from the National Academy of Sciences reviewed the Condon Report and approved its conclusions. "On the basis of present knowledge," noted the panel, "the least likely explanation of UFOs is the hypothesis of extraterrestrial visitations by intelligent beings." They agreed with Condon: UFOs did not warrant further scientific study.

In a press conference, January 11, 1969, Keyhoe complained that the committee had examined only fifty cases from 1947 to 1967, and those were hardly typical of the "reliable, unexplained" reports. NICAP had ten to fifteen thousand such cases in its files.

Hynek wrote in his review that he would never have wasted his time on nearly two-thirds of the cases studied by the committee. The Air Force consultant also noted that members of the committee sometimes stretched so far to explain a sighting they came up with solutions like this: "This unusual sighting should therefore be assigned to the category of some almost certainly natural phenomenon which is so rare that it apparently has never been reported before or since."

Dr. Peter Sturrock, professor of astrophysics and space science at Stanford, wrote a lengthy evaluation of the Condon Report for the Institute of Plasma Research. Sturrock concluded, "It is my opinion that the substance of the Condon Report presents a persuasive case for the view that there is some phenomenological fire hidden behind the smoke of UFO reports, and that the Report therefore *supports* the proposition that further scientific study of UFOs is in order."

On May 16, 1969, Roach, who had been responsible for the section on astronaut sightings, wrote to Hynek that he had attended a recent Condon lecture entitled "UFOs I Have Loved and Lost." "He was amusing, hilarious at times, but did not touch on the serious part of the investigation," said Roach. "The listeners must have gone away with the erroneous impression that his encounters with psychopaths or retardeds represented the esssence of the investigation rather than a peripheral aspect of the matter." Roach referred to "all the errors and comedies of the investigation," and ended with, "The fallibility of scientists has been revealed which is important and the public may now enter a new era of confusion."

Two years after the Condon Report, in November of 1970, a subcommittee on UFOs sponsored by the American Institute of Aeronautics and Astronautics found that many of Condon's conclusions were his own, not based on research in the report. Nor was there "a basis in the report for his prediction that nothing of scientific value will come of further studies." The subcommittee recommended increased study, finding it "difficult to ignore the small residue of well-documented but unexplainable cases which form the hard core of the UFO controversy."

"Nevertheless," Hynek recalled, "when the Condon Report came out in 1968, it was the kiss of death."

* * *

The Condon Report recommended that the Air Force's efforts at Project Blue Book be discontinued. One year later, December 17, 1969, the Secretary of the Air Force announced that the Air Force's twenty-two-year study of UFOs would be terminated. The Air Force "got out of the UFO business," folded Project Blue Book, and declassified all files: forty-two cubic feet of paper, over 80,000 pages. In twenty-two years the Air Force had investigated 12,618 reported sightings, only 701 of which remained unsolved. The rest the Air Force attributed to balloons, satellites, aircraft, lightning, reflections, stars, planets, the sun, the moon, weather conditions, or outright fabrications. Using the figures provided by the Air Force, once every eleven days for twenty-two years someone in the United States sighted a flying object that no one could explain.

But many people in the field had felt for some time that the Air Force and its Project Blue Book served only as a publicity front, that in fact the real investigation had been conducted by another agency or agencies. Bill Spaulding of Ground Saucer Watch examined the newly declassified Air Force files in the early seventies and came away feeling something was missing.

"It's always been our contention," said Spaulding, "that there was another agency or entity involved. In other words, the Air Force is not the bad guy. If you look at it logically you'll see that the Air Force projects consisted of about five people, including some secretaries, very miniscule, who did nothing. The Air Force went around and gathered information. But after reviewing all the Project Blue Book files, we came across none of the cases that people had given to us. Where were they? What we found out was that another agency was involved, so we said, 'To heck with this. Let's go after the CIA.' "

* * *

In 1975, under the newly revised Freedom of Information Act, Ground Saucer Watch filed a request with the CIA for one copy of the 1953 Robertson Panel Report. Responding to the request, the CIA declassified the controversial report, but stated that the CIA's *only* involvement with UFOs was the Robertson Panel.

"At no time prior to the formation of the Robertson Panel and subsequent to the issuance of the panel's report," read the reply, "has the CIA engaged in the study of the UFO phenomenon. The Robertson Panel Report is summation of the Agency's interest and involvement in this matter."

Three and a half years later, after extended litigation, the CIA was forced to admit to Ground Saucer Watch that it not only investigated the phenomenon before and long after the convening of the Robertson Panel, but that it possessed 412 UFO-related documents that had originated within the CIA, and another 199 documents that had originated with other government agencies. The CIA relinquished 900 pages of UFO sightings and internal policy on UFOs.

While the litigation between GSW and the CIA progressed through the legal system, an independent UFO researcher filed another Freedom of Information request, this one with the super-secret National Security Agency. He received this reply: "Regarding your inquiry about UFOs, please be advised that NSA does not have *any* interest in UFOs in *any* manner [emphasis in original]." But during its suit against the CIA, GSW learned that some of the CIA documents they sought had originated with NSA. After a new and again protracted legal battle NSA released only two of its admitted 239 documents relating to UFOs, a decision upheld by the courts for reasons of national security.

During the late 1970s and early 1980s, UFO groups and independent researchers utilizing the Freedom of Information Act prompted the release of 3,000 pages of previously classified material concerning UFOs—reports, correspondence, minutes, and memoranda—all pieces of a historical puzzle that when put together revealed over thirty years of interest in UFOs by the State Department, Army, Navy, Air Force, FBI, CIA, NSA, and Defense Intelligence Agency.

Among the thousands of pages of UFO-related documents researchers found many old and revealing memoranda such as this one concealed in CIA files since 1950. On November 21 of that year, an engineer named Wilbert B. Smith in the Canadian Department of Transport wrote a proposal for a study of the earth's magnetic field as a possible energy source. In the secret memo, he stated, "I made discreet enquiries through the Canadian Embassy staff in Washington who were able to obtain for me the following information:

a. The matter is the most highly classified subject in the United States Government, rating higher even than the H-bomb.
b. Flying saucers exist.
c. Their modus operandi is unknown but concentrated effort is being made by a small group headed by Doctor Vannevar Bush.
d. The entire matter is considered by the United States authorities to be of tremendous significance."

* * *

Since no one had ever uncovered a photo lab or darkroom where Eduard Meier might have developed and possibly fabricated his photographs, Elders and Welch wanted to know who processed his film. Perhaps that person could offer clues or even answers, making the testing of the photographs unnecessary. They discoverd that Meier had all of his film developed at a small photography and video shop in Wetzikon called Bär Photo, part of a downtown shopping strip about thirty or forty minutes from the farm. Bär Photo was owned by a couple in their mid-thirties, Beatrice and Willy Bär, each of whom during the interview appeared to be bright and well traveled, far more cosmopolitan than most of the people they had met at the farm. Each spoke English well.

When Meier had first brought in rolls of black-and-white film to be developed, Bär himself had done much of the processing.

"I never saw anything suspicious in the black-and-white film I developed," said Bär, "nor was I ever told to manipulate anything. A lot of people have suspected I did that, but no. When someone brings you pictures like this your first reaction automatically is, 'This is a lot of crap.' But he aroused my curiosity."

Meier had even invited Bär several times to accompany him on a contact to photograph the beamships if he desired, but Bär had declined. At the time he did not believe strongly in Meier's story, nor did he have time to drive and walk with Meier through the Swiss countryside late at night. He had been curious, but not curious enough.

When Meier had first brought his exposed film to Bär, the shop owner had studied the photographs closely with a magnifying glass. He was certain he would be able to recognize a double exposure because the portion exposed twice always appears "stronger." But he never saw any evidence that Meier had tinkered with the photographs.

Bär said, "My personal opinion was always, 'I don't know about UFOs, but the pictures are real.' You could drag me before a court of law and I would say the same thing I have told you."

During the interview Bär said he had always sold Meier equipment he could handle with one hand. That was the major selling point. Meier would come into the store and experiment for hours with every model until he found one that would be the easiest for him to use. Bär had once sold Meier an old 8mm camera made by Alcom that had been sitting around his shop for years; nobody wanted to buy it, but it was by far the easiest movie camera to use with one hand.

"If he had an accomplice," Bär pointed out, "he would

not have to try out all the models to see what could be used with one hand."

Beatrice Bär also knew Meier and often had spoken with him in the shop. Unknown to Meier she, too, had studied his photos.

"I don't believe in the same thing he does," she said. "But I always wondered just how he could do that, because the pictures looked real, they didn't look faked. As a rule, if you have a double exposure or any reproduction, you can see the outline, but with his pictures you could see nothing."

She and her husband often had talked about Meier, but neither understood how the man could create such authentic-looking photography. Beatrice herself had decided that Meier fabricated everything, but she couldn't see how he was doing it. Nor could she understand, with so many people traveling to the farm to visit Meier, and now so many actually living with the Meiers, how some of them could not know or even be involved in the hoax. She wondered how Meier could keep all of them quiet, especially the children.

"Children always talk," she said.

Both Willy and Beatrice Bär had learned nearly everything they knew about photography and developing from a younger man who several years before had been employed at the shop when it had a different owner, and who had encouraged the Bärs to buy the shop when it came up for sale in 1970. Fritz Kindliman, who recently turned thirty-one, had now worked there for ten years. He knew Meier better than anyone in the store, had handled and inspected hundreds of his photographs, and often had talked with him since Meier began bringing his film to Bär for processing in 1973.

Kindliman had been taking pictures since he was a small boy. When he turned sixteen and under the Swiss educational system had to select a profession for study and apprenticeship, he chose video and television. Whenever new equipment came out on the market he bought it so he could study how it worked. He now owned and could dismantle and reassemble many cameras, video, and 35mm.

Quiet, somewhat disheveled, with hair sticking up in the back, and appearing almost lost when out of the lab or not behind a camera, Kindliman met one morning with Elders and Welch in a small pastry shop a few doors down from Bär Photo. At first the conversation was of congenial things—Kindliman's interest in cameras, his years of experience at the Bär shop. Then, speaking through an interpreter, Elders asked Kindliman, "Did Mr. Meier ever ask you about darkroom techniques or film developing?"

Kindliman shook his head.

"Never?" said Elders.

Kindliman turned to the interpreter and said that Meier never asked *any* questions about such things. "Of course I must admit," he added, "in the beginning I was very critical when he came in with these pictures. But he kept bringing them in. Today I am convinced this is the real thing."

The photographer seemed equally positive that Meier had no color photo lab of his own hidden away somewhere. The processing and equipment were far too expensive and complex to be owned and operated by a single individual. Bär Photo itself had no such sophisticated laboratory. Every roll of film Meier brought to the shop, and often there were as many as four or five a week, Bär sent to one of three places: slides to Lausanne Kodak, Ektachrome to Studio 13 in Zurich, prints to Wädenswil Labor Pro-Cine.

Since Meier used both print and slide film, his negatives had to be sent to all three Swiss laboratories. Kindliman's job included scanning random pictures when they came back from the developing labs, checking through the packets to ensure the quality of the photos and slides they returned to their customers. He had examined many of Meier's photographs before Meier himself had seen them. And he was certain there had never been any of what he called "manipulation" of the photos.

Welch asked him why. *"Warum?"*

On the table in front of them lay a picture of Meier's they had brought to the interview, two beamships close up, one below the crest of a hill and one just above. Kindliman picked it up and immediately began to talk.

"If you wanted to superimpose those two UFOs on the landscape you would have to practice for a long time to get the upper one without any shadows on it. You must understand when you bring in a whole strip of film there are many pictures on that strip. If this shot had been manipulated you would assume that on that strip of film you would have several shots of the same scene but of different quality, because he's experimenting with that scene.

"Now if Herr Meier had come into the store just to order one picture and on the strip to the left and to the right there were the same scene with different lighting techniques, then I would have immediately noticed these pictures had been manipulated. But I never had the slightest suspicion the pictures had been manipulated. I exclude such a possibility. Whenever he brought in negatives to have prints made, the negatives were always in strips, not cut up."

Welch asked Kindliman if there was any way Meier could have manipulated some of these pictures without his being able to detect it. Kindliman became indignant.

"I can't imagine that," he said. "Absolutely not!"

Kindliman also said they had told Meier again and again to take better care of his negatives, because he would bring them in scratched and smudged.

Elders and Welch had surmised that when they got to Bär Photo they would discover that Meier frequently had been in asking about darkroom techniques. But according to the man in the shop who had spent the greatest amount of time with him, he never asked such questions. Kindliman told them that most of Meier's film was in slides and that if Meier had wanted to fake pictures of that size he would have needed specialized macro equipment, but Meier didn't have any.

"Had he ever asked me questions about macro technique or how to light macro shots, then I would have become suspicious," said Kindliman. "Had he asked me pointed questions, I might have studied those photos more carefully, but he never gave me reason to disbelieve him."

Perhaps the single thing that impressed Kindliman was Meier's 8mm films of the beamships—Meier's footage of the beamship that appears to cut in front of a tall pine causing it to sway, of the ship coming to a stop over Hasenbol, and of the craft that begins to dematerialize above a hillside and seems to be reappearing down below in the same frame.

Video and movie film had become Kindliman's specialty. He told Elders and Welch, "When I saw these shots they looked real to me."

* * *

Even on warm summer evenings, the large Meier kitchen with its many chairs continued to be the place for everyone to gather. After a dinner of boiled potatoes from the garden, with perhaps some cheese and a loaf of bread out of the oven, most everyone simply remained at the table, especially if there were guests. Chairs got rearranged, people tilted back or leaned on the table, and the conversation went on until the evening light showing through the kitchen windows first had softened to gray, then finally turned black.

"We had many such evenings," recalled Welch. "On one that I'll always remember we talked about the Pleiadians, what Meier had been told, their knowledge of their past, tracing it from Lyra, how they for the first time came in contact with Earth. I think we sat there spellbound for about two hours. And the way it came out of him was more than interesting. *He* found it interesting, and so he would highlight points that were interesting to him or somehow had surprised him, as a couple of things had.

"I looked at all of it in a dual sense: The question whether it was too far out to believe I felt we'd find the answer to later, so that wasn't important to me. At that time I was more interested in experiencing, watching, and hearing all of it, and I enjoyed the experience. And what was impressing me to no end was that a lot of what was coming out of Meier . . . was not Meier. It was alien to the man, and to his style of describing things. He was explaining something he'd been told by somebody else. Whoever was the source of all this description was very, very intelligent, very, very good at communicating a fact or an event. And very philosophical at times in an alien way, or highly technically accurate in a way that Meier didn't even seem to be aware of."

"We *are* the Pleiadians," Meier was explaining to the people at the table. "We came from a cross between the Pleiadians and the human beings from the earth."

"Why don't we live as long as they do?" asked Welch.

"We have to build up our age," said Meier, "like they had to do on their planets some millions or billion years ago. The age of a living form, especially of a human being, will evolve very slowly, like his wisdom and knowledge, and his technology. You can see here in Europe some twenty-five years ago we had an average age for the European people of seventy-two years. And now it's up to seventy-five years."

"What does Erra look like?" asked Elders.

Meier said he had never traveled there. "But it looks nearly like earth," he explained. "It's a little bit smaller than earth, and the buildings there are round. The vehicles have no wheels, they hover, and the work is done by robots and androids. The androids are half mechanical and half organic, and they are able to think by themselves, but humans oversee everything that's done. Each family is not more than five persons, the parents and a maximum of three children."

Meier told them that about three thousand ships from other star systems in the galaxy visit the earth each year.

"There's eight different human races that have stations here on earth," he claimed. "They are here exploring, they are here studying, they are here watching."

"Are any of them here to try to destroy us?" asked Elders.

"No," said Meier. "If a human race can cross a very, very great distance, maybe light years of space, they will not be coming here to make trouble or start a war. The earth human is a fighting creature—his whole life is based on fighting—so he thinks if there is a human race on another planet those creatures will be exactly the same as he is. But that isn't true."

If they so desired, the Pleiadians could destroy the earth in a matter of minutes, said Meier; they could have enslaved all earthlings thousands of years ago. Meier admitted that some of the other ships had picked up humans against their will, but he compared the situation to earth scientists and anthropologists who, upon discovering a primitive people still on earth, dispatch teams to study them and return them to the lab.

"Humans are humans," said Meier.

If the Pleiadians or other entities abducted earth humans, it served only to satisfy their legitimate curiosity. Occasionally a mistake might be made and an abducted human would die, much as earth doctors made mistakes causing people to die. But human life was never taken purposely.

Meier was certain that World War III would take place.

"That will be for sure," he said.

"When will it happen?" asked Welch.

"That's a good question," said Meier.

"Very soon?"

"It's not so far," replied Meier. "They know the exact dates, but it's not so good to know them."

"Won't the Pleiadians try to stop it?" asked Welch.

"It is impossible," said Meier. He told the people at the table that the Pleiadians are not allowed to interfere with the development of earth. "It is absolutely impossible to stop all these things. Some two thousand years ago, World War III was called by several prophets. Nobody heard them for two thousand years. And now it's really too late."

Such a holocaust could be prevented only by change, and change could be effected in only two ways: One was by teaching, by showing earth humans how to advance spiritually from within, which the Pleiadians desired to do; the other was to use force, which the Pleiadians forbid. They would not step in to prevent war unless our earth war threatened civilizations elsewhere. Though they possessed the power to stop the ultimate conflagration, they would stand idly by and watch us destroy ourselves if we chose to do so, even if a crazy man reached for the button. The Pleiadians attempted only to effect small changes in people of clear head and heart, by teaching and allowing the person to grow from the inside.

"If you travel into space," said Meier, "you will find humans wherever you go. And when they start to think, they need a teacher. If they have never seen a flower before, never heard anything about a flower, the one who knows the flower can teach them. And this is the way over the whole universe. The photographs are only to make people think, to show them something; people shall come for these pictures, but they shall study the teachings, and they shall come to know."

* * *

Meier told Welch of many things that had been explained to him by the Pleiadians, one of the most intriguing and controversial being perhaps the most fundamental to the Pleiadian presence on Earth.

With the Pleiades nearly five hundred light years from Earth, conventional Earth physics dictated that traveling at the greatest speed conceivable, the speed of light, a trip from the Pleiades to Earth and back again would require one thousand years. Yet Meier maintained that the Pleiadian propulsion system was capable of speeds many millions of times faster than light, and that Semjase frequently traveled back and forth between her home planet Erra and Earth. The Pleiadians, said Meier, made the trip in seven hours.

185

During the fourth contact and again in the eighth, Semjase had explained to Meier aspects of the propulsion system that enabled the Pleiadian beamships to transcend distance and the passage of time.

"For traveling through cosmic space," she said, "a drive is necessary which surpasses the speed of light many times over. But this propulsion can come into action only when the speed of light is already attained. This means then that a beamship needs at least two drives—a normal drive which provides acceleration up to the speed of light, and a second hyper-drive, as you would call it. With this we are able to paralyze time and space simultaneously," explained Semjase. "They collapse into null time and null space. And only when time and space have ceased to exist are we capable of traveling through distances of light years in a tiny particle of a second. This is done so quickly that living forms are not aware of it.

"The reason we need seven hours to reach Earth is because first we must fly far into space before we can convert to hyper-speed. We then comes back out of the hyper-space condition far outside of your solar system, and fly to here once more in normal drive.

"I am not allowed to give you any further details. But I can tell you that your advanced scientific circles are already working on systems known as light-emitting drives and 'tachyon' drives. The elemental principles are already known to them. The light-emitting drive serves as the normal propulsion system to move the ships to the limits of space and time. Once there, the tachyon drive is brought into action. This is the hyper-propulsion system, which is able to force space and time into hyper-space. We use other names, but the principles are exactly the same."

Before Stevens's first trip to Switzerland in 1977, Lou Zinsstag had sent him the contact notes pertaining to the Pleiadian propulsion system. But Stevens had never heard the term "tachyon." Nor had the Elders or Welch.

After Welch had read in the contact notes Semjase's explanation of Pleiadian propulsion to Meier, he questioned

the man often about the concept. Welch came away thinking that Meier knew more than he should, both for his
station in life and for the dearth of information on the
subject in all but the most sophisticated scientific circles.

"He wrote down in the notes what he had been told,"
said Welch, "and then he elaborated on what he understood
of the concept as a method of space travel. I saw those notes
in '78. We did learn later that for some period of time
specialists either connected with NASA or with companies
like General Dynamics had been quietly working on that as
a propulsion concept. What's interesting is that the man
who wrote the notes has a formal education equivalent to
the fifth or sixth grade. He does not live near major libraries, he does not live near major scientific centers, he
doesn't have immediate contacts in those fields. At the
time, we didn't know what 'tachyon' meant. Most *physicists*
didn't know what a tachyon was. And to apply the concept
of theoretical tachyon to space propulsion is a huge step to
make. There was no evidence that we could dig up that he
had collaborated with anybody on this.

"But the thing that was startling to me was that as
soon as we started to dig into that, all of a sudden something else would pop up, in the notes or through Billy, that
was equally sophisticated, unique, and advanced in a different field. In the notes there were conversations about the
universe and celestial mechanics, about healing methods
and advanced medical equipment that just did not make
sense coming from a man out in the remote countryside of
Switzerland. Most of it, though, I noticed in the way he
carried himself in conversations—the way he dealt with
knowledge. It all seemed out of context with his personality. It seemed as if the man had a tutor in various fields who
was one incredible tutor."

* * *

"After my first trip in the summer of '78," said Welch,
"we got together and decided there was a tremendous
amount of information here, a tremendous number of unan-

swered questions. We were intrigued, we were hooked at this point. Witnesses we had met seemed quite sincere as well as changed. That was the thing. They seemed changed. There was a sense of change in the area all around the Meier farmhouse, something that you couldn't put your finger on, just something you sensed. I can give you an analogy. Some of the people we met reflected the same kind of change you would detect in someone who's been on an operating table and has been termed technically dead for two or three minutes and then comes back. I had talked to two people like that, so I knew the difference. They have a light airiness about them, a sense of harmony about their lives that envelops you when you talk to them. I sensed that in some of the witnesses.

"When I left after that trip, I had the feeling, 'I don't know what it is, but something is going on. Something here is going on.' And I wouldn't have been satisfied if Meier himself all of a sudden had stood up in front of everybody and shocked them by saying, 'I faked everything!' I wouldn't have believed that, because he couldn't have known how."

NINE

Although little known in the United States before 1979, the case of Eduard Meier would emerge as one of the most controversial in the history of UFO phenomena. No case had ever offered so much evidence; in fact, Meier seemed to possess more evidence than nearly all previous UFO cases combined. But that evidence would be seen by few and studied by even fewer, because Meier's preposterous and sometimes misunderstood stories of traveling back in time to see Jesus and photographing the Eye of God would be laughed at and dismissed as nonsense—the same as Lee Elders had reacted before he had seen with his own eyes the conditions in which Meier lived, talked with the witnesses, and walked the sites. Meier's stories couldn't be true, but neither could the witnesses and the evidence be dismissed easily. Instead of space potatoes from the Moon and piano music from Saturn, Meier offered scientists what they had asked for for thirty-two years—something they could place under a microscope or enter into a computer and examine. And Lee Elders held all of it in his hands.

But in the late 1970s in the United States at least a dozen private groups vied for such evidence. The Aerial Phenomena Research Organization (APRO), headquartered in Tucson, and the Mutual UFO Network (MUFON), in Sequin, Texas, were the largest now that NICAP was defunct. Both organizations boasted several scientists and experts in various fields who lent prestige to the groups' activities and publications. But the research, the gathering of facts, the interviewing of the rancher who had observed the strange light in the night sky, often was conducted by volunteers whose only qualification was the dues they paid to be members of the organization.

"Hobbyists," Stevens called them. "Often their investigations are no more than meeting the witness in his living room and discussing his experience over tea or coffee."

Usually short-lived and poorly financed, most investigations generated one or two pieces of paper to be mailed to the organization's headquarters, which most often was the home of the director.

Though united in a common cause, this small community churned with dissension. Because each organization remained viable only through the energy, dues, and contributions of its members, keeping their interest high was important, and this often led to intense competition for the more compelling stories. Should one group discover an intriguing case with claims or photographs to captivate its membership, it would often conceal such discovery as long as possible. Debate over old cases raged for years. Newsletters and bulletins mailed to memberships of a few hundred or a few thousand became forums for attacking not only cases, but other ufologists. Emotions ran high and accusations were sometimes vicious.

When Stevens returned from Switzerland after meeting Eduard Meier in the fall of 1977, he felt the case was so big, complex, and potentially sensational that if he took it to one of these groups it would become embroiled in the politics of the UFO community. He wanted to avoid this. (Stevens had his own critics: One prominent ufologist, Stanton Friedman, had labeled him a case "collector, not investigator.") Stevens also knew that most ufologists still automatically dismissed contact cases, especially claims of repeated contact. But he felt that the Meier case had hard evidence and that this evidence needed more than the typical short-term, poorly financed investigation by one of the UFO groups. Instead, he had approached the Elders and Welch, who were experienced in investigation and the preservation of evidence, and, most important, had no connection with any UFO organization. Immediately, Elders had capped the case with a tight lid of security.

"I guess I was overly protective with this case in the beginning," he said later. "And rightfully so. I still wasn't totally convinced it was for real, but I'd be damned if I would let anybody get near the evidence. We're talking about hard evidence. I made a lot of enemies that way. Our problems really began right after that with the UFO community."

* * *

In the summer of 1978, Jim Dilettoso set out to explore, experiment, and talk to people about how the Meier evidence might be legitimately tested. If he was to organize the testing, he needed to know the latest equipment, the qualified scientists, and the proper procedures. He searched first for the experts. Then he spent a year writing and phoning them, sometimes interviewing them in person, before he understood what tests should be performed and what equipment should be used, and which scientists were not only knowledgeable, but also open-minded enough to analyze evidence associated with UFOs. After he felt he understood the procedures, he tried to locate and use the equipment at various labs and universities before he approached one of the scientists with the actual evidence in his hand.

"At times I cringed about it," said Welch. "It would have been much nicer to have somebody with a Ph.D. who'd spent five years in research at Harvard to be there carrying on that conversation for us. Also, I cringed many times because we couldn't be sitting there with a $20,000 check in our hand when approaching someone to ask to use their equipment or to do the work."

Once he understood what needed to be done, Dilettoso then had to convince the scientists themselves to perform the actual procedures on the metal, sound recording, and photographs, and that proved difficult. A scientist's reputation remains only as good as his credibility, and many if not most scientists felt their credibility would be seriously threatened if it were known they were studying UFOs. But after many tries, Dilettoso discovered an Achilles' heel he suspected might exist—the natural curiosity of the scientist.

* * *

Marcel Vogel was a research chemist, one of less than a dozen senior scientists at the IBM facility in San Jose that employed 9,000 people. The holder of thirty-two patents, he had worked for IBM for twenty-two years, inventing for the huge computer company the magnetic disk coating memory system still used in IBM disk memories throughout the world. Research begun in 1960 by Vogel also had introduced the use of liquid crystals for optical display. Now a specialist in the conversion of energy inside crystals, Vogel probed the interior of crystalline structures with the most complete optical microscopic equipment available in the world—a system of scanning electron microscopes costing $250,000.

In his forty years as a scientist, Vogel had received many unusual requests for his expertise, but the strangest came in mid-April 1979, in a phone call from Jim Dilettoso. Searching for scientists to examine the Meier evidence, Dilettoso had discovered Vogel at IBM and felt he represented the perfect blend of expertise and curiosity: Eminent in his field, he had a reputation for being open to new ideas, even those on the fringe of science. When Dilettoso contacted Vogel, the scientist seemed amused with the story, but intrigued as well. Stevens followed with a letter cataloguing the samples in his possession—various crystals that Meier had labeled as coming from certain planets in other star systems, and four states of metal used in forming the hull of the Pleiadian beamships.

"These specimens are available for any kind of non-destructive analysis," wrote Stevens.

Both men explained to Vogel that the samples had been entrusted to Stevens by a Swiss farmer named Eduard Meier, who claimed since 1975 to have met face-to-face over one hundred times with beings from the star cluster known as the Pleiades. "I am personally convinced that the contact is actually taking place," wrote Stevens, "and is still to this date proceeding on an irregular basis."

Skeptical but curious, Vogel agreed to conduct an analysis. Later he admitted, "I've had a rather negative feeling toward UFOs because, I said, 'Unless I have something physical that I can get my hands on, just reported sightings and things like that have no interest to me.' "

One Saturday morning, not long after he had agreed to examine the Meier evidence, Vogel found lying on his doorstep a small padded mailer addressed to him. Upon opening the package he was surprised to find a note from Stevens and four smaller packages, one enclosing a lavender crystal, two filled with darkened metal specimens, and the last containing a half-inch triangle appearing to be an alloy of silver and gold.

Vogel studied the samples in his hand and conducted elementary testing in his IBM laboratory. Except for its clarity and the beauty of its soft violet tinge, the amethyst crystal revealed no unusual properties. And the two metal specimens darkened by oxidation contained only small and impure quantities of aluminum and sulphur, with some silver, copper, and lead. But they held at least one surprise for him.

"When I touched the oxide with a stainless steel probe," Vogel later remembered, "red streaks appeared and the oxide coating disappeared. I just touched the metal like that, and it started to deoxidize and become a pure metal. I've never seen a phenomenon like that before. It's just something that was unusual."

Though the two darkened samples exhibited this unusual property, Vogel considered them no better than standard silver solder. "You could have gone to a jeweler and gotten a specimen of that," he said. "The other fragment that I had, the triangle, was different."

In the separate packages, Vogel had found handwritten notes with information about each specimen. The note enclosed with the triangle said that when the Pleiadians gave it to Meier in 1975, Meier recorded in the contact notes that they had warned: Earth scientists would easily be able to analyze the components of the alloy, which included the basic building blocks of the universe. But the alloy was bonded in a unique way involving seven separate development stages that by twentieth-century earth technology would be impossible to duplicate.

"This information," one of them told Meier, "can be only a suggestion to the earth scientists for the still distant future."

One evening, several days later, Vogel remained late at IBM to begin analyzing the burnished triangle. Placing the metal in the electron microscope, he turned on a video tape to record his analysis and peered through the lens. Though he had expected to encounter nothing new in the specimen, to his surprise he was looking at the most peculiar maze of elements he had ever seen.

* * *

Since arriving in Tucson in 1966, Stevens had investigated cases for the Aerial Phenomena Research Organization, sometimes piloting a private plane to the sites. Though he was friends with Jim and Coral Lorenzen, who had founded APRO in 1952, he told them nothing of the Meier case for over a year. "I didn't want them meddling in it yet," he said, "because I didn't know where it was going." But after visiting the farm and talking to Meier in April 1978, he and Elders had discussed bringing APRO in on the case: The UFO organization had connections in the science community that might prove useful in having the evidence analyzed.

"So we decided to invite APRO to come into the case with us," said Elders. "I really respected at that time the work they were doing, and so did Steve. They were the oldest and largest UFO group in the world, and they had a great reputation, they were dedicated, they had pioneered in a lot of areas. I liked Jim Lorenzen. And Jim was interested in the case, he seemed sincere."

Lorenzen said later he had "serious doubts" about the case. But he would reserve judgment until the evidence had been examined by "outside experts." For the present, he said, he considered Meier's photos to be "art." "They were exciting and interesting," he added, "but we didn't consider them proof of anything."

The alliance with APRO began with a basic misunderstanding. Lorenzen saw the gesture as an invitation to him to supervise the investigation so that the APRO stamp would make the efforts of Stevens and Intercep "beyond question."

"I got involved in this with the idea it was to be an objective investigation and that I was to have control of the investigation," said Lorenzen. "I would decide what tests would be done and what scientists and labs to use."

"Mostly," said Stevens, "he asked questions about where I was on the investigation. Had I tested this? Had I looked at it this way or that way? Did I ask this or that question? The only inclination he gave me that he was sympathetic to it was that he said several times, 'There seems to be an awful lot here for one party to fake. Either it's a big group with a big scam, or something is going on.' "

For a while Lorenzen met frequently with the investigators. He talked at length with the producer John Stefanelli and traveled to San Francisco to speak with Marcel Vogel, the scientist Dilettoso had discovered at IBM; he met with representatives of a computer company that manufactured image processing equipment for analyzing photographs. But as time went on, Stevens held back on much of the evidence and information coming from the case. He did not want to lose control to Lorenzen. Furthermore, Dilettoso was now digging into the science for them, and he had begun to establish his own contacts; they no longer needed APRO's connections in the science community.

At the same time, Lorenzen had been speaking with other ufologists who had European contacts, and one of them passed on a rumor that the whole case was a big joke, that each time the Americans left Switzerland to return home, the Meier group laughed behind their backs at how easily they had been fooled. Lorenzen also heard that affidavits from alleged witnesses not only failed to support Meier's claims, but actually refuted them.

"I think he used models," Lorenzen said later, "and he threw away those pictures that didn't turn out. See, they never checked out his avenues of developing and printing to see if they stood up. They never checked anything like that, which is one of the first things I would have checked." Lorenzen said that as far as he knew, no scientist ever analyzed the photographs.

Then, over a year into the investigation, Lorenzen and Elders had a disagreement.

"Lorenzen asked if we would cover his expenses to Europe," said Elders. "At that time, we were using our own money, Intercep money, to cover our segment of the investigation. Wendelle was using his retirement pay from the Air Force. So we were operating on the 'ten dollars a day through Europe' program to save money to try to conduct the investigation. We told APRO no, we couldn't do it. APRO said, 'Okay then, fine, we want all the evidence turned over to the APRO organization.' Hell, who needs someone to help you under those conditions? So we said, 'Thanks, but no thanks.' Made them mad."

"We all finally agreed," Stevens admitted later, "that we wouldn't discuss the facts in the case anymore with anybody outside our group, and if anybody pressed for answers, try to get out of it, and if we couldn't get out of it, to drag a hare across the trail and throw them off. It was probably not the best thing to do, but we were trying to keep people from stirring our pot at that time. We already were inside government laboratories, and we didn't need anybody else trying to help us get in there."

* * *

Before 1978 scientists had used image processing exclusively to extract data from a photograph everyone knew was legitimate: A satellite had beamed it back from the Moon or Mars; it was real. The challenge with the Meier photos was to detect possible fabrication. Dilettoso discovered a UFO group in Phoenix, Ground Saucer Watch, that claimed to have a reliable computer method for authenticating UFO photographs. Since 1974 they had received five hundred photographs from around the world, subjected them to their new process, and pronounced a large majority hoaxes. A few, less than 5 percent, they proclaimed to be genuine.

Unknown to Dilettoso, a West German researcher had sent ten Meier photos to GSW for analysis two years earlier. After analyzing the photos, GSW had reported: "All of the pictures are hoaxes and they should not be considered evidence of an extraordinary flying craft." Nearly every method of photo fakery possible had allegedly been employed by the one-armed Meier—a suspended model, the double exposure technique, the double print method. The West German UFO group had immediately ceased their investigation of the Meier case.

Later, Ground Saucer Watch had received a photograph of a disk-shaped craft taken by a man in Calgary, Canada. They analyzed the photograph and found it to be "genuine," which they announced publicly. Sometime later, through an intermediary, the man from Calgary sent a second photograph he had taken of the same disk on the same roll of film. GSW concluded that the photo "depicts the crudest attempt at a hoax that we have ever seen." Since that blatant contradiction was publicized, few people had given weight to the findings of the organization.

In his research of equipment and procedures, Dilettoso learned that GSW performed none of the alleged computer work. They sent all photographs to a firm in California, where technicians entered them into a computer by taking another picture with an inexpensive video camera, and applied basic software programs to enhance the photographs with bright colors. Then they took another picture off the computer screen and sent these pictures back to GSW to be studied with the naked eye. By then, the information in the original photograph had been greatly distorted.

"This frustrated Jim," said Welch, "it frustrated Steve and me. Because there was no structured approach. They could have been looking at stuff that came from a dirty lens."

"Or," said Dilettoso, "the angle of the light on the photo could be wrong and create surface reflection from the gloss on the picture. There's a hundred things that could happen. I spent a lot of time talking to GSW and found I wasn't going to get anything out of them. They really were playing with toys."

After GSW, it took Dilettoso little time to discover the father of image processing, Dr. Robert Nathan at NASA's Jet Propulsion Laboratory in Pasadena. Dr. Nathan had conceived image processing in the 1960s and developed it for nearly twenty years. Although other government labs now had comparable equipment, as well as scientists competent in image processing, JPL was considered first in the field. After several calls form Dilettoso and Stevens over a period of months, Nathan finally agreed to look at the photos, but he would not commit himself to examining them: The procedure was costly and time consuming, and though Nathan's job was to detect and analyze objects in space, whatever their nature, he had no time to waste. Still, he kept an open mind.

In his office, before even viewing the photographs, Nathan told Stevens and Dilettoso he would look at the photos as an individual, not as a scientist at JPL, and that any opinion he rendered would be his own, not that of the NASA facility. That made clear, Stevens pulled out several 11×14 prints he had had made of Meier photos and laid them on Nathan's desk. The scientist perused them, saying nothing. Then he reached for the phone and called the photo lab to tell them he was coming over. After looking at the photos for a few more minutes, he escorted Stevens and Dilettoso to the lab to have copies made of a set of transparencies also in Stevens's possession.

"We took the internegatives that I had to their processing facility," recalled Stevens. "And they made copies from those. They wanted to keep the internegatives, but we wouldn't let them, because every time somebody has kept one they end up talking with it in front of them and little spit balls fall on it, and when you put it under super magnification the next time you've got little blues in the picture."

Bob Post, the head of the photo lab where every JPL photo of planets, stars, asteroids, and comets was processed and printed, had worked there for twenty-two years. "Over the years of looking at photographs and judging photographs," he said, "you get to the point where you can see a lot of things in a photograph that the average person doesn't see."

About four o'clock in the afternoon, Nathan entered the lab and showed the large prints to Post. "I'd seen pictures of UFOs before," said Post, "and I looked at them as a bunch of bull. There's no definition to anything. But these were good. Whatever they were, they were good. You've got a nice spacecraft sitting there, you've got some good ground out here, you've got a sky with clouds in it once in a while, and you can see some detail. The pictures look good. Under further scrutiny you might find out, 'Yeah, they're fake.' But some of his pictures I thought were gorgeous, absolutely gorgeous, best stuff I've ever seen for UFO pictures.

From a photography standpoint, you couldn't see anything that was fake about them. That's what struck me. They looked like legitimate photographs. I thought, God, if this is real, this is going to be really something."

Nathan reserved judgment.

* * *

By the summer of 1979, the Elders, Welch, and Stevens had spent over $30,000 traveling to Switzerland to see Meier, traveling to San Francisco, Los Angeles, and other locales to speak with scientists and computer companies, and telephoning all over the United States. With Dilettoso beginning to open doors at major laboratories, they decided they needed more money if they were to continue investigating the case properly. A few scientists had conducted preliminary tests on some of the evidence, and so far they were getting interesting results, but nothing conclusive as yet. Without consulting Lorenzen further, Intercep formed Genesis III Publishing and produced *UFO . . . Contact from the Pleiades,* a large-format photo journal containing many of the Meier photos, a sampling of quotes by Semjase, a brief outline of Meier's experiences since 1975, astronomical and mythological information on the Pleiades, and some of the preliminary findings on the testing of the evidence. "Sort of a mix of what we had done up to that point," said Elders.

Seventy-one pages long, the Pleiades book claimed that a number of scientists had been consulted on the Meier evidence and that some now were conducting "a most exhaustive and painstakingly detailed investigation." But the text mentioned no names. The book displayed pictures of various people sitting around a table in the Meier kitchen and noted there were "a substantial number of local witnesses who had personally observed these remarkable events," though it identified no one in the pictures. The book informed that scientists were analyzing the Meier photos more thoroughly than any UFO photos had ever been analyzed, "utilizing additional, highly advanced procedures and technology drawn from sophisticated aerospace and nuclear medicine applications," but it included no signed reports or statements from the scientists. Near the end of the book was one page comprised of two short paragraphs entitled "Metal Samples Analysis." The first paragraph claimed: "From the beginning, unique qualities in the metal samples were detected." But the text referred to those who had performed the analysis only as "the scientists involved." Then it claimed that these scientists "had never seen anything like it before," and that "these detailed analyses continue today." The text failed to divulge even one source, yet the writing abounded in hyperbole.

Elders's earlier refusal to release any of the evidence to the UFO community had caused considerable controversy over the Meier case months before publication of the photo journal. Many ufologists thought Meier's claims of having traveled in space and time were outlandish; they laughed when he said that a tree in a photograph had later disappeared because Semjase had "erased its time," and reports constantly drifted back from Europe that someone had seen small models hanging in Meier's barn. With Intercep's extravagant claims now public and totally unsupported in the text of the photo journal, accusations from the UFO community increased and became more heated. While pretty to look at, alleged the kinder criticism, the pictures, and whatever other evidence the Elders and their group claimed to have, represented no proof of anything. Harsher critics screamed fraud.

Mutual UFO Network director Walt Andrus wrote in 1980 in the *MUFON UFO Journal* that the photo book produced by the Intercep group "is an outright fraud perpetrated upon the public for financial gain." He added: "A U.S. investigation had identified a balloon in several of the photographs that supports the model on a string while Billy Meier, with one arm operating his camera, moves through several different angles." Andrus lamented even mentioning the photo journal in his group's publication. "However," he wrote, "it is imperative that such opportunists be exposed."

A 1980 book review in *Fate* magazine concluded: "I think this book is nonsense—handsomely packaged, to be sure, but nonsense all the same." The reviewer, George Earley, later wrote in a spring 1981 edition of a UFO newsletter called *Saucer Smear* that what Stevens offered as proof was "cheap twaddle."

"Stevens well knows what constitutes legal and/or scientific proof here on planet Earth," he continued, "but he and his compatriots have consistently and persistently failed to provide any such proof. Until they do, they deserve every bit of criticism sent their way by the rest of us."

In the fall of 1979, Jim Lorenzen, who had had more exposure to the evidence than anyone outside the Intercep group, told the audience gathered at UFO '79, the APRO convention in San Diego, "My present disposition is that the Meier case is a hoax." Then he paused and added, "It's not that simple though." Some aspects of the case and some of the evidence presented, he felt, were "very difficult to explain." But too often Meier's inflated claims required Lorenzen to suspend common sense. He accused Stevens and the Intercep group of going to Meier "as skeptics and as investigators" but becoming "disciples spreading the word. . . . Part of it, I would say, is mysterious and I can't account for it," he concluded, "but that doesn't mean I have to buy the whole package."

In the *APRO Bulletin* of October 1979, Lorenzen's words were more pointed. Addressing Stevens he wrote: "I submit, seriously, that you and your associates have rushed to judgment on this matter because of a strong will to believe—a predisposition toward exotic explanations. . . . So far, each instance of evidence that Meier has offered, when pursued to its logical limit, ends up being a zero as far as compelling proof is concerned. Add any number of zeros and you still have zero."

One ufologist, Lucius Farish, a columnist for the *MU-*

FON UFO Journal, publicly defended Stevens and the Intercep group. "You are free to think anything you wish concerning the Meier case or Stevens's investigation of it," he wrote to the journal's editor. "However, the fact remains that you have no *proof* that the case is a hoax. I've heard all kinds of *accusations,* but I have yet to see one iota of real evidence. . . . When anyone takes thousands of dollars out of his own pocket to investigate UFOs, I think he deserves to be heard without a bunch of clowns harassing him because he showed them up at their own game."

Later, in a letter to another ufologist, Kal Korff, who more than anyone else had repeatedly attacked the Meier case, Farish wrote: "The opinions of persons who have never bothered to investigate the case and who are willing to accept negative statements concerning it without investigation are totally worthless. . . . I would say that 98% of the criticisms of the Meier case which I have read/heard are merely 'sour grapes'. . . ."

In the *MUFON UFO Journal* of December 1980, Korff published an article entitled "The Meier Incident: The Most Infamous Hoax in UFOlogy," which he later expanded into a booklet and distributed among other ufologists. Korff concluded: "After a careful review of all of the major purported events as stated by Genesis III and those individuals involved with the Meier case, it can be conclusively shown that none of the events as claimed contain the slightest shred of evidence to support their authenticity. Therefore it must be stated that the Meier case gives every appearance of being nothing more than a grandiose and elaborate hoax. It is certainly the most extravagant of all of the known contactee cases contained within the records of UFOlogy."

"At UFO '79 in San Diego," remembered Lee Elders, "the character assassination started against us. They started attacks that were unbelievable. They sent out flyers and brochures talking about this Meier hoax that we had perpetrated. We went through a bloody mess for a year and a half after that, so we quietly rallied our forces together. We're being attacked day and night for perpetrating 'the wildest hoax since time began,' and we can't lay this card on the table with IBM or any of the other labs. We don't want people bothering the scientists. So at that point we refused to release any more information on the case. We took it underground. And this haunted me for two years. I felt we had tangible evidence as an investigator. I didn't know if we could prove the case to be real, but I knew we had tangible evidence. Not one of these UFO people had ever been to Switzerland. They hadn't spent five minutes with Meier. None of them has been there. So how can they say it's a hoax? That's what frustrated me the most."

"Then," added Brit, "letters started coming in here saying, 'We want to see what you have. Send it to us.' We wrote back saying, 'No. If you want to see what we have, you come to Phoenix and look at it. It does not leave our possession.' So then everybody starts saying, 'They don't have anything. They're not going to let anyone see what they have because they don't have anything at all.' That's how this little merry-go-round works. I said, 'It's here, but if you want to see it you come here to see it.' None of them ever did."

* * *

While Dilettoso conducted his campaign with the scientists, Lee Elders returned from Switzerland with a new sound tape from Meier. Eva Bieri, one of the witnesses present when the sounds were recorded, had described to Elders the experience of listening to the sounds as a beamship, unseen, hovered overhead. An attractive Swiss woman in her mid-twenties, Eva had stood in a meadow only two miles from the farm, balancing her two-month-old son on her hip. Popi, a tape recorder in her hand, stood nearby. Near the edge of a pine forest 200 to 300 yards away, Meier had sat on his tractor, as another tape recorder turned in the small trailer behind it. Soon, Engelbert and Maria Wachter and others had joined them, and then everyone had watched the sky and waited.

Eva, who had sensitive ears, disliked loud music and

loud people. But when the deafening sounds suddenly filled the sky over her, she became angry not for her own discomfort, but because she felt it would harm the ears of her baby.

"On tape it sounds different than it really was," she said. "It was like the sky was full of sound, not from one place. The sound was everywhere, and we were thinking it must be very loud because people came from far away to see what had happened, and they were running, not walking."

Shrill and unnatural, seeming to echo from within as it rose and fell, the sound, though loud, seemed almost pleasant to Eva's ears. Her child did not cry, but only craned his neck and blinked his eyes and listened.

For years Dilettoso had worked at creating sound using digital sound synthesizers; whereas analyzing photos involved techniques new to him, he understood the analysis of sound. Through a former employer, Micor Corporation, he arranged one evening to examine the recording with a digital audio analyzer. But after taking the sounds apart he could not figure out how to duplicate them.

"That was the point at which I was blown away," he said. "To the ear they don't sound that unusual. It sounds like what you'd expect a sci-fi flying saucer to sound like. But upon analysis, they're continually shifting and changing, and combinations of them are getting louder and softer and doing things at such a rapid rate that even with a synthesizer being able to generate that many sounds it would be really, really complex."

But needing independent verification, Dilettoso sent the tape to Rob Shellman, a sound engineer with the United States Navy sonar sound laboratory in Groton, Connecticut. Also intrigued with their complexity, Shellman immediately eliminated one major possibility: Meier could not have used any electrical AC source to create the sounds.

"The equipment was set up to analyze for 50 or 60 hz line frequencies, which are common electrical outlets," Shellman wrote to Dilettoso. "If the device that generates the sound was an electric motor or machine the line frequencies would be evident. No such frequencies were detected."

Seeking further verification of what seemed to be an unusual recording, Stevens located in Los Angeles an electronics consultant and computer engineer, Nils Rognerud. A designer with a large electronics firm, Rognerud took the tape to a sound lab and converted the sounds to wavy lines on a spectrum analyzer. As he watched, the various frequencies vibrated up and down across the screen, converged into a thick zigzag, then split apart and converged again.

"I was being very skeptical from a scientific viewpoint," Rognerud said later, "but the sounds were unusual."

At a loss to explain them, Rognerud called in a second consultant, Steve Ambrose, who built custom microphones for rock stars and was the sound engineer for Stevie Wonder. Recently, Ambrose had built a tiny wireless radio receiver and speaker that fit inside Stevie Wonder's ear. The radio, called a Micro Monitor, was one of two inventions Ambrose had patented. He also toured regularly with Simon and Garfunkel, Engelbert Humperdinck, Diana Ross, and other popular singers as a sound specialist. He understood sound synthesizers and their capabilities. Rognerud had asked him to listen to the Meier recording to see if he thought Meier somehow had fabricated the sounds with a synthesizer.

Later Ambrose said, "Nils knew that if I thought it was a hoax I would just flatly say, 'I'm sorry, I could do this.' He's like that, too."

Over the phone Rognerud explained to Ambrose that the alleged source of the sounds was an interstellar beamship coming to earth from the Pleiades. He added that from everything he could discern the sounds seemed to be authentic. Such a strong endorsement from Rognerud piqued Ambrose's interest, but the recording still held surprises for him. After listening to it awhile and watching it on the spectrum analyzer, he told Rognerud the sounds could not possibly have been made with a synthesizer. They were analog, or natural, sounds, and he agreed with Rognerud that they seemed authentic. "If someone is perpetrating a hoax," he said, "they went to some length."

"Synthesizers use oscillators that are capable of making things that sound real," Ambrose explained later. "But the frequencies that this sound generated were so random and varied it was beyond the capabilities of an oscillator or even a group of oscillators. You'd have to use a microphone of some analog, natural sound like a lathe, metal cutting metal, which has low frequencies and high frequencies, and if you speeded it up or slowed it down you could get the various frequencies that would resemble what this had on it. But even then you'd have to take that and layer it several times, mixing one sound in with another, and this just didn't sound like something that had been layered, track upon track upon track. When you've dealt with recording and electronic sound you get to be able to hear what happens when you layer one sound on top of another. This was a single sound source recording that had an amazing frequency response."

Ambrose knew many people in Hollywood involved in creating special effects, and the sounds, he said, were something none of them could have conceived.

"How would you duplicate that sound?" he asked. "I'm not just talking about how it sounded to your ears, but how do you show those various things on a spectrum analyzer and on the 'scope that it was doing? It's one thing to make something that sounds like it, it's another thing to make something that sounds like it *and* has those consistent and random oscillations in it.

"If it is a hoax," he continued, "I'd like to meet the guy who did it, because he could probably make a lot of money in special effects."

* * *

Since the spring of 1977, the farm had been slowly transformed into a functional place complete with electricity and hot and cold running water. Finally the mud was gone; the water that had once spilled down the hillsides was now dammed, directed, and fashioned into small pools. Running in long, well-tended rows, a huge garden spread from the old carriage house along the path to Schmidruti. Pear and apple trees produced large fruit in the fall and provided fresh juices kept on the back porch in large glass jugs. At the entrance to the farmhouse, screen mesh covered the large aviary filled with canaries and finches, one snow-white, fluttering back and forth between nests made of little baskets. From the front porch came a constant chirping and twittering.

But one thing at the farm had not changed. It continued to attract large numbers of strangers—the religious, the scientific, the philosophical, the cynical, the merely curious—all wanting to speak with Meier. Families came, as well as priests, ufologists, film crews, couples on motorcycles, single women, reporters, and an occasional disciple searching for the Messiah. At dinner the Meier kitchen often filled with people they had never seen before, and because of Semjase's request that he educate earth humans on the existence of other races in the universe, Meier felt obligated to speak to them all.

In November 1978, after a dozen or more articles about Meier had appeared in the European press, *Der Spiegel,* the huge international magazine, had run an eleven-page cover story on UFOs: "Apparition or Reality? The UFOs Come." The magazine cover was a dramatic Meier photograph—a beamship accompanied by a remote-controlled craft, the latter just below the horizon.

The people who now sought out Meier came from all over the world. An old guest book signed by only a very few of the visitors bore addresses from Tahiti, Japan, France, Germany, Spain, Italy, Mexico, and Belgium. Actress Shirley MacLaine flew to Switzerland to spend five days with Meier, helping to weed the garden and trim tree branches by day, and at night probing Meier for answers about the universe. When MacLaine left she signed the guest book: "To Billy and his loving fight for all. Thank you for your dedication, your patience, and your LOVE. Always shine. Shirley."

Popi remained disgusted with the visitors. "I was fed up many times," she said later, "but we didn't have a choice. They would come into my house and say, 'Okay Billy, let's go.' Not a word to me. I got aggressive, I could not see why people could not understand when I told them that Billy was busy right now. They came here with their problems and Billy had to be here no matter what. He didn't care about his health, and the people didn't see that he needed time to relax, to take care of himself, and to be my husband. Nobody ever asked Billy, 'So you have a problem? Can we help you with anything?'

"I learned to accept the way it is. Von Däniken came. He wanted information. Billy talked to him. I was glad that I didn't have to speak with these famous people."

"We were there," recalled Lee Elders, "when cars came in from France, Holland, Denmark, from all over Europe. It created a nightmare for him."

"At the very beginning," added Brit, "Billy sincerely questioned his sanity. 'Why me? Why here? Why now?' Then he got to where it became fun. All of these people he'd never met before, coming to talk to him. Then the photographs hit the magazines, and all of a sudden he was swamped with people. They started lining up outside. Literally lining up. And that he didn't enjoy. People would say, 'Give me this photograph,' or 'Let me have that photograph.' Then they would disappear and he would never see them again. Here I think all of the fun left it, because half of everything got stolen. The kids were being harassed in school. His wife was unhappy, and he wasn't real happy. Because there was a constant flow of human bodies. Always."

Popi still would have nothing to do with any aspect of the contacts. She refused even to discuss them with her husband. "Popi was very jealous of the contacts anyway," said Brit, "not just the fact it was with a female space traveler, but also that Billy was doing something she couldn't be a part of, and that she, deep down inside, didn't want to be a part of. She didn't want anything to do with the contacts, she didn't want to know what was being said, she didn't want to see the photographs. And she didn't want to talk to the people who were invading her privacy. I've seen her take on everybody in the kitchen, tell them to get out, leave, leave the house, go away, she never wants to see them again. Because they were making demands on her husband, and in her mind that was separating her husband from her. She finally got to the point where she didn't care. She didn't care if anybody showed up, she didn't care if her house was a mess. She didn't care what happened to her kids, herself, or her husband. Everything around her was overrun with strangers."

* * *

Meier predictably had become a cult figure, visited by individuals searching for something to give life meaning. Some of those who had gravitated to him looking for an answer even took up residence at the farm, as rooms were completed and outbuildings renovated. They always wanted more contacts, notes, and photographs. The new people helped keep the farm going and assisted Meier in printing his contact notes, but now he spent much of his time and energy settling disputes among his "followers." Women frequently clashed with Popi, and men vied to become Meier's confidant. Even the contact notes had acquired a decidedly terrestrial tone, often concerned merely with the problems and personalities inhabiting the farm, and attributing conflict among the members to the acts of dark forces called the "Gizah people." The warm and stimulating, even magical atmosphere that many had experienced in Meier's presence began to erode with the arrival of more and more people.

Finally, rules had to be drawn, work schedules enforced, and dues collected from those who lived at the farm, as well as from regular visitors. Everyone remaining at the farm longer than thirty minutes was expected to work. And if anyone wanted to speak with Meier they either had to do so in the field as they worked next to him or in the kitchen after they had earned a piece of his time.

In the fall of 1979, with a Japanese production crew from the Nippon Television Network Corporation waiting in London, the Elders had traveled ahead to Schmidruti to see if Meier would agree to being interviewed for a documentary on his experiences. But when they arrived at the farm they found Meier locked in his office not speaking to anyone.

"He wouldn't come out of his office," Lee Elders remembered. "He wasn't eating. They would take a tray of food to the door and it would sit there. All he wanted was his cup of coffee and his cigarettes and 'leave me alone.' "

For three days Meier remained alone in the small room he used for an office. When he finally broke silence it was to send an urgent summons to Elders.

"What an experience that was. I'll never forget it as long as I live. I walked in, the room was dark, there was one little lamp on, and he was sitting there in the chair. We were about this far apart. And the light was on my side. I couldn't see him fully but he could see me. His hair was wild and he had this wild look in his eyes and he would just sit there. I mean he was just a beaten man, totally withdrawn, staring at me.

"Somewhere along in my life I was told that the first man that speaks under conditions like that loses. So I thought, I'll wait him out. I went through three cigarettes. Nothing. Him staring at me, and me looking at him and smoking a cigarette and waiting and waiting.

"Finally I knew he wasn't going to say anything, and I could have been there all day, so I said, 'How are you, Billy?' And he goes, 'Oh, Lee.' And then he poured his heart out to me for two hours. Talked and talked and talked about problems on the farm and how the pressure was getting to him, and he couldn't go on anymore and he was going to break the contacts. He says, 'I will break them. Break them.' He kept talking.

"So I sit for two hours in this darkened room listening to him and finally I said, 'How about some tea?' So I got up, went to the kitchen, got some tea, then went back over.

"I was there six hours total with the man. I did everything in my power to convince him to continue what he was doing. I'll never forget . . . it sounded hokey at the time, but in a way, when I started thinking about it, it wasn't that hokey because it worked. I drew the analogy of Michelangelo. I said, 'Look Billy, you're familiar with Michelangelo, aren't you?' He nods. 'Well, look at this man, look what he created, look what he did while he was on this planet, look at his artwork, look at the things that he accomplished, look at what he gave to humanity. You're doing the same thing. Your photographs are like Michelangelo, they're the best anybody's ever seen.' I said, 'You're contributing to raising the consciousness on this planet, and that's very important.'

"I went on and on. And he started listening, and then he started thinking about it. His problems were minute because he was accomplishing something great. See, by that time we had gone through a period where people were hounding us day and night over Volume I, letters from kids and letters from doctors and letters from people with terminal illnesses trying to get to the Pleiadians for help. We had undergone this onslaught of individuals. There was meaning behind it to them, and they weren't UFO nuts. It was sort of like hope during troubled times. So I knew what he was going through, but I also knew what it meant to these other people. Finally I said, 'Billy, I've got some Japanese waiting in London, what'll I tell them?' And he says, 'Bring them in.' "

* * *

While they waited for the film crew to arrive, Brit continued to record everyday life at the farm in her diary. "Popi fixed three-minute eggs, bread, sausage, cheese, enough for an army. Last night we had potatoes and cheese.

They laughed at us because we ate the potato skins—they peel theirs. I'm going to teach Popi how to fry eggs, make omelets and sausage the U.S. way."

One night eight people piled into a Land-Rover, and Meier drove on back trails across meadows to a small guest-house restaurant.

"Billy drives like a madman," wrote Brit, "lights off, shifts with his foot, laughs all the time, says he's protected, 'Don't worry,' At the restaurant Lee had his first coffee kirsch, we all joined in, had coffee kirsch, coffee schnapps. Came home same way—no lights, Billy shifting with his foot, 'Don't worry, we're protected.'

"Back home after a jigger of the strongest rum anyone could ever make, we all felt extremely 'relaxed.' Billy asked if we had ever seen this done before, and at that point he threw a spoon across the table and when I picked it up it was bent, twisted. Then he did one for Lee."

After Meier had bent the spoons, Brit said, "Are you the next so-called Prophet?"

"No," said Meier. "All people are prophets, and everyone has the power to bend spoons."

Meier explained that he used the force from the people around him and the force of his own mind in channeling it.

"I call them 'foolish turnarounds,'" he said. Then he held up one of the spoons he had bent. "This I do only for Brit."

"And between his thumb and index finger," Brit wrote in her diary, "he melted the spoon and broke it in half."

Lee still watched Meier closely, searching for a weak point or a clue. But Meier was so quick and so natural, Elders had yet to see anything suspicious or revealing. "I was fascinated with what he could do with a nail," said Elders, "with what he could do with a compass making it spin around without touching it. He'd say, 'It's just power of the mind,' so he didn't equate it to his Pleiadian contacts. It was something he had learned perhaps years ago, perhaps in India. But this fascinated me, because at this point I was pretty well convinced in my own mind that he was not hoaxing this thing through normal means."

* * *

Jun-Ichi Yaoi and the Japanese production crew arrived in Schmidruti the latter part of September to begin three weeks of filming. Their first night at the farm, they sat in the living room watching and filming Meier's 8mm footage of the beamships off a white screen. In the first sequence the ship darted back and forth over a farmhouse and a tall pine tree, and then appeared to cut quickly in front of the tree as the top branches suddenly bent as if caught in a backwash. Talking excitedly in Japanese, the crew had Meier run the sequence over and over as they focused on the top branches of the tree. Then while watching another series filmed at Hasenbol, one of the crew members noticed something unusual about a seeming reflection off the ship's flange. Meier ran it back, and the Japanese cameraman zoomed to the edge of the ship. There on the silver rim, like the slow brightening of a lighthouse beacon, a distinct red light flashed on and then off again.

During the day Elders and Welch accompanied the film crew to the sites where Meier's alleged contacts had taken place. They both had surmised for some time that if Meier's story were true, each of the landing sites would have some degree of radiation left behind by the beamship. The proper instrument at the right sensitivity might be able to detect that radiation. After several phone calls they located a gamma radiation detector at Wild-Heerbrügg, a precision instruments company in Switzerland. Similar to a Geiger counter, the instrument measures electromagnetic radiation, and Welch spoke to a physicist there who had used it many times.

"I told him what we were trying to determine," said Welch, "and he indicated that this would be the equipment to use."

The physicist told Welch that the instrument would

detect any artificially caused change in the molecular structure of grass and soil.

While the crew filmed Meier in a meadow not far from Hinwil, where Meier claimed the first Pleiadian beamship had landed and remained for an hour and a quarter nearly five years earlier, Elders and Welch set up the radiation detector. To establish a comparison, they first took readings in the grass of the surrounding area, which measured a low .00 to .05. Each time a stronger reading appeared on the dial, they marked the spot on the ground. But before they had finished taking readings in all of the areas, they noticed that the spots marked on the ground were beginning to form roughly the shape of a circle. Inside the circle the radiation level consistently measured .2, roughly 400 percent higher than the background measurements. And the readings inside the circle pulsated.

"It didn't go up and hang," remembered Welch. "It went up like this and then down a little bit, and then went back up, back down a little bit. We didn't expect this."

In diameter, the circle in which the readings pulsated and the radiation rose so much higher measured roughly twenty-one feet.

According to Welch's notes taken at the time of the measuring, "Immediately after that we went back to the hotel and I contacted the physicist who provided the equipment to determine if there was any significance at all to the findings, or if it was a calibration of the equipment that needed to be done. The physicist, who was somewhat reserved in his personality and approach, was surprised."

"Tell me again the background readings," said the physicist.

Welch read them over the phone.

"And the other readings?" asked the physicist.

"One point five, up to two point zero," said Welch.

"Where did you find these readings? Specifically."

As nearly as he could describe the area, Welch told the physicist its location. The physicist then told Welch that he and others had been using the equipment in his laboratory and in the field for about ten years, and it had always read accurately. No brand name appeared on the equipment, and the physicist could not remember its manufacturer.

When Welch suggested that either the readings were insignificant or the equipment needed calibration, the physicist dismissed both possibilities: The equipment was sound and the readings were indeed significant, since they represented gamma radiation levels of between 100 and 400 percent above the highest background levels.

The physicist recommended they immediately contact the Swiss Nuclear Safety Commission for further information and guidance, and allow their team to investigate. He did not know what the readings indicated, but he felt that a specialist should take them again and analyze them.

"He did not go into further detail," read Welch's notes, "except to explain what would be required to cause any such gamma radiation detection—an unnatural source strong enough to change the electromagnetic nature of every molecule where the readings were obtained." Like a paper clip that has been magnetized, articles near a strong electromagnetic field would acquire a "memory" of that force.

After this experience, they took the instrument to the Meier farm and got .00 readings in the vicinity, until they got within four hundred yards of the house, a giant circle. Within the circle, the needle suddenly jumped from .00 to .15.

"But it wasn't consistent," said Welch. "You'd be walking and there'd be no reading, and all of a sudden you'd get this jump. And it would hang at .15 for a second, and then it would start to go down."

At one alleged landing site at the edge of the forest below the farm, Welch again got sporadic readings up to .15. At another landing site in the gravel road leading to the front of the house, he got lightly pulsating readings from .05 all the way up to .2.

At this point they decided to check all of the articles

Meier carried to the contacts. They went into Meier's office and got his gun. First they took out the bullets and got no reading on those. When they asked Meier how long he had had the bullets, he said they had been purchased only recently. On the gun the meter went to .01. Meier's watch registered .05. A metal charm Meier kept in his pocket registered .1.

While checking the objects, they discovered that Meier himself gave off readings. His left shoulder fluctuated from .1 to .15, and his right arm from .05 to .1.

Welch again called the physicist at Wild-Heerbrügg.

"Did you slam a door on it?" asked the physicist. "Did you crush it, or anything like that?"

"Absolutely not," said Welch. "Is it something you have to handle like a feather? Because if that's the case, maybe a slight bump when you're picking it up out of its case could knock it off."

"No," said the physicist, "it's not like that. That's a steel plate you're hitting."

"So at this point," Welch remembered later, "I was very intrigued. He didn't have any answers. And we sure as hell did not want to go to the Swiss Nuclear Safety Commission."

After obtaining the unusual readings, Welch experimented with the instrument for a few days before they had to return it. He turned it on in his hotel room, while they were in restaurants, in open fields and forests; but each time, he recorded nothing near the readings he had gotten at the sites, at the farm, on the small articles, and on Meier himself.

* * *

Herbert Runkel rarely came to the farm now. Whereas the Hinwil house had been a place of intellectual freedom, and the farm in the early days a joy to help rebuild, the new religious "feel" of the group with their enforced meditation and their regulations had stifled what remained of that earlier atmosphere.

Meier had disenchanted Herbert two years earlier when he produced a series of photographs he said resulted from time travel with Semjase. The pictures showed the rubble of San Francisco following a massive earthquake that would occur sometime in the future. Later a friend of Herbert's discovered an article in *GEO* magazine that showed an artist's conception of what the long-predicted catastrophe might do to the city, and Meier's photographs obviously had been taken of this lifelike painting. With all of the beautiful photographs that no one seemed able to duplicate or explain, Herbert had been unable to understand why Meier would resort to such an obvious fabrication. Meier had said that the Pleiadians simply placed in the artist's mind an accurate picture of the real future, the same one Meier had photographed. And then the photographs had disappeared.

The pictures of San Francisco had confused Herbert because he had seen so many things for himself, some trivial, some remarkable, that contributed to a fascinating story he still could not explain. One October afternoon after he had been interviewed by the Japanese and they had departed, Herbert wanted to show Lee Elders a site that long ago had particularly intrigued him. He drove to the site, one that he and Harold had once visited with Meier shortly after Meier had had a contact there. Herbert stopped the car in a field crossed by railroad tracks, where he and Elders got out and walked down a dirt trail into the forest. After about a quarter of a mile they came to a secluded clearing the size of four or five football fields and surrounded by fir trees a hundred feet tall. A short way in from the meadow two trees in the forest bore large wounds frozen in sap and black from singeing.

Herbert told Elders that on the day he and Harold had come to the site with Meier three years earlier, they had wanted specifically to see these two trees: Meier allegedly had shot them with a laser gun the Pleiadians had demonstrated to him. And when Herbert and Harold had looked at the two trees that Herbert now pointed out to Elders, they could not figure out how Meier had created these marks that ate through the thick tree bark unless maybe he had used some kind of laser gun.

That day, while Herbert and Harold were studying the two trees, sometimes up close, sometimes stepping away to check distances, Meier had gone off nearby to look for mushrooms. At the edge of the clearing rambled a thicket of waist-high bushes. As he stepped all the way back to the meadow to eye one of the trees, Harold spotted from the corner of his eye a twig on a small bush. Something had snapped it in two. Something also had charred both of the broken tips. When Harold bent to examine the twig, he saw another one broken a few inches from the first. It, too, was charred. He called Herbert over and they discovered a perfectly straight line of broken twigs, each of them charred, that went through the tangle of thin branches, bush after bush after bush. It looked as though a narrow beam of intense heat had shot through the thicket.

Harold had called to Meier, who came over with his mushrooms to look at the small broken branches. After examining them for a moment, he said he remembered aiming the laser gun at the two tall pine trees, but not in the direction of the bushes. Maybe he had, he couldn't remember.

Three years later the charred branches no longer could be found, but Herbert had pictures of them he showed to Elders. The straight line that ran through the bushes, Herbert estimated, continued for at least a hundred feet.

Later in Munich, Elders also questioned Harold about the incident and Harold told him, "You could recognize the line of fire by the cracked branches and the blackened tips. It was so thin you could not do it with a welder."

At the site Elders had seen immediately that a bullet fired through the bushes would not leave the branch tips so finely charred, and the painstaking use of matches could not be carried out in a straight line. What mystified Elders even more was why Meier would go to so much trouble to fabricate such intricate evidence, when it seemed highly doubtful anyone would ever see it.

The trip that afternoon with Herbert typified how Elders and Welch spent most of their time in Switzerland—stumbling further and further into the unexplainable. The discovery of the charred twigs offered little concrete evidence that Meier's alleged contacts had taken place, but they were one more item on Welch's list of "gross consistencies."

* * *

While the Elders and Welch were in Switzerland, Stevens and Dilettoso traveled to Pasadena to meet with Dr. Nathan at the Jet Propulsion Laboratory. Since Nathan could not work from the prints Stevens had showed to him, he had instructed Bob Post at the photo lab to have 4×5 color film positives made from Stevens's internegatives. These copies then would be "digitized" and the information stored in a computer where Nathan could analyze it later.

Post asked an Englishwoman, Audrey Adkins, who had worked in the photo lab almost as long as he had, to remain after work to process the transparencies, and Stevens instructed her not to discard any of her test strips or rejected copies. But when Adkins retired to the darkroom, placed the first internegative in the enlarger, and brought the actual grain in the film into perfect focus with a 20X microscope, the picture itself remained blurred. As Adkins brought each of the internegatives into the finest focus possible, she thought to herself, If Dr. Nathan can make anything of these, he's lucky.

Both Post and Adkins skipped dinner that night to work on transferring the Meier photos from the internegatives to positive transparency film. After Adkins had finished her work around seven, she handed Stevens a large padded envelope and said to him, "This is all trash." She left the copies she had just made for Dr. Nathan.

The new transparencies revealed that Stevens's in-

ternegatives were several generations away from the originals. In fact, they appeared to be so inferior to the beautiful
prints Stevens had shown him at the outset that Nathan
immediately suspected Stevens of using him, of delib-
erately offering evidence that could not be tested.

"All I know is the negatives he gave us to work with
were already out of focus and that's all he would let us
have," said Nathan. "They had to be a different, later
generation, or a generation specifically made that was
intentionally out of focus. They couldn't have been used to
make the very high resolution prints he flashed by me. He
was not giving me his best data, he wasn't showing me
anything that I could work with."

"The key problem here," recalled Lee Elders, "was a
problem that originated with Meier himself. Because there
had been so much theft of the original material, we didn't
know if we had originals. If we had had the originals going
in, it would have made life much easier for us. But we
didn't. We knew we had a negative, but we didn't know how
far down it was. Is it first generation, fifth generation?"

Nathan placed the new negatives in a drawer and
never looked at them again.

"I was never impressed with the pictures," he said. "I
was very unhappy with them. At no time was I ever of the
feeling they were anything but a hoax. But don't forget, all
of my examination on this was extremely cursory. These
things have not really been given a good examination
because it isn't worth the time, from the quality of the
images given us, to do anything. I have no proof that this is
a fraud. But I have no proof that it is real. That's the second
statement that should always accompany the first."

* * *

For some time Lee Elders had been trying to track
down a key witness, Martin Sorge. Of the many Europeans
who had once traveled to Hinwil to investigate Meier's
early claims, Sorge repeatedly had been mentioned as the
chief detractor, the man who, some alleged, had exposed

Meier as a fraud. After finally locating Sorge by phone and arranging for an interview through an interpreter, the Elders drove to Locarno, a summer retreat on Lago Maggiore, one of many narrow lakes forming the border between Switzerland and Italy three hours south of Zurich. They found Sorge in a fine white house surrounded by summer hedges a few blocks up from the lakeshore.

Sorge was an articulate man in his late forties, and though his interests over the years had turned to psychology and the paranormal, he held a university degree in chemistry; he had published two books, one on hypnosis. Like many others in the summer of 1976, Sorge had read of Meier's claims of contact with extraterrestrials in a magazine, and, pulled by his own curiosity and the urging of a friend who had met Meier, he had traveled to Hinwil.

"I used to go there with my girlfriend at the time," he told the Elders, "and we would stay there for three or four days. As a personality I felt a certain fascination with the man." But Sorge had soon found himself in a quandary: On the one hand he thought Meier's pictures were convincing; on the other, he was skeptical. "So I wanted to be around to see what happened."

Sorge discovered that at the Meier house on Wihaldenstrasse the family was never alone. Always there was one, two, or three of the curious, often many more, squeezed into the modest living space.

"They stayed the whole night," he remembered, "or they left in the middle of the night, or they came in the middle of the night. And the whole atmosphere there was overshadowed by Billy's mission. He was like a dictator, he said what had to be done and that would have to be done. Even the needs of his family were overruled by his ever readiness to be at Semjase's call."

As he had watched and reflected on Meier, one thing had impressed Sorge above all others: the certainty with which Meier spoke. As Sorge put it, "The man appeared to be one with his story." He said he sometimes saw Meier so lost in his thoughts he could not communicate for days; he seemed filled with a power that originated from without, and this power so possessed him he was able to put people under a spell. Sorge recalled watching Meier point to the sky one night. "See that," Meier had said. Sorge himself had seen nothing. "But," he said, "I can imagine how he could persuade others to believe that they had."

Sorge remembered well the electric atmosphere that pervaded the Hinwil house when Meier was about to have a contact in those early days. There was always great excitement, he told the Elders. People hurried about, bringing Meier his gun, his hat, his boots, his walkie-talkie, his leather coat, preparing him to venture into the forest. Others brewed strong coffee, or warmed the engine of their cars. The ones to accompany Meier wondered if this might be the night they would see the beamship descend or glimpse the ethereal figure of Semjase.

The only nights that compared with these were the nights before publication of the pamphlet Meier called *Wassermannzeit, The Age of the Waterman,* who was Meier himself. On those nights Meier would be up all night, sweating in the lighted room on the third floor, feeding and pumping the printing machine furiously with one arm, not resting or even slackening his pace until the job was finished.

"It was unbelievable to see him running around this machine working it with one hand," said Sorge. "Real fast, real hard, like an obsessed person."

As Meier in a frenzy cranked out the pages of the pamphlet, music boomed from two speakers, the same pounding beat, over and over, causing the walls to quiver, a tempo that matched his own slamming of the press.

After describing his early experiences with Meier, Sorge began telling the story of how he had turned up the most damaging evidence anyone had ever discovered against Meier: several partially burned slides obviously taken of a model that looked similar to the beamships. It was the story the Elders had come to hear.

According to those in the UFO community who claimed

GARY KINDER

Meier was a fraud, Sorge had reached into a fire to rescue the slides before Meier could dispose of them. But when told of his alleged role in the story, Sorge said no, the incident had happened differently; he had never pulled anything from a fire. While in Hinwil, Sorge had shrewdly cultivated a friendship with Popi, surmising that the man's wife, if anyone, would know the truth behind the story, and that in the right situation she might reveal that truth.

"Billy and his wife always had many 'disturbances,' " he explained.

One day when Sorge was visiting, Popi had suddenly run from the house crying and screaming at her husband; when she returned hours later, she went to Sorge and secretly gave to him many color slides that had been charred by fire. "She had the feeling she had to confess to someone," thought Sorge.

When Sorge examined the partially burned slides he saw immediately they were of a model, either suspended in the setting or somehow superimposed. A prominent shadow appeared against the background. With proof that Meier had apparently experimented with models, and being himself skilled with his hands, Sorge had resolved to fabricate pictures of the same quality as Meier's better photographs.

"To prove it could be done," he said.

Sorge had studied the burned photos at length, then built a ten-inch model and photographed it with a plain background from different angles. Next he had gone into the forest and shot many scenes of trees, sky, and green rolling hills. Using two slide projectors, he had then cast one forest scene onto a silvered screen and simultaneously introduced another slide of the model he had constructed, centering the model in the background of forest. Then he had brought both slides into sharp focus and photographed the screen. As he spoke now of his photography experiment, he began laying before the Elders a sampling of his fabricated pictures.

Sorge's photographs showed a crude and somewhat stark beamship frozen in an otherwise familiar setting; but

224

they lacked the feel of Meier's, the natural relationship that appeared to exist between his background and his ships. They had no depth. Lou Zinsstag had referred to Sorge's photography experiments three years earlier in her final letter to Timothy Good: "A lot of them [former friends of Meier]," she had written, "even faked some ufo photos, doing pictures on a window pane, showing them around and telling everybody how easy this was. I've got two of those fakes. I fell for them only for a few seconds."

Sorge admitted that his pictures were of lesser quality than the ones Meier had produced, but his experiment convinced him that by superimposing projected images or using some similar technique Meier somehow could, and in fact did, fabricate this part of the evidence.

"I saw pictures of a UFO and it really was a model," he said. "In the first place I *saw* that it was a model, and in the second place I learned it from his wife. *She* said, 'Yes, he is working with models.'"

What Sorge didn't know is that long before he had seen the slides, Meier himself had shown them to Hans Schutz-bach, the one who had driven Meier to so many contacts and who had been with him the day the first sounds were recorded. According to Schutzbach, he had been in Meier's study one day in the early fall of 1976, when Meier presented the slides and explained to him that he had carved a model of one of the beamships and then tried to photograph it. In the pictures the model sat on three blocks of wood and lacked the luster and refined appearance of the glistening beamships in Meier's other photos. Meier said he thought the photographs should be destroyed to avoid confusion, but Schutzbach had persuaded him to keep them.

"I told him, 'These are an important document,'" Schutzbach had explained later. "'You can't throw them away.'"

Meier agreed and gave the slides to Schutzbach, who kept them safely in his apartment. Then one day Popi went to Schutzbach and asked that she be allowed to have the slides. A few weeks later, after fighting with her husband, she snatched up various documents, photographs, and slides, including those of the model, and threw them into the fireplace. Schutzbach said he had arrived at the house in time to see Meier himself stamp down the flames and then reach into the fire to save the slides. The next time Popi fought with her husband, Sorge had been visiting Hinwil with his girlfriend, and in a rage, instead of setting fire to the surviving slides, Popi had given them all to Sorge. This had caused problems, said Schutzbach, because Sorge had later written to Meier and promised to expose him as a fraud. When Popi denied knowing anything about how the slides had gotten into Sorge's hands Meier had threatened her, she pulled out his gun, and he took it away from her. Then Popi had tried to kill herself with pills.

Interested only in "scientific proof" supporting Meier's claims, once Sorge had seen the obviously contrived photographs and heard the accusations from Popi, he considered Meier a "swindler" and lost interest in the case. Since then, he had neither seen nor communicated with Meier; Meier, he said, was now far in his past. But his opinion of the man and the contacts curiously had changed.

"At that itme," he explained to the Elders, "I was not as far along as I am now. There is more behind it."

Sorge then paused for a long while as though he were organizing his thoughts. When he spoke again he said, "The result of my investigation is that these things can be made, but . . . now comes the big but . . . this is no proof that the other 'thing' does not exist. I doubt that these pictures are real, but that doesn't mean that all of the pictures are faked or that the story is a hoax."

Lee Elders wanted this statement clarified. Sorge answered immediately.

"Billy's intellect and his spiritual level are much below the message he preaches, therefore it is not possible that he could have invented this. So this indicates he must have gotten it from some other source. I am certain that these are messages from a spiritual being unseen by us but seen by him, coming from another world, and he's capable of hearing these messages."

The interpreter and Sorge talked back and forth in German, as the interpreter made sure he understood Sorge's position.

"I am certain he has these contacts," Sorge continued, "but not in the way he's telling us. He may receive them in the form of visions, the way mediums receive things. He may not even know himself if these visions are real. But for him it is reality, and to prove it he has to go out and build these things."

For technical reasons Sorge felt that Meier must have had at least one accomplice to help him, but he believed Meier actually had two or three, though he had no idea who they might have been.

"He is not flying away," he concluded, "and he is not meeting with Semjase, but he is able to put himself into a parallel world, and he has experiences in this parallel world. He fakes the evidence to make people understand his experiences."

TEN

Irina Froning, a tall, attractive blond woman in her mid-forties, sat in the silent back room of an office in San Pedro, California. It was night, and only lights shining softly on the plants enabled her to see. In the outer office, she could hear her friend, whom she was visiting for the weekend, typing reports and correspondence.

"It was Sunday evening," Irina later recalled, "and we were going to stay home, at her house, when my friend suddenly started. It was as if a bolt had struck her that she had to do some typing that night. So she said, 'Will you come with me?'"

Whenever she visited a new place, a home or office, Irina went immediately for the bookshelves to learn more about the person who lived or worked there. But on this night, as her friend typed, Irina wandered past the bookshelves to a small darkened doorway. She walked through the doorway, and in a back office, illuminated by the plant lights, she saw a credenza; on top of the credenza lay a large, square picture book entitled *UFO . . . Contact from the Pleiades*.

"I really was not interested in UFOs," she said. "I sat down and admired the plants, and then I thought, What am

228

I going to read? and that was the only book. So I put it on my lap. It was intriguing. But nothing really stunned me until I ran across that page in the middle of the book."

Her eyes focused immediately on the word "tachyon."

"This space being," she recalled, "is telling a man that earth scientists are now working on a 'tachyon' propulsion system. That blew my mind! Because for years David had been hugging the table with a pencil in his hand, working with the ideas coming to him about tachyons. He had just published a paper on tachyons! I said to myself, Nobody knows about this."

* * *

From Brit Elders's diary, February 20, 1980:

"Tempers flared tonight. Tom, Lee, Steve all arguing. Poor waitress must have thought they were going to blow. Odd thing, the three argued same issue, just different words. Point of problem: additional security needed. After all the trips/work convincing scientists it's okay to research, phone calls, etc., etc., no one willing to attach name to analysis. No one wants to release reports, only verbal. Too much going out of our office, not enough coming in. After three trips to San Jose we gained one video tape, lost one priceless metal sample. Photo tests jump ahead three feet, fall back two. Labs closed to UFO testing. Guys are using each other as verbal punching bags, venting frustration.

"Lee said, 'At least with a goddamn murder case you know you've got a crime. With a UFO case you don't know what you have.'

"Maybe our biggest problem: We're used to tangibles, bodies, bugs, etc. Can't touch a UFO. Metal confuses people. Photos representations only. Bottom line: There's no yes, no no. Round robin conversation finally brings out all tension.

"Reorganize thoughts, get out of frustration's way, proceed. (1) tighter security; (2) no open release of material or information to anyone; (3) one of us present for any analysis; (4) no more verbal reports; (5) low-key research, find the right ones for the right work; (6) no info to outsiders, gets too twisted; (7) everything done must be signed for, creates paper trail; (8) all work must be made known to Lee, he will coordinate and authorize research from here on.

"Suggest no discussion of UFOs until arrive, unless absolutely necessary. Has slammed too many doors in face in the past. Personal opinion: Wish more people with education, reputation, background, qualifications, had courage and curiosity to pursue subject. Tom says it's the nature of the beast.

"Finally all calm. Feel waterlogged from coffee, tired of sitting, 3:30 a.m., ready to sleep, much needed."

* * *

A year and a half into the investigation, caught between the antagonistic UFO community on one side and the reserved scientific community on the other, they had stalled. Until they could get all of the evidence thoroughly examined by qualified scientists, they had no defense against the attacks. The refusal of JPL's Dr. Nathan to analyze the photographs had discouraged them, even though results in other areas such as the sounds still looked promising. They now needed somehow to persuade more scientists to look at the evidence and to go on record. But one piece of evidence, the most important of all, had disappeared—the burnished triangle that had so intrigued Marcel Vogel at IBM. No one had any idea what had happened to the piece, and though it had disappeared almost from his very hands, Vogel seemed the most perplexed of all. One minute he had it, and the next minute it was gone. Though the fragment itself had disappeared, Vogel fortunately had already taped his entire analysis on video. The Elders now held that tape, and they concealed it, refusing to acknowledge its existence even in the face of endless attacks from the UFO community.

Colman VonKeviczky of Inter-Continental UFO Network (ICUFON) sent out a flyer to his membership claiming that UFO models had been found hanging in Meier's barn, and that a picture Meier claimed to be of an extraterrestrial named Asket was actually Meier's wife in a blond wig. Proclaiming the case a hoax, however, did not deter VonKeviczky from advertising at the bottom of the flyer's front page: eleven slides of original Meier photos for only $33; and, for an additional price, copies of Meier's contact notes.

The magazine *Second Look* in 1980 quoted Jim Lorenzen as saying that Eduard Meier was a totally unreliable witness because he "was jailed for thievery as a teenager, escaped from prison, joined the French Foreign Legion, deserted and served out the remainder of his jail term in Switzerland."

One reporter from the London publication *The Unexplained* wrote that Meier's story "has now become so bizarre that even the most gullible devotee of the extraterrestrial hypothesis ought to be feeling just the teeniest twinges of doubt." After dismissing the evidence as unconvincing, the writer said that Meier's story had "all the hallmarks of American George Adamski's extravaganzas, updated and technically sophisticated for a more demanding age."

After MUFON's Walt Andrus had called the Elders's photo journal an "outright fraud," a prominent ufologist, Bill Moore, distributed a letter among several ufologists pointing out that the Elders had failed to sue Andrus for the accusation. He added that "Andrus and all the rest of us would welcome with open arms [a lawsuit] since none of us believe they have any evidence which would stand up in court. On the other hand if they fail to sue, then they are in effect admitting that what Andrus has said is true. The legal precedent of 'in silence is consent' would certainly apply here, I believe." Then Moore closed: "I firmly believe that these people, down deep in their hearts, know exactly what the truth is in this matter. It is only their greed for money and profit that keeps them from telling it to the world. Think about it."

In another open letter, published in *Saucer Smear,* after accusing the Intercep group of suppressing some of Meier's more absurd statements, Moore wrote, "Let the record show that when confronted with a legitimate opportunity to present evidence to a qualified forum and thus settle the Meier controversy once and for all, [Intercep] has, by means of a conspicuous and revealing silence, patently refused to do so. The very fact that they chose not to reply at all speaks volumes."

"They're saying the case is a hoax," remembered Elders. "We're coming back and saying, 'We don't believe it's a hoax. We've got evidence that indicates there's something really happening.' They're saying, 'Prove it.' Well, they know we can't *prove* it. We tried for five years to prove it, and it probably never will be proven."

"We spent the first two years," said Brit, "trying to disprove it."

"And after two years," interjected Lee, "we discovered we couldn't prove it, so we said, 'To hell with it, let's try to learn from it.'

"This is the point," he continued. "I think the Lorenzens began APRO with dedication, as we did with this case, to try to get to the bottom of things. But I think after years of searching and years of frustration, they became jaded. Perhaps they became wise: They suddenly realized they'd never prove the existence of UFOs. So therefore, 'Let's just report the cases and forget it.' Because getting involved takes a lot of time and a lot of money, and nobody's going to believe it anyway. I think somewhere along the line people do become jaded, as we almost did with Meier. Throw in the towel, because you're tired of the hassle."

One night Lee Elders met Stevens at Picacho Peak, an extinct volcano that rises out of the desert floor halfway between Phoenix and Tucson. When the two men wanted to get away and go for a drive, they would meet in a park at the base of the peak and talk.

"So I met him that evening," recalled Elders, "and I was

really upset over what was happening. There was talk at
that time that we would get totally out of the case, because
I didn't want to get into mudslinging, I didn't want to get
into legal battles, I was tired of the character assassination,
tired of the cheap shots, tired of the attacks against the
case. So we met, and Steve gave me this book. He said, 'I
want you to read it. This problem is nothing new, it began
thirty years ago.' "

The book Stevens gave to Elders was *The Report on
Unidentified Flying Objects,* by Captain Edward J. Ruppelt,
still considered a classic on the subject. As head of Project
Blue Book for its first two years, Ruppelt had created the
term "UFO" for "Unidentified Flying Object" to replace
"flying saucer." After resigning his commission, he had
gone to work at Northrop Aircraft Company as a research
engineer and published his book in 1956. At Blue Book,
Ruppelt had spent two years talking to pilots, engineers,
generals, and scientists, and his book contained many
sightings, experiences, and other things he could not explain. But Stevens gave the book to Elders for what Ruppelt
had written in the foreword.

The report has been difficult to write because it involves
something that doesn't officially exist. It is well known that
ever since the first flying saucer was reported in June 1947
the Air Force has officially said that there is no proof that
such a thing as an interplanetary spaceship exists. But what
is not well known is that this conclusion is far from being
unanimous among the military and their scientific advisers
because of the one word, *proof;* so the UFO investigations
continue.

The hassle over the word 'proof' boils down to one
question: What constitutes proof? Does a UFO have to land
at the River Entrance to the Pentagon, near the Joint Chiefs
of Staff Offices? Or is it proof when a ground radar station
detects a UFO, sends a jet to intercept it, the jet pilot sees it,
and locks on with his radar, only to have the UFO streak
away at phenomenal speed? Is it proof when a jet pilot fires

at a UFO and sticks to his story even under the threat of court-martial?

The at times hotly debated answer to this question may be the answer to the question, "Do the UFOs really exist?"

Ironically, while the photo journal *UFO . . . Contact from the Pleiades* acted like a lightning rod drawing the wrath of ufologists, it began to serve as a calling card when asking scientists to examine the evidence. In time, it also became a beacon—an attractive coffee table display that occasionally intrigued a scientist, engineer, or special effects expert who then tracked down the Elders or Stevens, wanting to know more about the story. After nearly a year and a half of knocking on doors, in late 1979, 1980, and 1981, some new doors began to open: Besides doors at NASA's Jet Propulsion Laboratory and IBM, another door opened at Arizona State University, and one at the U.S. Geological Survey, then at Film Effects of Hollywood, and McDonnell Douglas Astronautics Company.

Probably as a category having the least probative value to a scientist, the photographs remained the most exciting and most controversial of the Meier evidence. But there would never be a definitive answer concerning their validity. Every scientist involved with photogrammetrics whom Dilettoso had spoken with had said at the outset that before they could render any conclusive statement they first would have to be assured that either the negative or the positive transparency to be examined was an original. Perhaps a first-generation copy would be sufficient for study, but anything lower than that would begin to leave room for the possibility of manipulation in the photograph. And no one knew the generation of the Meier photographs. But Dilettoso found two scientists willing to analyze them anyhow: They could always examine a photograph of lesser generation and likely detect a fabrication if it existed, but were they to find nothing, they could never be certain that a fabrication indeed had not taken place.

In late February 1981, with the photographs now properly "digitized" on magnetic tape at the University of Southern California's Image Processing Institute, Dilettoso made an appointment with Eric Eliason at the U.S. Geological Survey in Flagstaff, Arizona. For eight years Eliason had been a research computer scientist at USGS, developing image processing software so astrogeologists could analyze photographs of the planets beamed back from space. He had spent two years producing the intricate radar map of cloud-covered Venus acquired by Pioneer 10, and later applied his software in the processing of space photography beamed back by both Viking and Voyager.

Dilettoso arrived at Eliason's office after working hours with two of the Meier photos on magnetic tape. After Dilettoso's preliminary explanation of the photographs, Eliason took them to the computer room, mounted the magnetic tape into a tape drive, typed in the appropriate commands, then went to a library of programs that allowed him to turn the image, filter it, stretch the contrast, and perform other image enhancement techniques.

On the screen in the darkened room, Eliason brought up the edges of the craft extremely sharp and studied the precise point at which the image of the craft met the blue of the sky. Describing the test as "pretty sophisticated," he said he could not imagine anybody being able to fool it.

"One conclusion I made was that it certainly hadn't been dubbed in," Eliason said later. "There was just a natural transition. If you had a sharp contrast boundary, you might think, Well, that looks pretty hokey. But right along these boundaries there were no sharp breaks where you could see it had been somehow artificially dubbed. And if that dubbing was registered in the film, the computer would have seen it. We didn't see anything.

"That doesn't eliminate the idea of somebody taking a little model and throwing it out there," he added. "That's a hoax, but you couldn't tell that with image processing."

But Eliason wanted more information about the film.

"You need to start with the original if you're going to play games like this," he said. "So in a sense this is not really a scientifically valid statement."

Eliason's concern was that superimposure, double exposure, or any other laboratory technique used to fabricate a photograph *could* occur right at the limits of the film; then by carefully rephotographing the doctored print, any obvious contrast would now be gone.

What bothered Eliason, and had bothered other scientists as well, was being viewed as an authority figure. "I really don't like being in a position of so-called expert on things like this. The guy who came in here kind of struck me as whatever I said about a particular issue would be the all-encompassing truth. I don't like that because the world just isn't that way. There are too many uncertainties."

He cautioned Dilettoso that although he had expertise in image processing and worked with sophisticated equipment, his testing of the Meier photos could not be considered definitive. He needed concrete information about the film. "But the guy wanted so badly to believe that this was the real thing," said Eliason, "he went ahead and believed it anyway. There is no doubt about it," he continued, "it is emotionally charged. But it is intriguing, and I'm sure it's one of those cases you'll never know one way or the other. All I can say is that whatever I started with, I didn't see anything hokey going on there in terms of dubbing. If it was dubbed, it had to be pretty clever."

* * *

At Arizona State University in Tempe, just outside Phoenix, thirty-one-year-old Dr. Michael Malin taught in the Department of Geology. He had a degree in physics from Berkeley and a Ph.D. from Cal Tech in Planetary Sciences and Geology, and had written his doctoral thesis, much of which involved the science of image processing, on the analysis of spacecraft images of Mars. He then had worked at Jet Propulsion Laboratory for four years before joining the ASU staff in 1979, where he now taught Geology of the Moon, Geology of Mars, and Geomorphology.

A few weeks after Dilettoso spoke with Eric Eliason, he discovered Malin and the Image Processing Laboratory at ASU. With joint funding from NASA and the university, Malin and a colleague had acquired for the lab the equipment for analyzing spacecraft images. Local papers often carried articles about the analyses the two scientists performed on photographs beamed back from space, and Dilettoso happened to see one of the articles and called Malin.

At their first meeting in mid-May 1981, Dilettoso lay before Malin the array of photographs in the photo journal, plus digitized images of two of the Meier photographs. As Malin's business was the analysis of pictures, he found the photographs interesting, "very pretty, very clear, very nicely processed." And he liked to study photographs, so Dilettoso did not have to try to persuade him to look at them.

"These pictures are much nicer pictures of UFOs than any I'd ever seen before," Malin said later, "in terms of the number and the quality for that number. You can see they *look* like real objects. Not just on the impression level, but on a demonstrable level. They glint in the sun, there are distinguishable reflections in the metallic objects, things like that that make them much better pictures. I don't think there's any question that, at least in the things that I've ever seen, these are by far the best UFO pictures taken. Whether they're authentic or not, that's a totally different matter."

Malin tried to keep an open mind, willing to consider topics often avoided by his colleagues; but he demanded facts and rendered his opinions with cold objectivity. The senior science editor at *National Geographic* once remarked, "If Malin says it, you can believe it."

Like Eliason and others before him, Malin wanted far more information than Dilettoso could provide. He told Dilettoso he wanted to see "the stuff that actually went through the camera." He wanted the camera itself, to study the lens and metering system. Because of the apparent clarity within the image, he was not bothered by the focus on the camera being jammed just short of infinity.

"Absolutely not," he said. "It shouldn't have an effect on whether you're hoaxing it or not." But he wanted to know the shutter speed, the aperture setting, and where the lens *was* focused.

"The important thing would have been the original film," he said. "Without the very detailed information about the originals, there's almost nothing you can say."

One more thing he pointed out: Photographs are pretty, fun, and impressive. But photographs of *anything* are poor evidence. In a hierarchy of probative value, photographs and sound lie at the bottom, because they both are "a recording of an ephemeral event, subject to manipulation after the fact. The only real physical evidence," said Malin, "would be some physical manifestation that could be tested and measured and physically examined. If you had a piece of metal whose manufacture could not be done on earth, that would go a long way."

As Malin considered the photographs, he also sized up Dilettoso. His first impression was that the young technician was a smooth and fast talker.

"My guess is that he was using my name to JPL and their name to me in an attempt to get something done, but I don't fault him for that. I think he's a pretty bright guy. I think he was perhaps more in favor of this thing being real than he was in favor of debunking it. But he was quite bright, and obviously had worked around computers. For the most part, he knew what he wanted to say, and I don't think he misrepresented anything."

Dilettoso met with Malin several times, in the professor's office, in front of computer screens in the image processing facility, and once at his own studio in Phoenix, where Malin had driven to see the image processing system Dilettoso had assembled for himself during the course of his research on the Meier case. Malin was impressed with the system. Dilettoso's computer setup, an estimated $50,000 worth of equipment, was as sophisticated as what Malin regularly worked with at ASU's image processing center.

"I'm not sure that he could do with it what I could do with it," said Malin, "but he could do things with it." And Malin felt that he himself could do "some real science" on the equipment.

Back in his own lab, Malin entered the digitized images Dilettoso had given him into the computer and began studying them with Dilettoso, and sometimes Stevens, present.

"I zoomed up a given section and then just looked for edges," he said. "I looked for contrast differences between various parts of the sky. I looked at the color of the sky reflected in the object versus the sky immediately around it. People say the sky is blue, but it isn't uniformly blue. So I did things like that. And what I found was that the quality of the data he gave me was insufficient to do a detailed analysis, a numerical analysis, of what these things were. But to the level of the quality of the data he gave me, I could not see anything obviously wrong with the images. Couldn't see any hoax to it. There was a proper amount of blurring of edges and distance fading and things like that. To the level that I saw it, I can say that the thing was not a photographic fake. But that doesn't mean that it wasn't a photographic fake. If I had the details of everything I wanted I might still say there is no obvious thing in it that is fake. But that's 'photographically fake.' It could still be an object twenty feet across held up by a helicopter above it on four strings.

"I wouldn't know what would motivate someone to fake them so I don't know how much trouble it's worth, what they expect to get in return. But my opinion would be that it would probably take more than a little camera and more than sending it to the local drugstore. It requires a lot of time. A person's got to want to do this.

"If they are hoaxes then I am intrigued by the quality of the hoax. How did he do it? I'm always interested in seeing a master at work. On the other hand if they're real, then I also have an academic interest in that my own research is involved in exploration of other planets. And if there were other organisms visiting our planet, they must be doing that for the same reason we explore other planets. Why do we explore other planets? We have a need to expand the sphere of human perception and thought and so on. Maybe that's what aliens do as well. So either way I win. If they're a hoax I win by learning a neat technique. If they're not a hoax I win by having potential colleagues from another planet.

"I find the photographs themselves credible," he concluded. "They're good photographs. They appear to represent real phenomena. The story that some farmer in Switzerland is on a first-name basis with dozens of aliens who come and visit him . . . I find that incredible. But I find the photographs more credible. They're reasonable evidence of something. What that something is I don't know."

* * *

Though Dr. Nathan at the Jet Propulsion Laboratory had refused to analyze the Meier photos because they provided him with too little information, he consented one morning to view several of the Meier films recorded on a half-inch video cassette. The first sequence was black and white, a beamship moving from side to side above a tall evergreen. At one point the ship appeared to cut in front of the tree, and the upper branches at the same instant blew as if caught in a sudden stiff wind or a backwash. Nathan laughed.

"That's pathetic! Ha, ha, ha. Oh, for God's sake! Look at that thing oscillating! Did you see that? That's the response you'd expect of an extremely light, small object that doesn't have any serious amount of mass associated with it."

To Nathan the object seemed to be oscillating on a very short tether from a point just above its dome. But it would take "a tremendous amount of analysis" to determine that. "My concern," said Nathan, "is that if we show him at any time involved with a hoax, then it's all a hoax. All you have to do is catch him in one lie and the whole thing goes to hell."

Two sequences later, a beamship seemed to disappear from a point fifty feet above a hillside and reappear only a few feet above the ground almost in the same frame. As far as Nathan was concerned it could be a model tethered on a long pole held by an assistant standing behind the photographer. The sites, however, had been described as wide open, with no place to hang models or to stand in such a position to extend a long-enough pole into the scene. Nathan said it could be a helicopter.

Then three ships hovering behind tree limbs appeared in the sky.

"Oh boy," laughed Nathan, "look at that."

He surmised they were small objects perhaps ten feet beyond the branches, and possibly suspended from a long pole with something like a puppeteer's wrench.

With his arms folded across his chest, he stood and watched a few more sequences on the television monitor until he saw one where the ship flies in front of snowcapped mountains at Hasenbol and comes to an abrupt halt. It then hovers motionless.

"The concern here," said Nathan, "is how he could very steadily move the object from one side of the scene to the other and have it come to an abrupt halt without it appearing to swing. If it were hanging from a long string, and you went ahead and moved the pole and then brought it to a halt, the whole object would tend to move back and forth. But it doesn't."

An assistant asked, "Do you think it could be tethered from someplace?"

"I have no idea," said Nathan. "He would still have to be awfully clever, because that's a very steady holding. It would have to be a very, very good tethering."

"I could imagine him filling a weather balloon with helium," speculated the assistant, "and then dropping a piece of monofilament, tying it to the object, and then dropping another piece of monofilament from the object and holding that from the ground."

"It would have to be a set of balloons," said Nathan, "because he's able to make the thing go back and forth and it doesn't blow like this off the boom. So it's got to be held rigid somehow, from a point right above the object. Apparently he's a sharp guy, very clever. So he should be given some points for effort."

Another intriguing aspect of the Hasenbol sequence appeared subtly in the lower right corner of the film—the branch of a pine tree blown continuously by a stiff wind as the ship hovers motionless over the valley.

"If this is a hoax," Nathan remarked, "and it looks like it is to me but I have no proof, this is very carefully done. Tremendous amount of effort. An awful lot of work for one guy."

Nathan suggested that maybe Meier was utilizing something like a clothesline with two poles set about twenty feet apart and a model operated by pulleys. "The camera can be alone," he noted, "and he can be the one all by himself moving the string."

But how did Meier transport all that equipment to the site and get those poles in the ground so they provided steady support by himself without being seen?

"That's his problem," said Nathan. "I'm sure he's clever. He's sharp. He's a sharp guy. *We're* still challenging whether or not this is a hoax. And whether or not that kind of thing is involved is no longer a scientific question. Now you have to bring in people with a detective mentality."

* * *

"My training has always been not to make models which are features in themselves, but rather something that melts into the woodwork so people don't notice."

Wally Gentleman had been involved with special effects for over thirty-five years. As a teenager in England he had begun his film career developing techniques for "shooting down planes" by using photographic images on a dome.

242

He studied animation and eventually joined the special effects team at the famous Pinewood Studios in Buckinghamshire, working with rear projection and using photographic means to create backgrounds and avoid expensive sets. From England he emigrated to Canada in 1957 to serve on the National Film Board for ten years as director of special effects.

While in Canada in 1961, Gentleman made a short film of mostly visual effects titled *Universe,* which was later discovered by Stanley Kubrick, who contacted Gentleman: He wanted to utilize the techniques Gentleman had created for *Universe* in his new film *2001.* For the next year and a half, Gentleman had served as director of special photographic effects for the Kubrick film. In 1977 he moved to Hollywood and, among other projects, served as an expert visually re-creating actual flying saucer reports on the new Jack Webb series *Project UFO.*

"You can build a model to fit a certain background, even though it's a scale size," Gentleman said. "These are called 'foreground hanging miniatures' in the trade. And if you do it very skillfully, no one can tell the difference. But the skill that you need for that is really quite specific, because when you reduce the size of a model you are still building with full-sized textured pieces of wood, plastic, whatever. The trick is to render a model with the right microscopic *textures* that will fit the true scale of the situation. And then you have to worry about things like the scale of movements, the movement of the background, the simultaneous activity that's going on. Models that are done badly show up like a sore thumb."

In early 1980, Bill Jenkins, who hosted a popular Saturday night talk show on KABC radio, Los Angeles, called Gentleman.

"I have some interesting stuff to show you," he said. "Can you tell me if it's authentic?"

At the time, Gentleman worked for Film Effects of Hollywood. When Jenkins brought by the photo journal, *UFO . . . Contact from the Pleiades,* Gentleman perused the photos and told Jenkins, "I'd like very much to see more of this."

With Jenkins's help, Gentleman located the Elders in Phoenix and a few weeks later flew over to meet them and to view their video tape of Meier's movie footage. After watching each of the eight segments several times, he said to the Elders, "They have a ring of authenticity. But I'd like to examine them to be really sure."

In addition to examining the films, Gentleman subjected several of the Meier photos to "perspective interlock," a drawing board geometric analysis which he had applied in the independent frame process at Pinewood Studios. If Meier maintained that the beamships he had photographed measured approximately twenty-one feet in diameter, Gentleman could take the size of a known object in the scene, a measured tree trunk for instance, and locate where in the scene a beamship of that size would have to be. The photograph could appear to be authentic, but perspective interlock would expose subtle inconsistencies. Placing the photos on his drawing board and then tracing perspective lines, Gentleman calculated that the beamships were exactly as Meier had said they were, in size and location.

"My big problem area with the Meier pictures," said Gentleman, "is that I have never seen an original negative. And without that I could never really be sure that it had not been doctored in any way at all. But given my particular background, I know it would take an expert of many years of experience even to doctor a picture to make it look authentic."

Holding one of the Meier photos in his hand, Gentleman said, "My greatest problem is that for anybody faking this [he points to the photograph], the shadow that is thrown onto that tree is correct. There are many things that are correct on many of the shots. Therefore, if somebody is faking them they have an expert there. And being an expert myself, I know that that expert knowledge is very hard to come by. So I say, 'Well, is that expert knowledge there or isn't it there?' Because if the expert knowledge isn't there, this has got to be real."

Gentleman explained that if you throw a model into a scene it will be frozen by the camera in a certain position, and the scale of the lighting on the model's surface (the angles and intensity of reflection) will indicate its small size and its relatively close proximity to the camera. Besides, he could see no way for a one-armed man to throw three or four models into the air at once and photograph them.

"Some of them are behind the twigs on a tree," he noted. "You've got to be some special effects man to do that, I can tell you. And the objects that were behind the tree appeared to be at the right distance for ships that were a long way away. That's called 'aerial perspective.' When you look at mountains you see different colors that deepen in blue as you go farther away, and all of these photographs had that aerial perspective indicating distance. If you threw a lot of little silver things in the air at once, they'd all be lit within the space that you could throw them, which might be, what, twenty feet? But these certainly had the aerial perspective in the change of hue and tone on them. If the photographs were a 'cheat,' they were superbly cheated, but I don't think they were."

After studying the films, Gentleman concluded that considering the expertise necessary, the logistics, and the expense, a one-armed man with no assistance could not possibly have produced the footage.

"That's the bottom line of everything," he said. "This Meier really had to have a fleet of clever assistants, at least fifteen people, who would know what the interface reflections of a shiny object were at certain times of the day, how to support these objects so that wires are not seen, how to rig it, how to watch it and stand by with their little airguns to spray the strings when they begin showing up.

"What we would do is go out and shoot the scene, and then bring it back to the studio, and then shoot the object onto that film by duplication processes, which is a *very* sophisticated procedure. It's difficult to do on 35mm, even worse with the 8mm film he was using. And the equipment was totally out of his means. If somebody wanted me to cheat something along those lines, $30,000 would probably do it, but this is in a studio where the equipment exists. The equipment would cost another $50,000.

"I think the one telling part of all this is that a single man with one arm, if he indeed was on his own, could not have done it. I think it would be well nigh miraculous for a person with even two arms to do that sort of work by himself up on a mountaintop. Even if you get a balloon and you hang your object on a fine piece of thread underneath, it's going to blow in any direction it wants to go. And with a lot of those pictures where you've got three or four flying saucers, you would need balloons with strings of varying length, otherwise you could pick out where the string comes from. It would be very difficult to do those shots in that sort of condition outside. And the fall of the land makes it very risky to do anything like that. It's all that sort of complication that leads me to think that the objects he's photographed and filmed were there independently and he simply snapped the shutter."

* * *

Irina Froning, the woman who had discovered the photo journal on Meier in her friend's office late one night, was married to H. David Froning, Jr., an astronautical engineer at McDonnell Douglas Corporation for twenty-five years who worked primarily in the highly classified field of military defense. A staff manager, he had helped to develop missiles for ballistic missile defense, and had done exploratory research to develop ideas and technology for advanced spacecraft design. A longtime member of the British Interplanetary Society and the American Institute of Aeronautics and Astronautics, Froning had presented many papers on interstellar flight at technical conferences in Europe and the United States.

The idea of actually transcending vast interstellar distances had intrigued Froning for fifteen years. Searching for a way to take humankind beyond the speed of light, he spent much of his spare time examining Einstein's theories of relativity and considering new ways to encompass those theories in a more general law, much as Einstein's laws of relativity had not violated, but encompassed Newton's laws of motion.

As far back as 1966, Froning, among others, had maintained that the barriers of space and time were not insurmountable, that someday humankind would indeed surpass the speed of light. In an article he wrote that year, he pointed out that only twenty years earlier hardly a scientist or engineer believed that man could break the sound barrier and survive. Many pilots had been killed trying. Yet, predicted Froning, in the late 1980s hypersonic airliners would fly from New York to Madrid in less than an hour, or five times faster than the speed of sound.*

In his early research, Froning immediately had concluded that rockets consuming terrestrial fuel would be too heavy and costly to achieve the speed of light. He also had considered and discarded the feasibility of interstellar ramjets that would scoop up hydrogen atoms and convert them to fuel as the craft traveled through cosmic space: The "scoop" would have to measure sixty miles in diameter. But Froning continued to search.

When Irina returned home that Monday, David was still out of town. Looking for the photo journal she had seen at her friend's office, she called around to several bookstores before locating a copy. When her husband returned home she presented it to him before saying hello.

"I guess I was never so impressed by a book," said David. "If what this Meier is saying is just a hoax, he's being cued by some very knowledgeable scientists."

Later he said he felt "numb." "But it was exciting," he

---

*In 1986, President Reagan announced plans to develop the technology for a hypersonic airliner called "The Orient Express."

added. "Kind of like a tingling and a numbing at the same time. It was a revelation. All of a sudden many things made sense. It had never occurred to me that tachyons might exist completely outside the dimension of time."

Froning had designed a theoretical quantum ramjet that could power starships to nearly light speed in a matter of hours by ubiquitous energy pulses that some scientists believe exist in the "fabric" of space. He also had theorized on the other side of the light barrier and had developed a conceptual model of what a craft might look like traveling faster than the speed of light.

"But I didn't have anything to tie these two concepts together," he said. "What hung me up was the seeming impossibility of being able to cover these tremendous inter-stellar distances within a matter of minutes, rather than centuries here on earth. Then I read the Meier book, and suddenly it all seemed plausible."

Within two weeks, Froning conceived a possible way to reach the speed of light and then make the transition to faster-than-light travel. *Most people think that faster-than-light speeds occur on our normal space-time realm of existence,* he explained. "But when Meier mentioned that the trip took seven hours and the longest part lasted only several seconds, it occurred to me that during that interval almost no time at all passes. And this gave me the further idea that you could actually arc above our space-time plane of existence and travel trillions of miles through space with only several seconds passing. I had never thought of that possibility."

With the help of a bookstore owner, Froning located Wendelle Stevens in Tucson and called him for additional information on the reputed propulsion system. One thing impressed him about the more detailed contact notes sent by Stevens: The voice of Semjase addressed each of the major scientific requirements to accelerate to the speed of light, make the jump or hyper-leap, and then decelerate.

"Though she doesn't say specifically how it's done," Froning recalled, "she gets technical enough to satisfy me as a scientist. And that's very convincing when someone does that."

What further impressed Froning was that almost a year before Irina discovered the photo journal, he had calculated the propulsion efficiency of his new quantum ramjet and determined that typical times for such a craft to reach light speed would be about four hours. According to Meier's figures, the Pleiadian ships required approximately 3.5 hours to accelerate to the speed of light, only seconds to traverse a distance of nearly five hundred light years, and then another 3.5 hours to decelerate and fly to earth. The credibility of Meier's numbers amazed Froning. To arrive at his figures, Froning had utilized complex formulas involving acceleration rates. Then he discovered that not only did Meier claim it required 3.5 hours for the Pleiadian beamships to reach the speed of light, but that at that point the ships would have traveled approximately 92 million miles. That figure, too, was within 20 percent of his own previous calculations.

"I think it would be very improbable for someone with Meier's educational background to hit on this combination of figures and have them be within a scientifically acceptable range," said Froning. "He would have to be coached by someone who's very knowledgeable in the sciences, who has knowledge of special relativity and of flight mechanics to know what kinds of times and distances make sense. If this is a hoax, it has to be with the assistance of someone like myself who could account for the plausible things that take place.

"I've only discussed this Meier case with scientists who are fairly open-minded about interstellar flight, but I'll tell you, the majority of them think it's credible and agree with at least part, or sometimes all, of the things talked about by the Pleiadians."

* * *

Before the golden-silver triangle had disappeared from the possession of Marcel Vogel, the IBM scientist had placed it under his $250,000 scanning electron microscope and turned on a video tape to record his findings. The tiny specimen held very pure silver, and "very, very pure" aluminum, plus potassium, calcium, chromium, copper, argon, bromium, chlorine, iron, sulphur, and silicon. One microscopic area revealed "an enormous mélange of almost all of the elements in the periodic table." And each was exceedingly pure.

"It's an unusual combination," Vogel said later, "but I would not in any way, shape, or form say that this would make it extraterrestrial."

What intrigued Vogel more than the number of elements and their purity was their discreteness: Each pure element was bonded to each of the others, yet somehow retained its own identity.

"It is uncanny when you look at the juxtaposition of the metals," he said as he looked through the microscope and talked out his findings for the video tape. "One layer against another is very pure, but they do not interpenetrate. You have a combination of metals and non-metals together, very tightly bonded. I don't know of anybody even contemplating doing something like this."

In one small area in the middle of the sample blown up five hundred times, he found two parallel grooves joined by furrows, precise hairlines somehow micro-machined into the metal. But even more surprising to him was that the major element present in that small area was the rare-earth metal thulium.

"It is totally unexpected," he said. "Thulium was only purified during World War II as a by-product of atomic energy work, and only in minute quantities. It is exceedingly expensive, far beyond platinum, and rare to come by. Someone would have to have an extensive metallurgical knowledge even to be aware of a composition of this type."

The magnification of the half-inch piece went from 500 to 1,600, and Vogel saw things he had never seen before. "A whole new world appears in the specimen. There are structures within structures—very, very unusual. At lower magnification one just sees a metallic surface. Now one sees a structure composed of various types of interlacing areas. This is very exciting."

Vogel probed deeper and deeper into the metal.

"We are now at over 2,500 diameters and one can see birefringent structures. Very exciting! It is very unusual for a metal to have these birefringent areas. When you first take a section and grind it off, it looks like a metal, it has the lustery appearance of metal, but now when you take it and go under the polarized light you find that, yes, it is metal, but at the same time . . . it is crystal!"

For hours, Vogel continued to roam through the interior of this tiny specimen, fascinated by what he saw. The next morning, he called a research scientist at NASA's Ames Research Center, Dr. Richard Haines.

"Why don't you come down," he said. "I want to show you something."

"He gave me just enough information on the phone to tantalize me," recalled Haines. "So I went down."

Vogel's office was next to the stairs on the second floor of one of the many buildings at the IBM Research Center. When Haines entered the office, Vogel said, "I want to show you something." Then he reached into his pocket for a small plastic bag in which he had carefully placed the triangle fragment the night before.

"He reached in his pocket," recalled Haines, "and couldn't find it . . . he looked at me with a blank expression I will never forget, he was flabbergasted. He's either a very good actor or he was telling the truth, and I think he was telling the truth."

Somewhere between the lab and Vogel's office the small metal fragment had disappeared. "He said he must have misplaced it somewhere. So we frantically looked all over the place. He checked his desk in his main office, and we went into the lab and looked around and couldn't find it there. He apologized profusely because he felt that he had gotten me all the way down there just to see the metal that now he couldn't produce. He did show me some photographs, color photographs, that he had taken of the sample and he alluded to something anomalous about the specimen. That's one of the reasons I went down. Because that's quite an offer, to have somebody like that with that kind of reputation making a claim like that."

Vogel never recovered the lost piece of metal, nor could he explain its disappearance. He hoped that Stevens could provide him with another, but that was the only sample that allegedly represented one of the final steps in the manufacture of the beamship hull.

"I needed additional pieces to look at to be sure there was something really unique," said Vogel. "I was enthusiastic. I was emotionally wound up in the study of it because it was an ideal challenge, something that many scientists would have very eagerly gone into. What was unusual was the purity of the individual spots of metals in the tiny specimen. Their discreteness. That's what intrigued me and that's why I wanted more specimens to look at. I would have gone much further into metallurgical analysis, looking at bending action and melting characteristics. I wanted a second opinion from another person at MIT, so we could compare notes on this before we put anything into print. It was a virgin opportunity, and I had gone to NASA to elicit as well the support of their own scientists who were interested, because here was a bit of material that could be looked at. I had many contacts within IBM who were deeply interested in exploring this with me. I could have had about an eight- or nine-man team. But I shut it all down."

The disappearance of the unusual metal disappointed Vogel, but he was equally disappointed that Stevens and Elders, eager to establish support for the case, had published his preliminary findings in their photo journal before he had been able to complete the testing, and without giving him an opportunity to review for accuracy what they had written.

"It was garbled-up bits and pieces of remarks," he said later, "not a cohesive way of presenting anything. It was technically wrong, and I resented it. It's unfortunate because I was willing to use all of the technology I had to find a real answer to this."

Vogel lost his enthusiasm for the project. "Not because of the metal," he said later, "but the way people acted." Of course, the metal was now gone anyway.

"I was enthusiastic," concluded Vogel, "I was interested, I went through a lot of effort. But the case is incomplete. That's the best way you can report it."

Just after the metal sample had disappeared, and before the photo journal had been published, the Japanese crew from Nippon Television had flown to San Jose to film Vogel for their documentary on the Meier case. Vogel had spoken openly with interviewer Jun-Ichi Yaoi about the results of his initial findings.

"I cannot explain the type of material I had," he told Yaoi. "By any known combination of materials I could not put it together myself as a scientist. With any technology that I know of, we could not achieve this on this planet! I showed it to one of my friends, who is a metallurgist, and he shook his head and said, 'I don't see how this can be put together.' That is where we are right now. And I think it is important that those of us who are in the scientific world sit down and do some serious study on these things instead of putting it off as people's imagination."

EPILOGUE

Long before the Air Force terminated Project Blue Book, citizens of this country and others claimed to have been abducted by strange-looking but apparently merely curious entities and taken aboard their disk-shaped craft. Even as far back as the fifties, respected citizens, including police officers and ministers, many of them shaken, had reported to authorities disturbing experiences where they had observed creatures in or near what appeared to be a spacelike craft. Sometimes to support their claims they pointed to pod marks and broken tree limbs, and they told of car engines that had died and then sprung to life. But they insisted on anonymity. The first publicized abduction, that of Betty and Barney Hill, remained unknown even to the abductees themselves until over two years after the abduction.

The Hills' experience had occurred on a September night in 1961, as they traveled toward home through a deserted stretch of highway in the White Mountains of New Hampshire. They noticed a bright light, seeming at first to be a star, that came closer and closer until it was huge, disk-shaped, and hovering only fifty feet from where Barney had stopped the car. He got out a pair of binoculars and approached the object on foot. Through the lenses he could

255

see clearly a row of windows and behind them six beings watching him. From that point the Hills remembered nothing, except a strange beeping sound that seemed to fill the car as they drove off. When they arrived home, they found peculiar shiny spots the size of silver dollars on the trunk of their car; Barney had an unusual mark on his groin; and two hours had passed that they could not account for.

Then the Hills began suffering inexplicable anxiety attacks and nightmarish dreams about flying saucers, until finally, two years later, they sought help from a Boston psychiatrist, Dr. Benjamin Simon. Under hypnosis the Hills revealed a detailed story in which the beings observed by Barney through the binoculars had directed them off the road and into their ship, where they examined Betty and Barney, including a "pregnancy test" with a thin needle inserted into Betty's navel. While regressed Betty alternately sobbed and spoke firmly. Barney screamed and trembled, "What do they want? What do they *want!*" And, "I've never seen eyes slanted like that!"

One night three years after the first regression, Dr. Simon invited Allen Hynek to observe the Hills under hypnosis and ask them questions. The session lasted for an hour and a half. Afterward, on January 5, 1967, Hynek wrote of his experience in a letter to Edward Condon: "I asked them to relive the episode, and they did so, talking to each other, presumably reliving the scene under total recall, including such little asides as remarks to the dog, etc. I have a tape of this and there is no question of the terror in Barney's voice when he views his object through binoculars. Whatever it was, tangible or imaginary, these people were terrified. Your committee should hear these tapes." They never did.

Twelve years after the Hill experience, Charles Hickson, forty-two, and Calvin Parker, nineteen, two shipyard workers in Pascagoula, Mississippi, were fishing off a dilapidated pier one night when a glowing craft suddenly appeared behind them expelling three mummylike creatures who levitated upright, floated them back to the craft, examined each under intense light, then returned them to the dock. Deputy Sheriff Glenn Ryder answered Hickson's call to the sheriff's office and picked up the two men. Parker was crying.

"They convinced me something happened to them," Ryder recalled in an interview later. "Especially the boy. He was scared to death. There's no way he could have acted that out. He kept saying, 'They're gonna come back and get us. They're gonna come back and get us. We gotta get outta here.' He wouldn't sit down. He was just standing up shaking the whole time. Never would sit down."

Ryder and the sheriff interviewed Hickson and Parker for over an hour, then purposely left the two men alone in an office for five minutes while a concealed tape recorder continued to turn. They expected to record Hickson and Parker snickering over how they had fooled two people so far. Instead, they heard Hickson say, "Calvin, you okay, hoss?"

"Tellya," said Parker, "I'm scared to death. This evenin' I like to had a heart attack, I ain't shittin' ya."

"I know," said Hickson.

"I came damn near to dyin'.'"

"I know, it scares me to death, too, son."

"I'm just damn near cryin' right now." said Parker. His voice trembled. "Reckon why they just picked us up?"

"I don't know, I don't know," said Hickson. "I'm telling you, man, I can't take much more of that."

"I'm just damn near crazy," Parker seemed to say to himself.

Hickson said, "When they brought you out of that thing, *goddamn!* I like to never in hell got you straightened out, man!"

"My damn arms," said Parker, "my arms, they just froze up and I couldn't move. Just like I stepped on a damn rattlesnake."

"I've never seen nothin' like that before in my life," said Hickson. "You can't make people believe—"

"Did you see how that damn door come right open in

front of us all of a sudden?" Parker interrupted him.

"I don't know how it opened, son," said Hickson, "I don't know."

"All I see was this here zzzzzzip, then looked around, them damn blue lights and them sonsabitches, just like that, they come out." Parker started to panic. "I gotta go to the house. I am done sittin' here gettin' so damn sick right now, I ain't shittin' ya. I gotta go to the house."

Hickson left the room to get the sheriff and Parker began praying. "It's just hard to believe . . . Oh God, it's awful . . . I know there's a God up there . . ." he babbled. The last thing heard on the tape was Parker saying, "Why did it have to happen to me?" Then Ryder and the sheriff returned and found Parker raking the walls with his fingernails.

In 1975, the third in the trio of famous American abduction cases occurred in the mountain forests of eastern Arizona just north of the Fort Apache Indian Reservation. Returning home along an old logging road a seven-man timber cutting crew encountered a saucer-shaped yellowish glow not a hundred feet away. Travis Walton, twenty-two, riding shotgun in the truck, jumped out and ran toward the object. Suddenly, a bolt of blue-green light hit him in the chest, knocking him into the air and back ten feet. Mike Rogers, the crew foreman driving the truck, hit the accelerator. About twenty minutes later the crew returned, but Walton's body was gone.

When Rogers and his crew reported the incident to the county sheriff's office they found themselves suspected of murder, and the sheriff had each examined by a polygraph expert flown in from Phoenix. One of the questions was: "Did you tell the truth about actually seeing a UFO last Wednesday when Travis Walton disappeared?" All six answered yes. The examiner concluded that five of the young men had told the truth. In his formal report, the examiner wrote, "These polygraph examinations prove that these five men did see some object that they believe to be a UFO and that Travis Walton was not injured or murdered by any of these men, on that Wednesday (5 November 1975). If an actual UFO did not exist and the UFO is a manmade hoax, five of these men had no prior knowledge of a hoax." The results on the sixth were "inconclusive."

Five days after his disappearance, Walton reappeared collapsed in a telephone booth at a small-town filling station. He said he remembered crouching behind a log to get a look at the glowing object, and that when he stood up he was hit by a "physical blow" that knocked him unconscious. He had awakened on a table on board the craft, surrounded by humanoids dressed in brownish-orange, whom he pushed away, and escaped to the ship's interior. There an entity appearing to be human found him and escorted him to a room in a much larger ship where two other humans, a man and a woman, laid him on a table and placed a mask over his face. When Walton again regained consciousness, he was lying on the pavement at the side of the road, watching the lighted bottom of the craft rise into a black sky. Walton flunked one polygraph exam and passed another.

In the past several years, hundreds of people, perhaps thousands, have claimed either to have been abducted or to be in contact with space beings, or both. And increasingly, these abductees and contactees are being thought of less as crazy people and more as a manifestation of a little understood but widespread and growing phenomenon. As a group they exhibit no mental deficiencies. The subject of a recent doctoral thesis by Dr. June Parnell at the University of Wyoming, 225 persons who claimed to have experienced highly unusual UFO sightings and/or to have been in communication with UFO occupants surprisingly were found to be above average in intelligence, assertive, experimental in their thinking, reserved, defensive, self-sufficient, resourceful, honest, and, most significant, devoid of mental disorders. Yet, although they suffer from no psychoses, and often have good jobs, families, and respect in the community, some claim to hear voices inside their heads instructing them. But most of these stories go no further than the office of a therapist where the individual showed up one day unable to explain strange dreams, small incisions or puncture wounds on his or her body, and a peculiar loss of time associated with the chance sighting of a UFO. Many have had contact experiences, ones they cannot explain, and they tell stories similar to Meier's but have no proof, only bizarre and detailed accounts of abductions that have surfaced during hypnotic regression. The number of such claims has increased so dramatically over the last several years that a few sociologists and psychologists now feel the answer to the UFO enigma lies in their study and understanding.

* * *

Attempting to understand the intense nature of the ten-year-old phenomenon of UFOs, Jung wrote in his essay *Flying Saucers* almost thirty years ago: "In the threatening situation of the world today, when people are beginning to see that everything is at stake, the projection-creating fantasy soars beyond the realm of earthly organizations and powers into the heavens, into interstellar space, where the rulers of human fate, the gods, once had their abode in the planets. Our earthly world is split into two halves, and nobody knows where a helpful solution is to come from."

Jung foresaw the end of an era, the dawning of a new age; and flying saucers somehow symbolized the transition. Suddenly a significant number of his patients had begun speaking to him of dreams in which inexplicable circular shapes descended from heaven. And he read of many others all over the world who reported seeing similar shapes in a daytime sky. He postulated that if the will were strong the awakened mind could conjure circular shapes that to the eye appeared as flying saucers, much as the palms of faithful Christians had been known to bleed spontaneously. And either these visions or the presence of an actual physical object, or both, could be the catalyst for what he called a "visionary rumour." But why this sudden need for the masses to clothe unexplainable things in extraterrestrial garb? Perhaps the omniscient God of the prophets like Moses and Jesus, once so radical in the eyes of Greco-Roman paganism, no longer fulfilled man's spiritual needs; perhaps this intense, unconscious desire to believe in the existence of flying saucers signaled a wrenching shift in religious paradigms. But—and this is where Jung disqualified himself—the breakdown of religious paradigms and flying saucers in dreams do not explain the trained fighter pilot who chases a silvery fifty-foot disk confirmed on radar, only to have the disk suddenly accelerate to a speed of several thousand miles an hour, execute a 90-degree turn, and quietly disappear.

After three years of research I have concluded that UFOs exist: Something we cannot explain indeed sails through our skies from time to time. This does not mean that representatives of extraterrestrial societies visit us, though there is some evidence to suggest that. I find it difficult to believe that anyone who looks seriously and objectively at the evidence—secret government documents that only recently have been discovered, the writings of and interviews with the coterie of scientists who have investigated the phenomenon, the reports themselves—can come away insisting the whole matter takes seed in the human mind. Though I have sampled only a small portion of the literature written by debunkers like Phil Klass and Robert Sheaffer, I find their arguments strained and unpersuasive, often more convoluted and difficult to believe than the sightings themselves.

On the other hand I empathize with the scientist who refuses to become involved. Never has there been a more frustrating subject, where questions abound, and answers only shimmer in the distance. With our recently acquired knowledge of the origin of the unvierse, the birth-and-death cycle of star systems, and the evolution of life on our own planet, many, if not most, scientists now believe that intelligent life probably exists on other planets in our own galaxy. However, many of these same scientists also believe that travel in space is impossible: The galaxy is simply too vast. In winter 1986, I spent several days with NASA scientists who are engaged in the Search for ExtraTerrestrial Intelligence (SETI) at Ames Research Center in California. The SETI people theorize that since alien civilizations cannot travel in space they communicate with one another across interstellar distances with speed-of-light radio waves. The scientists now search for such magnetic waves in the galactic "neighborhood" out to a distance of a hundred light years. Meanwhile, things no one can explain still dart through our earthly atmosphere. Maybe someday they will turn out to be, as many have suggested, merely a misunderstood natural phenomenon. In April 1984, Allen Hynek, in a column for *OMNI* magazine, even suggested that the seemingly solid, yet ephemeral nature of UFOs might best be explained as "an interface between our reality and a parallel reality, the door to another dimension. Surely," he added, "we haven't had our last revolution in scientific thought."

And where does Meier fit into all of this? I don't know. I would not call him a prophet, though he may be. I would not rule out impostor, though I have no proof. I know that if you boiled the story in a kettle you would find a hard residue composed of two things: One would be Meier's ravings about time travel, space travel, philosophy, and religion; the other would be the comments by the scientists and engineers impressed with the evidence he has produced. I can't believe the former, nor can I dismiss the latter.

"We can't prove the case is real," Lee Elders said to me in an interview in 1984. "We just can't do it. We can't prove that the metals are from a Pleiadian beamship, only that they are unusual. We can't *prove* anything. There are still things I question about the case," he added. "I don't know how to explain it."

"It took us two years," said Brit, "to figure out you're never going to prove it and you're never going to disprove it, it's just there."

When I met Meier in the spring of 1984, I saw a tired man with a deeply lined face who walked with a shuffle. His bright green, once playful eyes, described to me by so many people, had turned weary; and the beard he had begun to grow in the summer of 1978 was now curly and half gray, and fell nearly to his waist. Only forty-seven, he looked to be at least twenty years older. People at the farm told me he rarely slept, he had ghost pains in his missing arm, and he saw well out of only one eye. In the fall of 1982, Meier was in the bathroom early in the morning when he slipped and hit his head. A doctor diagnosed the injury as a severe concussion.

Meier still lives on the farm in Schmidruti, and people still come to visit. But rarely does he speak with anyone. When visitors drive up the gravel path, he may slip his index finger beside the sheer curtain in the parlor and peek out; more likely he will continue to stare at the television screen. Others at the farm usually intercept the visitors and talk with them about Meier and his experiences and show them photographs from several large albums, and then send them on their way. I was at the farm for three weeks in the spring of 1984 and again for two weeks that fall; in the spring of 1985 I lived in Switzerland for two months, traveling frequently to the farm. In all that time I rarely saw Meier anywhere but on that sofa in the parlor in front of the television.

Though years had passed since Meier left the farm for a contact, he told me the Pleiadians still spoke with him, and had even appeared in his office several times. But since it was customary for them to run things in cycles of eleven years, even that would end in 1986. "At present," he told me, "there isn't much happening in my head."

I doubted Meier's story from the beginning, but only for the typical reason: It couldn't be true. Two years later, out of frustration, I jerked open my file drawers, emptied everything into large cardboard boxes, and carried them into the basement of my office building. I could find no answers. The photoanalysis came up inconclusive because originals could not be studied. The unusual metal sample had disappeared. Except for the Intercep group, almost everyone I interviewed in the UFO community warned that I was wasting my time on an obvious hoax. But in Switzerland and again in Munich, I talked for days with Herbert Runkel, and I saw a sincere, curious, and intelligent man truly baffled by his experiences with Meier. His friend Harold impressed me the same way. With my translator Frank Stuckert I spoke often with the people at the farm about their myriad and unusual experiences; I walked the sites in the hills, and I talked at length with the people at Bär Photo. I spoke with village administrators, interviewed neighbors, and explored the old Hinwil house from the basement to the attic. I found the alleged detractors Martin Sorge and Hans Schutzbach: Sorge now believed the contacts had actually taken place, though in a different fashion; Schutzbach remained convinced that Meier had faked everything, but after two years of searching he had "found out nothing but a lot of ideas." He couldn't explain the landing tracks, photographs, or sound recordings, and still had no idea who even one accomplice might have been. He told me, "Around Billy the oddest things always happened." I met several intelligent and well educated adults who rarely visited the farm but who told me their lives had been changed upon meeting Meier. One afternoon, as I sat out front of the farmhouse talking with Meier, a taxi pulled up next to the aviary, and out stepped two Japanese women who had seen the television documentary on the Meier story. They had flown twenty-two hours from Tokyo. As the older woman stood next to the taxi, both hands enveloped the stem of a red rose.

The scientists who had examined the evidence cautioned against premature conclusions, but the evidence impressed most of them. That, of course, does not make Meier's story real, but having experienced the setting in Switzerland I, like others before me, could not understand how Meier could have created sophisticated special effects in his photography. Then there were the sounds, metal, landing tracks, films, the explanation of the beamship propulsion system, all of which lent credibility to the story.

Yet Meier's contrived photos of the San Francisco earthquake and his other outlandish claims tore at that credibility. He may simply be one of the finest illusionists the world has ever known, possessing not the power but the skill to persuade others to see things that did not happen and do not exist. Perhaps he has no such ability; perhaps beings on a much higher plane have selected him and controlled him and used him for reasons far beyond our comprehension. I do know this: Trying to make sense of it all has been the most difficult thing I will ever do. Finally I realized, as the Elders had years before, that the truth of the Meier contacts will never be known.

AUTHOR'S NOTE

During my research into the Meier story I located certain persons who had not been interviewed in the original investigation, but whose participation I felt was relevant to a retelling of the story. At the same time, I wanted to avoid the confusion of introducing myself as a character. So, for purposes of clarity and continuity, I have in two instances attributed scenes from my own interviews to characters in the story. The interviews with Willy Bär, Beatrice Bär, and Fritz Kindliman, all of Bär Photo, which I attribute to Lee Elders and Tom Welch, I actually conducted myself with a translator in the late spring of 1985. The interview with Martin Sorge in Locarno, which in the book appears as an interview by Lee and Brit Elders, in fact occurred only in my presence and that of my translator's, also in late spring 1985.

In 1983, two years after the completion of the Meier investigation, the prosecutor's office of Pima County, Arizona, charged Wendelle Stevens with child molestation. Stevens pleaded guilty and as of this writing is incarcerated in the Arizona state penal system. I believe that these charges, though serious, are irrelevant to the Meier investigation; but I pass the information along to the reader so that he or she may judge accordingly.

After completing the manuscript I mailed to each of the scientists, engineers, and the special effects expert a packet which included everything in the manuscript pertaining to each. I asked that each make any corrections, technical or otherwise, he cared to make. Either by phone or by mail each of the scientists responded. Some made minor changes; some changed nothing at all. Everything concerning the scientific analyses of the evidence appears in the book exactly as the scientists themselves have authorized it to appear.